Big Book of Scrap **Crochet** PROJECTS™

Edited by Vicki Blizzard

HOUSE of WHITE BIRCHES
PUBLISHERS
SINCE 1947

Big Book of Scrap Crochet Projects

Editor: Vicki Blizzard
Managing Editor: Jacqueline Stetter
Associate Editor: Cathy Reef
Technical Editor: Agnes Russell
Book and Cover Design: Jessi Butler
Copy Editor: Mary Martin
Publications Coordinator: Tanya Turner

Photography: Tammy Christian, Jeff Chilcote,
Denise Fosnaugh, Kelly Heydinger, Nancy Sharp
Photography Assistant: Linda Quinlan

Publishing Services Manager: Brenda Gallmeyer
Graphic Arts Supervisor: Ronda Bechinski
Graphic Artist: Amy S. Lin
Production Assistants: Janet Bowers, Marj Morgan
Traffic Coordinator: Sandra Beres
Technical Artists: Chad Summers, Liz Morgan, Mitch Moss

Chief Executive Officer: John Robinson
Publishing Marketing Director: David McKee
Book Marketing Manager: Craig Scott
Product Development Director: Vivian Rothe
Publishing Services Director: Brenda R. Wendling

Printed in the United States of America
First Printing: 2003
Library of Congress Number: 2001097996
ISBN: 1-882138-94-5

Hello, Friends

As avid crocheters, what's the one thing we all have in common? Scrap threads and yarns, of course! Little bits of this and that in pretty, bright colors or soft textures—little bits that we just can't bear to throw away and that get saved in hopes that we'll find the perfect pattern in which to use them.

We gave our talented team of designers a specific challenge when we asked for projects for this book: Make a great project that will appeal to our readers, and, oh yes, use only bits and pieces of yarn—no more than one skein of a particular color.

We think they've done a wonderful job! The projects in this book range from wearables to home decor. Along with fun projects such as place mats and toys, there are more fulfilling projects, such as afghans and a gorgeous collection of Christmas ornaments. Lots of the projects are portable, too, so you can take your crochet with you on your various travels around town.

We've also provided designer tips throughout the book, on topics such as working with multiple strands and making tassels. Be sure to look for them!

Start sorting through your scraps! We're sure you'll find just the right project to use up your bits and pieces of yarn and thread!

Happy stitching!

Vicki Blizzard

Contents

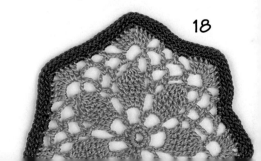

Chapter 4
Artistic Scraps

Chapter 5
Bazaar Quickies

138

Chapter 6
Playtime Friends

Chapter 7
Afghan Jamboree

180

Kitchen Colors

Warm, cozy and always filled with delicious aromas, the kitchen is, for most families, the gathering place. Fill your kitchen with pretty crocheted accents to add to that cozy, home-sweet-home feel!

Summer Place Mat Set

Designs by Michele Wilcox

Skill Level: Beginner

Size

Place mat: 14¾ x 11¼ inches

Coaster: 5½ inches in diameter, excluding leaves

Napkin ring: 2¾ inches in diameter, excluding flowers

Materials

- Elmore-Pisgah Peaches & Crème worsted weight cotton yarn: 2 oz light green #55, 1 oz each persimmon #33 and cream #3
- Size H/8 crochet hook or size needed to obtain gauge
- Tapestry needle

Gauge

4 sts = 1 inch; 6 rows = 2 inches
Check gauge to save time.

Pattern Notes

Weave in loose ends as work progresses.

Join rnds with a sl st unless otherwise stated.

Place Mat

Row 1: With light green, ch 53, sc in 4th ch from hook, dc in next ch, [sc in next ch, dc in next ch] rep across, turn.

Row 2: Ch 2 (counts as first dc throughout), [sc in sc, dc in dc] rep across, fasten off, turn.

Row 3: Attach cream, ch 2, [sc in sc, dc in dc] rep across, turn.

Row 4: Rep Row 2.

Row 5: With light green, rep Row 3.

Row 6: Rep Row 2.

Row 7: With persimmon, rep Row 3.

Row 8: Rep Row 2.

Rows 9 & 10: Rep Rows 5 and 6.

Rows 11–26: Rep Rows 3–10.

Rows 27–30: Rep Rows 3–6, at the end of Row 30, do not fasten off light green.

Rnd 31: Ch 1, sc evenly sp around outer edge, working 3 sc in each corner st, join in beg sc, fasten off.

Rnd 32: Attach cream, ch 1, sc in same sc as beg ch-1, sc in each of next 2 sc, ch 2, sl st in 2nd ch from hook, [sc in each of next 3 sc, ch 2, sl st in 2nd ch from hook] rep around, join in beg sc, fasten off.

Coaster

Rnd 1: With cream, ch 2, 6 sc in 2nd ch from hook, join in beg sc. (6 sc)

Rnd 2: Ch 1, 2 sc in each sc around, join in beg sc. (12 sc)

Rnd 3: Ch 1, [sc in next sc, 2 sc in next sc] rep around, join in beg sc. (18 sc)

Rnd 4: Ch 1, [sc in each of next 2 sc, 2 sc in next sc] rep around, join in beg sc. (24 sc)

Rnd 5: Ch 1, [sc in each of next 3 sc, 2 sc in next sc] rep around, join in beg sc. (30 sc)

Rnd 6: Ch 1, [sc in each of next 4 sc, 2 sc in next sc] rep around, join in beg sc. (36 sc)

Rnd 7: Ch 1, [sc in each of next 5 sc, 2 sc in next sc] rep around, join in beg sc, fasten off. (42 sc)

Rnd 8: Attach persimmon with a sl st in any sc, *[ch 1, hdc] in same st as sl st, 2 dc in next st, [hdc, ch 1, sl st] in next st, sl st in next st, rep from * around, fasten off. (7 petals)

Leaf

Make 2

Rnd 1: With light green, ch 8, sc in 2nd ch from hook, hdc in each of next 2 chs, dc in each of next 3 chs, 7 dc in last ch, working on opposite side of foundation ch, dc in each of next 3 chs, hdc in each of next 2 chs, sc in next ch, join in beg sc, fasten off.

This pretty floral set is sure to brighten your table any time of the year. Add a vase of fresh flowers for a summer picnic in the middle of winter!

Using photo as a guide overlap edge of leaves and sew tog; sew leaves under flower petals.

Napkin Ring

Row 1: With light green, ch 6, sc in 2nd ch from hook, sc in each rem ch across, turn. (5 sc)

Rows 2–24: Ch 1, sc in each sc across, turn, at the end of Row 24, leaving a length of yarn, fasten off.

Flower

Note: Make 2 each cream and persimmon.

Rnd 1: Ch 2, 6 sc in 2nd ch from hook, join in beg sc. (6 sc)

Rnd 2: [Ch 1, 3 dc in same sc as beg ch-1, ch 1, sl st in next sc] rep around, join, fasten off.

Alternating flower colors, sew flower to napkin ring, leaving 1½ inches of napkin ring bare. With rem length, sew ends of napkin ring tog. ✂

Country Heart Table Set

Designs by Donna Collinsworth

Gauge

3 hdc = 1 inch; 2 hdc rnds = 1 inch
Check gauge to save time.

Pattern Notes

Weave in loose ends as work progresses.

Materials listed make 2 each place mats and coasters.

Work with 1 strand each lilac and Aran held tog throughout.

Sl st to join each rnd in top of first hdc unless otherwise indicated.

Pattern Stitch

Hdc dec: [Yo, insert hook in next st, yo, draw lp through] twice, yo, draw through all 5 lps on hook.

Place Mat

Rnd 1: With 1 strand each color held tog, ch 12, hdc in 2nd ch from hook, hdc in each of next 4 chs, sk 1 ch, hdc in each of next 5 chs, working on opposite side of foundation ch, hdc in each of next 5 chs, [hdc, ch 1, hdc] in next ch, hdc in each of next 5 chs, join, turn. (22 sts)

Rnd 2: Ch 1, 2 hdc in each of next 2 sts, hdc in each rem st across to ch-1 sp, [hdc, ch 1, hdc] in ch-1 sp, hdc in each of next 4 sts, 2 hdc in each of next 3 sts, hdc in each of next 3 sts, hdc dec over next 2 sts, hdc in each of next 3 sts, 2 hdc in next st, join, turn. (30 sts)

Rnd 3: Ch 1, 2 hdc in each of next 2 sts, hdc in each of next 3 sts, hdc dec over next 2 sts, hdc in each of next 4 sts, 2 hdc in each of next 4 sts, hdc in each rem st to ch-1 sp, [hdc, ch 1, hdc] in ch-1 sp, hdc in each of next 7 sts, 2 hdc in each of next 2 sts, join, turn. (39 sts)

Rnd 4: Ch 1, 2 hdc in each of next 3 sts, hdc in each rem st to ch-1 sp, [hdc, ch 1, hdc] in ch-1 sp, hdc in each of next 10 sts, 2 hdc in each of next 5 sts, hdc in each of next 4 sts, hdc dec over next 2 sts, hdc in each of next 4 sts, 2 hdc in each of next 2 sts, join, turn. (51 sts)

Rnd 5: Ch 1, [2 hdc in next st, hdc in next st] 3 times, hdc in each of next 2 sts, hdc dec over next 2 sts, hdc in each of next 3 sts, [2 hdc in next st, hdc in next st] 6 times, hdc in each rem st to ch-1 sp, [dc, ch 1, dc] in ch-1 sp, hdc in each of next 9 sts, [2 hdc in next st, hdc in next st] 3 times, join, turn.

Set the table with this charming place mat set and enjoy a quiet cup of tea with the morning sunrise!

Rnd 6: Ch 1, hdc in each st to ch-1 sp, [dc, ch 1, dc] in ch-1 sp, hdc in each of next 30 sts, hdc dec over next 2 sts, hdc in each rem st around, join, turn.

Rnd 7: Ch 1, [2 dc in next st, dc in each of next 2 sts] twice, hdc in each of next 4 sts, hdc dec over next 2 sts, hdc in each of next 4 sts, [2 dc in next st, dc in each of next 2 sts] 4 times, hdc in each rem st to ch-1 sp, [dc, ch 1, dc] in ch-1 sp, hdc in each of next 14 sts, [2 dc in next st, dc in each of next 2 sts] twice, sl st to join in top of first dc, turn.

Rnd 8: Ch 1, [2 dc in next st, dc in each of next 2 sts] twice, hdc in each st to ch-1 sp, [dc, ch 1, dc] in ch-1 sp, hdc in each of next 17 sts, [2 dc in next st, dc in each of next 2 sts] 4 times, hdc in each of next 6 sts, hdc dec over next 2 sts, hdc in each of next 6 sts, [2 dc in next st, dc in each of next 2 sts] twice, sl st to join in top of beg dc, turn. (81 sts)

Rnd 9: Ch 1, [2 dc in next st, dc in each of next 2 sts] 3 times, hdc in each of next 4 sts, hdc dec over next 2 sts, [2 dc in next st, dc in each of next 2 sts] 6 times, hdc in each st to ch-1 sp, [dc, ch 1, dc] in ch-1 sp, hdc in each of next 6 sts, [2 dc in next st, dc in each of next 2 sts] 3 times, sl st to join in top of beg dc, turn.

Rnd 10: Ch 1, [2 dc in next st, dc in each of next 2 sts] 3 times, hdc in each st to ch-1 sp, [dc, ch 1, dc] in ch-1 sp, hdc in each of next 24 sts, [2 dc in next st, dc in each of next 2 sts] 6 times, hdc in each of next 5 sts, sl st in each of next 3 sts, hdc in each of next 5 sts, [2 dc in next st, dc in each of next 2 sts] 3 times, sl st to join in top of beg dc, fasten off. (106 sts)

Coaster

Rnds 1 & 2: Rep Rnds 1 and 2 of place mat.

Rnd 3: Ch 1, 2 hdc in each of next 2 sts, hdc in each of next 3 sts, sl st in each of next 3 sts, hdc in each of next 3 sts, 2 hdc in each of next 4 sts, hdc in each rem st to ch-1 sp, [dc, ch 1, dc] in ch-1 sp, hdc in each of next 7 sts, 2 hdc in each of next 2 sts, join, fasten off. ✂

Mexican Serape Place Mat & Napkin Ring

Designs by Charlene Finiello

Skill Level: Beginner

Size

Place mat: 15½ x 11½ inches

Napkin ring: 1¾ x 2½ inches

Materials

- Worsted weight yarn: 3 oz black, assorted amounts variegated
- Size H/8 crochet hook or size needed to obtain gauge
- 6-inch square of cardboard
- 2 safety pins
- Tapestry needle

Gauge

4 sc = 1 inch; 5 sc rows = 1½ inches Check gauge to save time.

Pattern Notes

Weave in loose ends as work progresses.

Each row of place mat requires approximately 4⅓ yards of yarn.

Place mat can be made larger by adding chs for desired width of mat.

Napkin Ring

Row 1 (RS): With black, ch 21, sc in 2nd ch from hook, sc in each rem ch across, fasten off. (20 sc)

Row 2 (RS): Working in back lps only, attach variegated in first sc of previous row, ch 1, sc in each st across, turn.

Row 3 (WS): Ch 1, working in front lps only, sc in each st across, turn.

Row 4 (RS): Ch 1, working in front lps only, sc in each st across, fasten off.

Row 5 (RS): Working in back lps only attach black in first sc of previous row, ch 1, sc in each st across, fasten off. (20 sc)

Place Mat

Foundation (RS): With black, ch 60, leaving a 3-inch length, fasten off.

Row 1 (RS): Leaving a 3-inch length of yarn, attach variegated in first ch of Row 1, ch 1, working over rem length of yarn at each end, sc in each ch across, leaving a 3-inch length, fasten off. (60 sc)

Row 2 (RS): Leaving a 3-inch length of yarn, attach black in first sc of previous row, ch 1, working over rem length at each end and working in back lps only, sc in each st across, leaving a 3-inch length, fasten off.

Row 3 (RS): Leaving a 3-inch length of yarn, attach variegated in first sc of previous row, ch 1, working over rem length at each end and working in back lps only, sc in each st across, leaving a 3-inch length, fasten off.

[Rep Rows 2 and 3] 17 times.

Border

Note: With WS tog, fold napkin ring in half; With safety pin, secure open edge of napkin ring centered on left edge of place mat.

It's fiesta time! Delight your family and friends and turn fajita night into a real south-of-the-border celebration!

Rnd 1 (RS): Working in both lps of each sc st, attach black in first sc of last row of place mat, ch 1, sc in each sc across top, ending with 3 sc in corner st, working down left edge, sc in each row across, working through all thicknesses across napkin ring and ending with 3 sc in corner st, working across opposite side of foundation ch, sc in each ch, ending with 3 sc in corner st, working across right edge, sc in each row across, ending with 2 sc in same sc as beg sc, sl st to join in beg sc, fasten off.

Remove safety pins.

Fringe

Fringe is worked in each sc st on each end of place mat only. Wind black yarn several times around cardboard. Cut at both ends to produce 6-inch lengths. Fold 1 strand in half; insert hook from WS to RS and draw yarn through at fold to form a lp on hook. Draw cut ends through lp on hook and pull gently to secure. When completed, trim ends evenly. ✂

Fruit Napkin Rings

Designs by Cynthia See

Gauge

4 dc = 1 inch

Check gauge to save time.

Pattern Notes

Weave in loose ends as work progresses.

Join rnds with a sl st unless otherwise stated.

Cherries Napkin Ring

Rnd 1: With gray, ch 20, join to form a ring, ch 3 (counts as first dc throughout), dc in each ch around, join in 3rd ch of beg ch-3. (20 dc)

Rnds 2 & 3: Ch 3, dc in each dc around, join in 3rd ch of beg ch-3. At the end of Rnd 3, fasten off.

Cherry

Make 2

Rnd 1 (WS): With red, ch 3, join to form a ring, ch 1, 6 sc in ring, join in beg sc. (6 sc)

Rnd 2: Ch 1, 2 sc in each sc around. (12 sc)

Rnds 3 & 4: Ch 1, sc in each sc around, join in beg sc.

Rnds 5 & 6: Ch 1, [sc dec over next 2 sc] rep around, join in beg sc, at the end of Rnd 6, fasten off. (3 sc)

Rnd 7: Attach dark green in top of cherry, ch 7, sc in 2nd ch from hook, sc in each of next 2 chs, ch 7, sl st in top of 2nd cherry, fasten off.

Leaf

Make 2

Rnd 1: With dark green, ch 7, sc in 2nd ch from hook, hdc in next ch, dc in next ch, tr in each of next 2 chs, 4 dc in last ch, working on opposite side of foundation ch, tr in each of next 2 chs, dc in next ch, hdc in next ch, sc in last ch, join in beg sc, fasten off.

Sew leaves to napkin ring, sew sc sts of stem of Rnd 7 centered between leaves.

Grapevine Napkin Ring

Rnds 1–3: With rose, rep Rnds 1–3 of cherries napkin ring. (20 dc)

Leaf

Make 2

Row 1: With dark green, ch 7, sl st in 2nd ch from hook, sk next 2 chs, 3 tr in next ch, tr in next ch, 4 tr in last ch, turn.

Row 2: Ch 1, sl st into 3rd tr, ch 4, sl st in 2nd ch from hook, 2 dc in same tr as ch-4, 1 dc in each of next 2 tr, 3 dc in next tr, turn.

Row 3: Ch 1, sl st into 3rd dc, ch 3, sl st in 2nd ch from hook, hdc in same dc as ch-3, hdc in next st, 2 hdc in next st, turn.

Row 4: Ch 1, sl st in 2nd hdc, ch 4, sl st in 3rd ch from hook, ch 1, sl st in next hdc, fasten off.

Row 5: Attach dark green in center of foundation ch of first leaf, ch 8, sc in 2nd ch from hook, sc in each of next 3 chs, ch 3, sl st in center of opposite side of foundation ch of 2nd leaf, fasten off.

A charming touch to any table setting, these delightful napkin rings are easy to make. Crochet a set for yourself and another set to give as a gift!

Grapes

Row 1: With navy, ch 10, 5 dc in 4th ch from hook, draw up a lp, remove hook, insert hook in top of 10th ch, pick up dropped lp, draw through st on hook, [ch 1, sk 1 ch, 6 dc in next ch, draw up a lp, remove hook, insert hook in first dc of 6-dc group, pick up dropped lp, draw through st on hook] 3 times, turn. (4 pc)

Row 2: Sl st into ch-1 sp, ch 3 (counts as first dc throughout), 5 dc in same ch-1 sp, draw up a lp, remove hook, insert hook in top of beg ch-3, pick up dropped lp, draw through st on hook (beg pc), [ch 1, 6 dc in next ch-1 sp, draw up a lp, remove hook, insert hook in first dc of 6-dc group, pick up dropped lp, draw through st on hook (pc)] twice, turn. (3 pc)

Row 3: Sl st into ch-1 sp, beg pc in same ch-1 sp, ch 1, pc in next ch-1 sp, turn. (2 pc)

Row 4: Sl st into ch-1 sp, beg pc in

same ch-1 sp, fasten off. (1 pc)
Sew leaves and grapes to napkin ring.

Raspberry Napkin Ring

Rnds 1–3: With rose, rep Rnds 1–3 of cherries napkin ring. (20 dc)

Leaf

Make 2

Rows 1–4: Rep Rows 1–4 of leaf for grapevine napkin ring.

Raspberry

Make 2

Rnd 1: With burgundy, ch 3, join to form a ring, ch 3 (counts as first dc throughout), 3 dc in ring, draw up a lp, remove hook, insert hook in top of beg ch-3, pick up dropped lp, draw through st on hook (beg pc), ch 1, [4 dc in ring, draw up a lp, remove hook, insert hook in first dc of 4-dc group, pick up dropped lp, draw through st on hook (pc), ch 1] twice, join in 3rd ch of beg pc. (3 pc)

Rnd 2: Sl st into ch-1 sp, [beg pc, ch 1, pc, ch 1] in same ch-1 sp, [pc, ch 1] twice in each of next 2 ch-1 sps, join in top of beg pc. (6 pc)

Rnd 3: Sl st into ch-1 sp, ch 2 (counts as first hdc), pc in next ch-1 sp, [hdc in next ch-1 sp, pc in next ch-1 sp] twice, join in 2nd ch of beg ch-2, fasten off. (3 pc; 3 hdc)

Rnd 4: Attach dark green in 2nd of beg ch-2 of previous rnd, ch 1, sc in same st, ch 3, sc in 2nd ch from hook, sc in next ch, sc in top of next pc, ch 3, sc in 2nd ch from hook, sc in next ch, [sc in next hdc, ch 3, sc in 2nd ch from hook, sc in next ch, sk next pc] twice, join in beg sc. (4 sc)

Rnd 5: Working in the 4 sc sts worked in previous rnd only, not the sc sts worked across the ch-3 sps, [sc dec over next 2 sc] twice, join in beg sc, fasten off. (2 sc)

Stem

Row 1: Attach dark green to center top of Rnd 5 of first raspberry, ch 7, sc in 2nd ch from hook, sc in each of next 2 chs, ch 7, sl st in top of Rnd 5 of 2nd raspberry, fasten off.

Sew leaves and raspberries to napkin ring. ✂

Rainbow Stripes Table Runner

Design by Shirley Patterson

Skill Level: Beginner

Size: 15 x 18 inches

Materials

- Crochet cotton size 10: 75 yds red, 50 yds each orange, green, purple, dark blue, light blue and goldenrod
- Size 5 steel crochet hook or size needed to obtain gauge
- Tapestry needle

Gauge

Rows 1–4 = 1 inch; 8 sts = 1 inch
Check gauge to save time.

Pattern Notes

Weave in loose ends as work progresses.

Join rnds with a sl st unless otherwise stated.

Pattern Stitches

Picot (p): Ch 3, sl st in top of last st.

3-tr cl: *Yo hook twice, insert hook in indicated st, yo, draw up a lp, [yo, draw through 2 lps on hook] twice, rep from * twice, yo, draw through rem 4 lps on hook.

Beg 3-tr cl: Ch 3 (counts as first tr), *yo hook twice, insert hook in indicated st, yo, draw up a lp, [yo, draw through 2 lps on hook] twice, rep from * once, yo, draw through all 3 lps on hook.

Runner

Row 1: With orange, ch 201, hdc in 2nd ch from hook, hdc in each rem ch across, turn. (200 hdc)

Row 2: Ch 4 (counts as first tr throughout), [sk next st, tr in next st, tr in skipped st] rep across to last st, tr in last st, turn. (200 tr)

Row 3: Ch 1, hdc in each tr across, fasten off, turn.

Row 4: Attach green, ch 1, hdc in each hdc across, turn.

Rows 5 & 6: Rep Rows 2 and 3.

Row 7: With red, rep Row 4.

Rows 8 & 9: Rep Rows 2 and 3.

Row 10: With purple, rep Row 4.

Rows 11 & 12: Rep Rows 2 and 3.

Row 13: With dark blue, rep Row 4.

Rows 14 & 15: Rep Row 2 and 3.

Row 16: With light blue, rep Row 4.

Rows 17 & 18: Rep Rows 2 and 3.

Row 19: With goldenrod, rep Row 4.

Rows 20 & 21: Rep Rows 2 and 3.

Row 22: With orange, rep Row 4.

Rows 23–43: Rep Rows 2–22.

Rows 44–54: Rep Rows 2–12.

Border

Rnd 1: Attach red in first st of previous row, ch 1, 3 sc in same st (for corner), sc across edge to last st, 3 sc in last st (for corner), sc evenly sp down side edge, working across opposite side of foundation ch, 3 sc in first ch, sc in each rem ch across edge to last ch, 3 sc in last ch, sc evenly sp across last edge, join in beg sc.

Rnd 2: Ch 1, †*sc in first sc of 3-sc corner group, ch 3, sk next sc, sc in 3rd sc of corner *, [ch 5, sk 3 or 4 sc sts, sc in next st] rep across edge to have 40 ch-5 sps across edge, rep from * to * (for corner), [ch 5, sk 3 or 4 sc sts, sc in next st] rep across edge to have 18 ch-5 sps across edge, rep from † around, join in beg sc.

Made with scraps of leftover thread in a rainbow of colors, this colorful table runner is fun to crochet and even more fun to use!

Rnd 3: Sl st into corner ch-3 sp, ch 9 (counts as first tr, ch-5), tr in same corner ch sp, ch 7, [sc in next ch sp, ch 7] rep across edge, *[tr, ch 5, tr] in corner ch-3 sp, ch 7, [sc in next ch sp, ch 7] rep across edge, rep from * around, join in 4th ch of beg ch-9.

Rnd 4: Sl st into corner ch-5 sp, beg 3-tr cl in corner sp, *[{ch 2, 3-tr cl} 5 times] in same corner ch-5 sp, sc in next ch sp, p, [ch 7, sc in next ch sp, p] rep across edge to next corner ch-5 sp **, 3-tr cl in next corner ch-5 sp, rep from * around, ending last rep at **, join in top of beg 3-tr cl.

Rnd 5: Sl st into ch-2 sp, *sc p in ch-2 sp, ch 3, [sc in next ch-2 sp, p, ch 3] 4 times, [ch 7, sc in next ch sp, p] rep across edge to last ch sp before corner, ch 3, rep from * around, join in beg sc, fasten off. ✂

Coaster Crazy

Designs by Rose Pirrone

Protect your furniture by serving up your favorite beverages on these delightful coasters. In an array of styles and sizes, you can crochet a truly unique plaid coaster or any of the others in a variety of colors!

Gauge

5 dc = ½ inch; 2 dc rnds = ½ inch

Check gauge to save time.

Pattern Notes

Weave in loose ends as work progresses.

Join rnds with a sl st unless otherwise stated.

Ch-3 counts as first dc throughout.

Pattern Stitches

5-dc cl: [Yo hook, insert hook in indicated st, yo, draw up a lp, yo, draw through 2 lps on hook] 5 times, yo, draw through all 6 lps on hook.

Beg 5-dc cl: Ch 2 (counts as first dc), [yo, insert hook in indicated st, yo, draw up a lp, yo, draw through 2 lps on hook] 4 times, yo, draw through all 5 lps on hook.

2-dc cl: [Yo hook, insert hook in indicated st, yo, draw up a lp, yo, draw through 2 lps on hook] twice, yo, draw through all 3 lps on hook.

Seven-sided Coaster

Rnd 1: With MC, ch 6, join to form a ring, ch 1, 12 sc in ring, join in beg sc. (12 sc)

Rnd 2: Ch 1, sc in same st as beg ch-1, [ch 7, sk 1 sc, sc in next sc] 5 times, ch 3, dc in beg sc to form last sp. (6 ch sps)

Rnd 3: Ch 3, 4 dc in same sp, ch 3, [5 dc in next ch-7 sp, ch 3] rep around, join in 3rd ch of beg ch-3. (30 dc)

Rnd 4: Ch 3, dc in each of next 4 dc, ch 3, sc in next ch-3 sp, ch 3, [dc in each of next 5 dc, ch 3, sc in next ch-3 sp, ch 3] rep around, join in 3rd ch of beg ch-3.

Rnd 5: Beg 5-dc cl over next 5 dc, *ch 5, sc in next ch-3 sp, ch 5, sc in next ch-3 sp **, ch 5, 5-dc cl over next 5 dc, rep from * around, ending last rep at **, ch 2, dc in top of beg cl.

Rnd 6: Ch 1, sc in same ch sp, [ch 5, sc in next ch-5 sp] rep around, ending with ch 2, dc in beg sc. (18 ch sps)

Rnd 7: Ch 1, sc in same ch sp, *ch 3, [4 dc, ch 2, 4 dc] in next ch-5 sp, ch 3, sc in next ch-5 sp, ch 3 **, sc in next ch-5 sp, rep from * around, ending last rep at **, join in beg sc, fasten off.

Rnd 8: Attach A in first ch-3 sp of previous rnd, ch 1, 3 sc in same ch-3 sp, *sc in each of next 4 dc, 3 sc in ch-2 sp, sc in each of next 4 dc **, 3 sc in each of next 3 ch-3 sps, rep from * around, ending last rep at **, 3 sc in each of next 2 ch-3 sps, join in back lp only of beg sc.

Rnd 9: Ch 1, working in back lps

only, sc in each st around, join in beg sc, fasten off.

Octagonal Coaster

Rnd 1: With MC, ch 6, join to form a ring, ch 3, 15 dc in ring, join in 3rd ch of beg ch-3. (16 dc)

Rnd 2: Ch 1, sc in same st as beg ch-1, *ch 4, 2-dc cl in 4th ch from hook, ch 5, 2-dc cl in 4th ch from hook, ch 1, sk 1 dc **, sc in next dc, rep from * around, join in beg sc, fasten off.

Rnd 3: Attach A in ch-1 sp between first 2 cls, ch 1, sc in same sp, ch 7, [sc in ch-1 sp between next 2 cls, ch 7] rep around, join in beg sc.

Rnd 4: Ch 1, [sc in sc, 9 sc in next ch-7 sp] rep around, join in back lp only of beg sc. (80 sc)

Rnd 5: Working in back lps only, ch 3, dc in each of next 4 sts, [3 dc in next st, dc in each of next 9 sts] rep around, ending with dc in

each of last 4 sts, join in 3rd ch of beg ch-3.

Rnd 6: Working in back lps only this rnd, ch 3, dc in each st around, working 3 dc in center dc of each 3-dc group, join in 3rd ch of beg ch-3.

Rnd 7: Attach MC to center dc of any 3-dc group, ch 1, sc in same center dc, ch 3, sk 1 st, [sc in next st, ch 3, sk 1 st] rep around, join in beg sc, fasten off.

Plaid Coaster

Rnd 1 (RS): With MC, ch 7, join to form a ring, ch 3, 15 dc in ring, join in 3rd ch of beg ch-3. (16 dc)

Rnd 2 (RS): Ch 3, 2 dc in same st, [hdc in each of next 3 sts, 5 dc in next st] 3 times, hdc in each of next 3 sts, 2 dc in same st as beg ch-3, join in 3rd ch of beg ch-3.

Rnd 3 (RS): Ch 8 (counts as first dc, ch-5), dc in same st as beg ch-8, *[ch 1, sk 1 st, dc in next st] 3 times, ch 1,

sk 1 st **,
[dc, ch 5, dc] in
next st, rep from * around, ending last rep at **, join in 3rd ch of beg ch-8, turn. (4 ch-5 sps; 16 ch-1 sps)

Rnd 4 (WS): Ch 3, *[dc in next ch-1 sp, dc in next dc] 4 times, ch 2, 5 dc in 3rd ch of next ch-5 sp, ch 2, dc in next dc, rep from * around, ending with ch 2, join in 3rd ch of beg ch-3, fasten off, turn.

Rnd 5 (RS): Attach A to center dc of any 5-dc corner group, ch 3, 2 dc in same st, *dc in each of next 2 dc,

Continued on page 27

Floral Coaster Set

Designs by Lillian Gimmelli

Skill Level: Beginner

Size

Centerpiece: 8½ inches in diameter, excluding leaves

Coaster: 3¼ inches in diameter, excluding leaves

Materials

- DMC pearl crochet cotton size 8: 10 grams each very light shell pink #224 (A), rose #335 (B), salmon #760 (C)
- DMC Cébélia crochet cotton size 20: 10 grams light aquamarine #992 (D)
- Size 10 steel crochet hook or size needed to obtain gauge
- Tapestry needle

Gauge

7 dc = 1 inch

Check gauge to save time.

Pattern Notes

Weave in loose ends as work progresses.

Join rnds with a sl st unless otherwise stated.

Ch-3 counts as first dc throughout.

Centerpiece Motif

Note: Make 6 each A and B, and 1 C.

Rnd 1 (RS): With motif color, ch 7, join to form a ring, ch 3, 24 dc in ring, join in 3rd ch of beg ch-3. (25 dc)

Rnd 2: Ch 3, dc in same st as beg ch-3, [dc in next dc, 2 dc in next dc] rep around, join in 3rd ch of beg ch-3. (38 dc)

Rnd 3: Ch 8, sk next 2 dc, [sc in next dc, ch 8, sk next 2 dc] rep around, join in first ch of beg ch-8. (13 ch-8 lps)

Rnd 4: Sl st into center of ch-8 sp, ch 1, sc in same sp, ch 8, [sc in next ch-8 sp, ch 8] rep around, join in beg sc.

Rnds 5 & 6: Rep Rnd 4.

Rnd 7: Ch 1, 8 hdc over each ch-8 sp, join in first hdc, fasten off. (112 hdc)

Using photo as a guide, sew 7 motifs tog to form a circle with C at center, alternating A and B around outer edge of C.

Rem 6 motifs are for coasters.

Leaf

Make 36 half leaves

Row 1: With D, ch 4, 3 hdc in 4th ch from hook, turn. (4 hdc)

Row 2: Ch 2 (does not count as a hdc st throughout), 2 hdc in first st, hdc in each of next 2 hdc, 2 hdc in last hdc, turn. (6 hdc)

Rows 3–7: Ch 2, 2 hdc in first hdc, hdc in each rem hdc across to last hdc, 2 hdc in last hdc, turn. (16 hdc)

At the end of Row 7, fasten off.

Sew 2 half leaves tog across Row 7 to form a complete leaf.

Using photo as a guide, sew 2 sets of 3 leaves on side edge of centerpiece. Sew 2 leaves to each coaster. ✄

A bright arrangement of motifs creates a floral centerpiece with matching floral coasters perfect for time visiting with friends!

Ode to a Crochet Designer

By Shirley Patterson

Creativity is the plan,
Reaching for thread with hook in hand.
Ovals and squares come into mind,
Cubes and oblongs to design.
Hoping each project will turn out fine.
Even House of White Birches thinks it's divine.
Thus nothing so time-consuming,
As having to watch for the mailman coming.
Open the envelope, take a look.
Oh! Send your design, we want it for our book!
Knowing the thrill that comes from this sale.
Start more projects, wait for the mail!

Dainty Floral Coasters

Designs by Gloria Graham

Skill Level: Beginner

Size: 5½ inches in diameter

Materials

- Worsted weight 4-ply cotton yarn: 10 yds ivory, 12 yds each pink, peach, yellow and light blue, 30 yds light green
- Size G/6 crochet hook or size needed to obtain gauge
- Tapestry needle

Gauge

Rnds 1 and 2 = 1¼ inches

Check gauge to save time.

Pattern Notes

Weave in loose ends as work progresses.

Join rnds with a sl st unless otherwise stated.

Materials listed will make a set of 4 coasters.

Center

Rnd 1 (RS): With ivory ch 5, sl st to join to form a ring, ch 1, 6 sc in ring, join in beg sc. (6 sc)

Rnd 2: Ch 1, 2 sc in each sc around, join in beg sc, fasten off. (12 sc)

Flower petals

Note: Make 1 each pink, peach, yellow and light blue.

Rnd 3: Attach flower color, ch 1, sc in same sc as beg ch-1, ch 2, [sc in next sc, ch 2] rep around, join in beg sc. (12 ch-2 sps)

Rnd 4: Sl st into ch-2 sp, ch 1, sc in same ch-2 sp, 5 dc in next ch-2 sp, [sc in next ch-2 sp, 5 dc in next ch-2 sp] rep around, join in beg sc, fasten off. (6 petals)

Rnd 5: Ch 1, beg in same sc as beg ch-1, [sc in next sc, hdc in next dc, dc in next dc, 3 dc in next dc, dc in next dc, hdc in next dc] rep around, join in beg sc, fasten off. (48 sts)

Leaf Trim

Rnd 6: Working in back lps only, attach light green with a sl st in center dc of 3-dc group of previous rnd, *hdc in next dc, dc in next dc, 2 tr in next hdc, ch 2, sl st in top of last tr, sk next sc, 2 tr in next hdc, dc in next dc, hdc in next dc **, sl st in next dc, rep from * around, ending last rep at **, join in same dc as beg sl st, fasten off. ✄

Crochet these pretty coasters in a variety of floral colors for yourself or someone you love!

Floral Tissue Box Cover

Design by Margaret Nobles

Skill Level: Beginner

Size: 4½ x 4½ x 5½ inches; fits boutique-style tissue box

Materials

- Baby sport weight yarn: 2 oz each lime green, turquoise and multicolor
- Size H/8 crochet hook or size needed to obtain gauge
- Yarn needle

Gauge

Motif = 1¼ inches square; 4 sc = 1 inch

Check gauge to save time.

Pattern Notes

Weave in loose ends as work progresses.

Join rnds with a sl st unless otherwise stated.

Pattern Stitches

Beg pc: Ch 3, 4 dc in same st, remove hook, insert hook in top of beg ch-3, pick up dropped lp and draw through st on hook.

Popcorn (pc): 5 dc in indicated st, remove hook, insert hook in first dc of 5-dc group, pick up dropped lp and draw through st on hook.

Shell: [2 dc, ch 2, 2 dc] in indicated st.

Motif

Note: Make 12 with lime green and 12 with turquoise centers.

Rnd 1 (RS): With lime green or (turquoise), ch 5, sl st to join to form a ring, beg pc in ring, ch 2, [pc in ring, ch 2] 3 times, join in top of beg pc, fasten off. (4 pc; 4 ch-2 sps)

Rnd 2 (RS): Attach multicolor in any ch-2 sp, ch 3 (counts as first dc throughout), dc in same sp, ch 1, *shell in top of next pc, ch 1 **, 2 dc in next ch-2 sp, rep from * around, ending last rep at **, join in 3rd ch of beg ch-3, fasten off.

Top Section

Note: Make 1 each lime green and turquoise.

Row 1: Ch 17, sc in 2nd ch from hook, sc in each rem ch across, turn. (16 sc)

Row 2–8: Ch 1, sc in each sc across, turn. (16 sc)

Row 9: Ch 1, sc in each of next 4 sc, turn.

Row 10: Ch 1, sc in each of next 4 sc, fasten off.

Finishing

With yarn needle and multicolor yarn, st motifs tog, alternating center colors and making 3 rows of 8 blocks each. Sew ends tog to form sides.

Holding Row 10 of first top section to Row 8 of 2nd top section, sew across the 4 sts. Sew opposite edge in same manner, leaving opening for the tissues at center.

Matching corners of top to motifs, sew top to sides.

Attach multicolor to bottom edge of sides, ch 1, sc evenly sp around bottom edge, join in beg sc, fasten off.

Attach multicolor to top edge at joining of top and sides, ch 1, reverse sc evenly sp around top, join in beg reverse sc, fasten off.

Attach multicolor at edge of opening, ch 1, reverse sc evenly sp around, join in beg reverse sc, fasten off. Place cover over tissue box. ✂

Have fun with color combinations or select colors to match your decor. Crochet just one or one for every room!

Blue Skies Pot Holder

Design by Rose Pirrone

Skill Level: Beginner

Size: 8 x 8½ inches

Materials

- Worsted weight 4-ply cotton: 2 oz dark blue, ½ oz each yellow and off-white
- Size G/6 crochet hook or size needed to obtain gauge
- Tapestry needle

Gauge

7 sc = 1 inch
Check gauge to save time.

Pattern Note

Weave in loose ends as work progresses.

Pattern Stitch

Long sc: [Insert hook in indicated st, yo, draw up a lp level with working row, yo, draw through both lps on hook] 3 times in same st.

Pot Holder

Row 1: With dark blue, ch 31, sc in 2nd ch from hook, sc in each rem ch across, turn. (30 sc)

Row 2: Ch 1, sc in each sc across, turn.

Row 3: Ch 1, sc in each sc across, drop dark blue, do not fasten off, do not turn.

Row 4 (RS): Attach yellow in 2nd sc at beg of previous row, [long sc in corresponding sc of row below, sk next 2 sc] 10 times, fasten off.

Row 5: Pick up dropped lp of dark blue, ch 1, sk first dark blue sc of previous sc row, sc in each of next 29 yellow sc, sk next yellow sc, sc in last blue sc, turn.

Rows 6 & 7: Ch 1, sc in each sc across, turn.

Row 8: Rep Row 3.

Row 9: With off-white, rep Row 4.

Rows 10–13: Rep Rows 5–8.
[Rep Rows 4–13] twice.
[Rep Rows 4–10] once.

Fluffy white clouds against a sun-filled blue sky are reflected in this delightful pot holder!

Border

Rnd 1: Attach dark blue in any st away from corner, ch 1, sc evenly sp around outer edge, working 3 corners with 2 sc and 4th corner with [sc, ch 12, sl st in first ch of ch-12, sc] in corner st, sl st to join in beg sc, fasten off. ✂

Floral Hot Pad

Design by Michele Wilcox

Skill Level: Beginner

Size: 10½ inches

Materials

- Elmore-Pisgah Peaches & Crème worsted weight cotton yarn (2.5 oz per ball): 1 skein white #1, 1 oz each cream #3, persimmon #33 and apple green #51

- Size K/10½ crochet hook or size needed to obtain gauge

- Tapestry needle

Turn a basket of scraps into a pretty and practical hot pad! Use it at home, or give it as a sure-to-be-appreciated hostess gift!

Gauge

Rnds 1 and 2 of hot pad = 4 inches; 2 sc rnds = 1 inch
Check gauge to save time.

Pattern Notes

Weave in loose ends as work progresses.

Join rnds with a sl st unless otherwise stated.

Hot Pad

Rnd 1: With white, ch 5, join to form a ring, ch 3 (counts as first dc throughout), 11 dc in ring, join in 3rd ch of beg ch-3. (12 dc)

Rnd 2: Ch 3, dc in same st as beg ch-3, 2 dc in each dc around, join in 3rd ch of beg ch-3. (24 dc)

Rnd 3: Ch 3, 2 dc in next dc, [dc in next dc, 2 dc in next dc] rep around, join in 3rd ch of beg ch-3. (36 dc)

Rnd 4: Ch 1, sc in same st as beg ch-1, sc in each of next 4 dc, 2 sc in next dc, [sc in each of next 5 dc, 2 sc in next dc] rep around, join in beg sc. (42 sc)

Rnd 5: Ch 1, sc in same st as beg ch-1, sc in each of next 5 sc, 2 sc in next sc, [sc in each of next 6 sc, 2 sc in next sc] rep around, join in beg sc. (48 sc)

Rnd 6: Ch 1, sc in same sc as beg ch-1, sc in each of next 6 sc, 2 sc in next sc, [sc in each of next 7 sc, 2 sc in next sc] rep around, join in beg sc. (54 sc)

Rnd 7: Ch 1, sc in same sc as beg ch-1, sc in each of next 7 sc, 2 sc in next sc, [sc in each of next 8 sc, 2 sc in next sc] rep around, join in beg sc. (60 sc)

Rnd 8: Ch 1, sc in same sc as beg ch-1, ch 3, sk 1 sc, [sc in next sc, ch 3, sk 1 sc] rep around, join in beg sc.

Rnd 9: Ch 1, [4 sc in next ch-3 sp] rep around, join in beg sc, fasten off.

Leaf

Make 6

Rnd 1: With apple green, ch 5, sc in 2nd ch from hook, hdc in each of next 2 chs, 5 hdc in last ch, working on opposite side of foundation ch,

Continued on page 31

Christmas Star Hot Pad

Design by Connie Folse

Gauge

5 dc rnds = 3 inches; 3 sc rnds = 1 inch

Check gauge to save time.

Pattern Notes

Weave in loose ends as work progresses.

Join each rnd with a sl st unless otherwise stated.

Ch-3 counts as first dc throughout.

Front

Rnd 1 (RS): With white, ch 2, 6 sc in 2nd ch from hook, join in beg sc. (6 sc)

Rnd 2: Ch 1, 2 sc in each sc around, join in beg sc. (12 sc)

Rnd 3: Ch 1, [sc in next sc, 2 sc in next sc] rep around, join in beg sc. (18 sc)

Rnd 4: Ch 1, [sc in each of next 2 sc, 2 sc in next sc] rep around, join in beg sc. (24 sc)

Rnd 5: Ch 1, [sc in next sc, ch 10, sk next 3 sc] rep around, join in beg sc. (6 sc; 6 ch-10 sps)

Serve up your holiday favorites on this festive hot pad!

Rnd 6: Ch 1, [sk sc, work 12 sc over ch-10 sp] rep around, join in beg sc. (72 sc)

Rnd 7: Sl st in next 5 sc, ch 3, 2 dc in next sc, 3 dc in next sc, ch 8, [3 dc in 6th sc of next 12-sc group, 3 dc in next sc, ch 8] rep around, join in 3rd ch of beg ch-3.

Rnd 8: Ch 1, sc in each of next 6 dc, 8 sc over ch-8 sp] rep around, join in beg sc, fasten off. (84 sc)

Rnd 9: Attach red in first sc of previous rnd, ch 1, sc in each sc around, join in beg sc, fasten off. (84 sc)

Rnd 10 (RS): Attach green in first sc of previous rnd, ch 1, [sc in each of next 6 sc, 2 sc in next sc] rep around, join in beg sc, fasten off, turn. (96 sc)

Rnd 11 (WS): Attach red in first sc of previous rnd, ch 1, sc in same sc, tr in next sc, [sc in next sc, tr in

next sc] rep around, join in beg sc, fasten off.

Back

Rnds 1–4: With green, rep Rnds 1–4 of front. (24 sc)

Rnd 5 (RS): Ch 3, dc in each of next 2 sc, 2 dc in next sc, [dc in each of next 3 sc, 2 dc in next sc] rep around, join in 3rd ch of beg ch-3. (30 dc)

Rnd 6: Ch 3, dc in each of next 3 dc, 2 dc in next dc, [dc in each of next 4 dc, 2 dc in next dc] rep around, join in 3rd ch of beg ch-3. (36 dc)

Rnd 7: Ch 3, dc in next dc, 2 dc in next dc, [dc in each of next 2 dc, 2 dc in next dc] rep around, join in 3rd ch of beg ch-3. (48 dc)

Rnd 8: Ch 3, dc in each of next 2 dc, 2 dc in next dc, [dc in each of next 3 dc, 2 dc in next dc] rep around, join in 3rd ch of beg

ch-3. (60 dc)

Rnd 9: Ch 3, dc in each of next 3 dc, 2 dc in next dc, [dc in each of next 4 dc, 2 dc in next dc] rep around, join in 3rd ch of beg ch-3. (72 dc)

Rnd 10: Ch 3, dc in each of next 4 dc, 2 dc in next dc, [dc in each of next 5 dc, 2 dc in next dc] rep around, join in 3rd ch of beg ch-3. (84 dc)

Rnd 11: Ch 3, dc in each of next 5 dc, 2 dc in next dc, [dc in each of next 6 dc, 2 dc in next dc] rep around, join in 3rd ch of beg ch-3. (96 dc)

Rnd 12: Holding both pieces with WS tog, matching sts and working through both thicknesses, ch 1, sc in each st around, join in beg sc, ch 8 (for hanger), sl st in same st as joining st, fasten off. ✄

Coaster Crazy

Continued from page 19

ch 2, dc in each of next 9 dc, ch 2, dc in each of next 2 dc **, 5 dc in next dc, rep from * around, ending last rep at **, 2 dc in same st as beg ch-3, join in 3rd ch of beg ch-3, turn.

Rnd 6 (WS): Ch 3, 3 dc in same st, *dc in each of next 4 dc, ch 2, dc in each of next 9 dc, ch 2, dc in each of next 4 dc **, 7 dc in next center corner st, rep from * around, ending last rep at **, 3 dc in same st as beg ch-3, join in 3rd ch of beg ch-3, fasten off, turn.

Rnd 7 (RS): Attach MC in center dc of any corner 7-dc group, ch 1, 2 sc in same st as beg ch-1, sc in each rem dc around, working 2 sc in each ch-2 sp and 3 sc in center sc of each corner 3-sc group around, ending with sc in same st as beg 2-sc, join in beg sc.

Rnd 8: Ch 1, working in back lps

only, 2 sc in same st as beg ch-1, sc in each rem st around, working 3 sc in center sc of each corner 3-sc group, ending with sc in same corner as beg 2-sc, join in beg sc, fasten off.

Weaving

Thread needle with 3 strands of B each 12 inches in length. Leaving same length at each end, weave through first row of open sps on 1 side of coaster beg under first bar. Cut thread.

Thread needle with another 3 strands of B, weave through the same row of sps beg over first bar.

Cut 4 strands of B each 7 inches in length, draw through first sp at end of same row of open sps and pull ends even.

To form tassel, gather all strands tog; tie an overhand knot close to edge, pulling each strand separately

to tighten knot. Cut ends of thread to ¾ inch from knot.

Rep tassel on opposite end of same row.

Weave through each of the rem 3 rows of sps in same manner, attaching a tassel at each end of weave. ✄

Ladybug Hot Pad

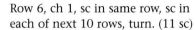

Design by Michele Wilcox

Skill Level: Beginner

Size: 8¾ x 10 inches

Materials

- Elmore-Pisgah Peaches & Crème worsted weight cotton yarn: 1½ balls red #95, ½ ball black #2
- Size K/10½ crochet hook or size needed to obtain gauge
- Tapestry needle

Gauge

5 sc = 2 inches
Check gauge to save time.

Pattern Notes

Weave in loose ends as work progresses.

Join rnds with a sl st unless otherwise stated.

Front

Body

Row 1: With red, ch 11, sc in 2nd ch from hook, sc in each rem ch across, turn. (10 sc)

Rows 2–5: Ch 1, 2 sc in first sc, sc in each sc across to last sc, 2 sc in last sc, turn. (18 sc)

Row 6: Ch 1, sc in each sc across, turn.

Rows 7–10: Rep Row 6. At the end of Row 10, fasten off.

Row 11: Attach black, ch 1, sc in each sc across, fasten off, turn.

Row 12: Attach red, ch 1, sc in each sc across, turn. (18 sc)

Rows 13–16: Rep Row 6.

Rows 17–20: Ch 1, sc dec over next 2 sc, sc in each sc across to last 2 sc, sc dec over next 2 sc, turn. (10 sc)

Row 21: Rep Row 6, fasten off.

Head

Row 1: Attach black in side edge of Row 6, ch 1, sc in same row, sc in each of next 10 rows, turn. (11 sc)

Rows 2–5: Ch 1, sc dec over next 2 sc, sc in each sc across to last 2 sc, sc dec over next 2 sc, turn. (3 sc)

Trim

Rnd 1: Working around outer edge, sc evenly sp around, changing color as needed, join in beg sc, fasten off.

Give your table a touch of whimsy! This charming little lady will be good company at any meal!

Spot

Make 6

Rnd 1: With black, ch 2, 6 sc in 2nd ch from hook, join in beg sc, fasten off.

Sew 3 spots on each side of front body.

Back

Body

Rows 1–5: Rep Rows 1–5 of front body. (18 sc)

Row 6: Ch 1, sc in each sc across, turn.

Rows 7–16: Rep Row 6.

Rows 17–21: Rep Rows 17–21 of front body.

Head

Rows 1–5: Rep Rows 1–5 of front head.

Trim

Rnd 1: Rep Rnd 1 of front trim.

Finishing

Holding front and back WS tog and working through both thicknesses, attach red, ch 1, sc evenly sp around, changing to black around head, join in beg sc, fasten off. ✂

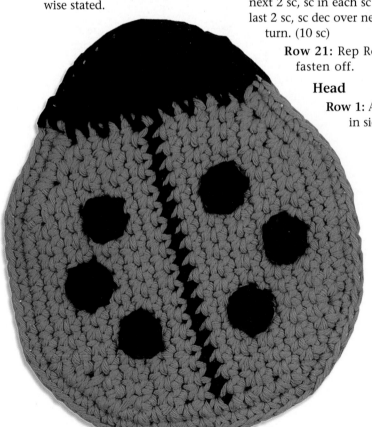

Cherry Jubilee Dish Towel

Design by Rose Pirrone

Add a cheery touch to your kitchen with this vibrant cherry-motif dish towel!

Gauge

Leaf = 1¼ inches long; Rnds 1–4 of cherry = 1 inch

Check gauge to save time.

Pattern Notes

Weave in loose ends as work progresses.

Join rnds with a sl st unless otherwise stated.

Cherry

Make 3

Rnd 1: With red, ch 2, 7 sc in 2nd ch from hook, join in beg sc. (7 sc)

Rnd 2: Ch 1, 3 sc in first sc, [sc, hdc] in next sc, 2 dc in each of next 3 sc, [hdc, sc] in next sc, 3 sc in next sc, do not join, turn. (16 sts)

Rnd 3: Ch 1, [sc in next st, 2 sc in next st] rep around, turn. (24 sc)

Rnd 4: Ch 1, sc in each sc around, sc in base of Rnd 2 to close the gap, sl st in first sc, fasten off.

Stem

Make 3

Row 1: Attach green to top of cherry, ch 18, sl st in 2nd ch from hook, sl st in each rem ch across, sl st in top of cherry, fasten off.

Leaf

Make 3

Rnd 1: With green, ch 12, sc in 2nd ch from hook, sc in next ch, hdc in next ch, dc in each of next 5 chs, hdc in next ch, sc in each of next 2 chs, ch 2, sl st in 2nd ch from hook, working on opposite side of foundation ch, sc in each of next 2 chs, hdc in next ch, dc in each of next 5 chs, hdc in next ch, sc in each of next 2 chs, join in beg sc, fasten off.

Finishing

Using photo as a guide, sew cherries with stems and leaves to towel.

With embroidery needle and red, embroider blanket st along bottom edge of towel with sts approximately ⅜ inch apart. ✄

Delightful Dishcloths

Designs by Michele Wilcox

Variegated Cotton Dishcloth

Skill Level: Beginner

Size: 12½ x 13½ inches

Materials

- Elmore-Pisgah Peaches & Crème worsted weight cotton yarn: 1½ balls potpourri ombre #178, ½ ball ecru #4

- Size G/6 crochet hook or size needed to obtain gauge

- Tapestry needle

Gauge

4 rows = 3 inches
Check gauge to save time.

Pattern Note

Weave in loose ends as work progresses.

Dishcloth

Row 1: With potpourri ombre, ch 30, 2 dc in 4th ch from hook, [sk 1 ch, 2 dc in next ch] rep across to last 2 chs, sk 1 ch, dc in last ch, turn. (28 dc)

Rows 2–15: Ch 3 (counts as first dc throughout), [2 dc in sp between next 2-dc groups] 13 times, dc in top of turning ch, turn. (28 dc)

At the end of Row 15, fasten off.

Edging

Rnd 1: Attach ecru in any corner st, ch 1, *[sc, ch 2, sc] in corner st, work 26 sc across edge, rep from * around, join in beg sc.

Rnd 2: Sl st into corner ch-2 sp, *[ch 4, sl st in 3rd ch from hook, sc] in corner ch-2 sp, [ch 3, sk next sc, sc in next sc] rep across to next corner ch-2 sp, sl st in corner ch-2 sp, rep from * around, fasten off.

Sunny Days Dishcloth

Skill Level: Beginner

Size: 12 inches square

Materials

- Elmore-Pisgah Peaches & Crème worsted weight cotton yarn: 1½ oz yellow #10, 1 oz each cream #3 and sunburst #11

- Size G/6 crochet hook or size needed to obtain gauge.

- Tapestry needle

Gauge

4 dc rnds = 3 inches
Check gauge to save time.

Pattern Notes

Weave in loose ends as work progresses.

Sl st to join each rnd in 3rd ch of beg ch-3.

Dishcloth

Rnd 1 (RS): With yellow, ch 4, sl st to join to form a ring, ch 3 (counts as first dc throughout), 2 dc in ring, ch 2, [3 dc in ring, ch 2] 3 times, join, fasten off.

Rnd 2: Attach cream in any corner ch-2 sp, [ch 3, 2 dc, ch 2, 3 dc] in same corner sp, ch 1, [{3 dc, ch 2, 3 dc} in next corner ch-2 sp, ch 1] rep around, join, fasten off.

Rnd 3: Attach sunburst in any corner ch-2 sp, [ch 3, 2 dc, ch 2, 3 dc] in same corner sp, *ch 1, 3 dc in next ch-1 sp, ch 1 **, [3 dc, ch 2, 3 dc] in next corner ch-2 sp, rep from * around, ending last rep at **, join, fasten off.

Note: *For Rnds 4–10 maintain the same color sequence.*

Rnds 4–10: Attach yarn in corner ch-2 sp, [ch 3, 2 dc, ch 2, 3 dc] in corner sp, *ch 1, [3 dc in next ch-1 sp, ch 1] rep across to next corner ch-2 sp **, [3 dc, ch 2, 3 dc] in corner ch-2 sp, rep from * around, ending last rep at **, join, fasten off; at the end of Rnd 10, do not fasten off.

Rnd 11: Sl st into corner ch-2 sp, ch 1, *[hdc, 3 dc, ch 2, sc in 2nd ch from hook, 3 dc, hdc] in corner ch-2 sp, sk next dc, sk next dc, sc in each of next 2 dc, [{hdc, dc, ch 2, sc in 2nd ch from hook, dc, hdc} in next ch-1 sp, sk next dc, sc in each of next 2 dc] rep across to next corner ch-2 sp, rep from * around, join in beg hdc, fasten off. ✂

You can never have enough dishcloths! Each is pretty enough to make the job more enjoyable and sturdy enough to hold up to the task!

Floral Hot Pad

Continued from page 25

hdc in each of next 2 chs, sc in next ch, join in beg sc, fasten off.

Flower

Rnd 1: With cream, ch 2, 6 sc in 2nd ch from hook, join in beg sc. (6 sc)

Rnd 2: Ch 1, 2 sc in each sc around, join in beg sc. (12 sc)

Rnd 3: Ch 1, [sc in next sc, 2 sc in next sc] rep around, join in beg sc. (18 sc)

Rnd 4: Ch 1, [sc in each of next 2 sc, 2 sc in next sc] rep around, join in beg sc, fasten off. (24 sc)

Row 5: Attach persimmon in next sc of Rnd 4, ch 1, sc in same sc as beg ch-1, sc in each of next 3 sc, turn. (4 sc)

Row 6: Ch 1, sc in each of next 4 sc, turn.

Row 7: Ch 1, [sc dec over next 2 sc] twice, fasten off.

[Rep Rows 5–7] 5 times. (6 petals)

Rnd 8: Attach persimmon in first sc of any Row 7 of petals, ch 1, 2 sc in each of next 2 sc at top of petal, sc evenly sp around petal, working sl st between each petal and 2 sc in each of 2 sc at top of each petal, join in beg sc, fasten off.

Sew flower centered to hot pad. Sew a leaf to hot pad between each petal. ✂

Foot-Warming Rugs

Add a designer touch to your home while warming the toes of those you love! This collection of rugs will appeal to all personalities and styles. They're quick and fun to stitch, too—the perfect project for beginning or experienced crocheters!

American Pride Rug

Design by Janet Rehfeldt

Gauge

4 rows = 1 inch
Check gauge to save time.

Pattern Notes

Weave in loose ends as work progresses.

Join rnds with a sl st unless otherwise stated.

Rug

Row 1 (WS): With larger hook and MC, ch 68, working in bottom lp of ch, sl st in 2nd ch from hook, [dc in next ch, sl st in next ch] rep across, turn. (67 sts)

Row 2 (RS): Ch 1, sc in first sl st, [sl st in next dc, sc in next sl st] rep across, turn.

Row 3: Ch 1, sl st in first sc, [sl st in next st, dc in next st] rep across to last 2 sts, sl st in last 2 sts, turn.

Row 4: Ch 1, sc in first sl st, [sc in next sl st, sl st in next dc] rep across to last 2 sts, sc in last 2 sl sts, changing to B in last st, turn.

Row 5: Ch 1, sl st in first sl st, [dc in next st, sl st in next st] rep across, turn.

Row 6: Ch 1, sc in first sl st, [sl st in next dc, sc in next sl st] rep across, turn.

Row 7: Ch 1, sl st in first sc, [sl st in next st, dc in next st] rep across to last 2 sts, sl st in last 2 sts, turn.

Row 8: Ch 1, sc in first sl st, [sc in next sl st, sl st in next dc] rep across to last 2 sts, sc in last 2 sl sts, changing color in last st to the next color in the color sequence, turn.

Not the normal striped pattern, this rotating sequence of colors gives this patriotic rug a truly unique look!

Rep Rows 5–8 for established pattern st, changing color every 4 rows using the following color sequence: [4 rows each of A, B, MC, A, MC, B] 4 times. [4 rows each of A, B and MC] once.

Edging

Rnd 1 (RS): With smaller hook, attach B, ch 1, sc evenly sp around outer edge, working 3 sc in each corner st, join in beg sc.

Rnd 2 (RS): Ch 1, reverse sc in each sc around, working 2 reverse sc sts in each center corner sc, join in beg reverse sc, fasten off.

Block rug to size. ✂

American Flag Rug

Design by Michele Wilcox

Skill Level: Beginner

Size: 17 x 25½ inches

Materials

- Elmore-Pisgah Peaches & Crème worsted weight cotton yarn (2½ oz per ball): 2 balls each red #95, delft blue #28 and white #1, 3 oz yellow #10
- Size K/10½ crochet hook or size needed to obtain gauge
- Size F/5 crochet hook
- Tapestry needle

Gauge

Star = 2 inches in diameter; 3 cl sts = 3½ inches

Check gauge to save time.

Pattern Notes

Weave in loose ends as work progresses.

Join rnds with a sl st unless otherwise stated.

Pattern Stitch

Cl st: [Sc, hdc, dc] in indicated st.

Rug

Row 1: With larger hook and 2 strands of red held tog, ch 63, [hdc, dc] in 3rd ch from hook, [sk 2 chs, {sc, hdc, dc} in next ch] 19 times, sk 1 ch, sc in last ch, turn. (20 cl sts)

Row 2: Ch 2, [hdc, dc] in same sc as beg ch-2, [sk 2 sts, cl st in next sc] rep across to last 3 sts, sk next 2 sts, sc in top of turning ch, fasten off, turn.

Row 3: Attach 2 strands of white, ch 2, [hdc, dc] in same sc as beg ch-2, [sk 2 sts, cl st in next sc] rep across to last 3 sts, sk next 2 sts, sc in top of turning ch, turn.

Row 4: Rep Row 2.

Row 5: Attach 2 strands of red, rep Row 3.

Row 6: Rep Row 2.

Rows 7–12: Rep Rows 3–6.

Row 13: Attach 2 strands of delft blue, work 9 cl sts, fasten off delft blue, attach 2 strands of red, work 10 cl sts, turn.

Row 14: Work 11 cl sts with red, fasten off red, attach 2 strands delft blue, work 8 cl sts, turn.

Row 15: Work 9 cl sts with delft blue, fasten off delft blue, attach 2 strands of white, work 10 cl sts, turn.

Row 16: Work 11 cl sts with white, fasten off white, attach 2 strands delft blue, work 8 cl sts, turn.

Rows 17–26: Continue to rep color sequence of Rows 13–16, at the end of Row 26, fasten off.

Edging

Rnd 1 (RS): Attach 2 strands of yellow in any st, ch 1, sc evenly sp around outer edge, working 3 sc in each corner st, join in beg sc.

Show your American pride with this patriotic project! It's perfect for hanging on a wall or using as a rug!

Rnd 2: Ch 1, sc in same sc as beg ch-1, ch 5, [sc in next sc, ch 5] rep around, join in beg sc, fasten off.

Star

Make 18

Rnd 1: Working with smaller hook and 1 strand of white, ch 2, 5 sc in 2nd ch from hook, join in beg sc. (5 sc)

Rnd 2: Sl st in next sc, [ch 3, sl st in 2nd ch from hook, sc in next ch, sl st in next sc] 5 times, fasten off.

Using photo as a guide, sew stars to delft blue section of flag. ✄

Cozy Pet Bed

Design by JoHanna Dzikowski

Skill Level: Beginner

Size: 17 inches in diameter

Materials

- Worsted weight yarn:
  8 oz each black and gray,
  8 oz assorted colors

- Size K/10½ crochet hook
  or size needed to obtain
  gauge

- Fiberfill

- Tapestry needle

Gauge

5 dc = 2 inches; 2 dc rnds =
2 inches; 5 sc rnds = 2 inches
Check gauge to save time.

Pattern Notes

Weave in loose ends as work
progresses.

Join rnds with a sl st unless
otherwise stated.

Work with 1 strand each black, gray and scrap color held tog throughout.

Tube

Rnd 1: Holding 3 strands tog, ch 25, join to form a ring, ch 3 (counts as first dc throughout), dc in each ch around, join in 3rd ch of beg ch-3. (25 dc)

Rnd 2: Ch 3, dc in each dc around, join in 3rd ch of beg ch-3.

Rnds 3–52: Rep Rnd 2, changing scrap-yarn color every 4 rnds.

Fold tube flat across; working through both thicknesses, sl st across, fasten off.

Stuff tube lightly with fiberfill and sew opposite end closed. Sew ends tog to form a circle.

Base

Rnd 1: Holding 3 strands of yarn tog, ch 6, join to form a ring, ch 1, 12 sc in ring, join in beg sc. (12 sc)

Rnd 2: Ch 1, [sc in next sc, 2 sc in next sc] rep around, join in beg sc. (18 sc)

Rnds 3 & 4: Rep Rnd 2. (40 sc)

Rnd 5: Ch 1, sc in each sc around, join in beg sc.

Rnds 6 & 7: Rep Rnd 5.

Rnd 8: Ch 1, [sc in each of next 5 sc, 2 sc in next sc] rep around, join in beg sc. (46 sc)

Rnds 9 & 10: Rep Rnd 8. (61 sc)

Pamper your loyal and loving furry friends with this cozy pet bed!

Rnd 11: Rep Rnd 8. (71 sc)

Rnd 12: Rep Rnd 5.

Rnd 13: Rep Rnd 8. (82 sc)

Rnd 14: Rep Rnd 5.

Rnd 15: Rep Rnd 8. (95 sc)

Rnd 16: Rep Rnd 5, fasten off.

Thread needle with 2 strands of yarn; sew beg ch-3 sts around bottom of tube to Rnd 16 of base. ✄

Scrap Country Rug

Design by Tammy Hildebrand

Skill Level: Beginner

Size: 24 x 34½ inches

Materials

- Worsted weight yarn:
  8 oz cream (MC), 6 oz
  assorted scrap colors (CC)
- Size N/15 crochet hook
  or size needed to obtain
  gauge
- Tapestry needle

Gauge

Square = 7½ inches

Check gauge to save time.

Pattern Notes

Weave in loose ends as work progresses.

Work with 2 strands of the same color held tog throughout.

Each square uses MC and 3 different CC yarns. Never use the same CC more than once in a square.

Join rnds with a sl st unless otherwise stated.

Square

Make 12

Rnd 1: With CC, ch 4, join to form a ring, ch 3 (counts as first dc throughout), 15 dc in ring, join in 3rd ch of beg ch-3. (16 dc)

Rnd 2: Attach a different CC with a sl st in any st, [ch 3, 2 dc, ch 2, 3 dc] in same st, sk next 3 sts, [{3 dc, ch 2, 3 dc} in next st, sk next 3 sts] 3 times, join in 3rd ch of beg ch-3, fasten off.

Rnd 3: Attach MC in any ch-2 corner sp, ch 3, 4 dc in same ch-2 sp, *sk next st, sc in next st, 3 dc in sp between groups of sts, sk next st,

sc in next st **, 5 dc in next ch-2 sp, rep from * around, ending last rep at **, join in 3rd ch of beg ch-3, fasten off.

Rnd 4: Attach a different CC in first dc of any 5-dc group, ch 1, sc in same dc, sc in each of next 4 dc, *fpdc around center dc of Rnd 2 directly below sc of previous rnd, sc in each of next 3 sts, fpdc around next center dc of Rnd 2 directly below sc of previous rnd **, sc in each of next 5 dc, rep from * around, ending last rep at **, join in beg sc, fasten off.

Rnd 5: Attach MC in center sc of any 5-sc group, ch 1, [sc, ch 3, sc, ch 5, sc, ch 3, sc] in same st (for corner), *[sk next st, {sc, ch 3, sc} in next st] 4 times, sk next st **, [sc, ch 3, sc, ch 5, sc, ch 3, sc] in center st of next 5-sc group (for corner), rep from * around, ending last rep at **, join in beg sc, fasten off.

Notes: *For ch-3 joining: Ch 1, drop lp from hook, insert hook in center ch of corresponding ch-3 sp on previous square, pick up dropped lp, draw through, ch 1.*

For ch-5 joining: Ch 2, drop lp from hook, insert hook in center ch of corresponding ch-5 on previous square, pick up dropped lp, draw through, ch 2.

One-side joining

Rnd 5: Attach MC in center sc of any 5-sc group, ch 1, [sc, ch 3, sc, ch-5 joining, sc, ch-3 joining, sc] in same sc, [sk next st, {sc, ch-3 joining, sc} in next st] 4 times, sk next st, [sc, ch-3 joining, sc, ch-5 joining, sc, ch 3, sc] in next st, *[sk

next st, {sc, ch 3, sc} in next st] 4 times, sk next st **, [sc, ch 3, sc, ch 5, sc, ch 3, sc] in next center sc, rep from * around, ending last rep at **, join in beg sc, fasten off.

Two-side joining

Rnd 5: Attach MC in center sc of any corner 5-sc group, ch 1, [sc, ch 3, sc, ch-5 joining, sc, ch-3 joining, sc] in same st, [sk next st, {sc, ch-3 joining, sc} in next st] 4 times, sk

Chase away the winter chill and warm your toes with this charming country rug!

next st, [sc, ch-3 joining, sc, ch-5 joining, sc, ch-3 joining, sc] in next center sc, [sk next st, {sc, ch-3 joining, sc} in next st] 4 times, sk next st, [sc, ch-3 joining, sc, ch-5 joining, sc, ch 3, sc] in next center sc, [sk next st, {sc, ch 3, sc} in next st] 4 times, sk next st, [sc, ch 3, sc, ch 5, sc, ch 3, sc] in next center sc, [sk next st, {sc, ch 3, sc} in next st] 4 times, join in beg sc, fasten off.

Join squares in 3 rows of 4 squares each.

Border

Rnd 1: Attach MC in any corner ch-5 sp, ch 3, 6 dc in same ch sp, sc in next ch-3 sp, 3 sc in each of next 4 ch-3 sps, sc in next ch-3 sp, [7 dc in next ch-5 sp (or joining of 2 ch-5 sps), sc in next ch-3 sp, 3 sc in each of next 4 ch-3 sps, sc in next ch-3 sp] rep around outer edge, join in 3rd ch of beg ch-3, fasten off. (14 groups 7-dc) ✂

V-Stitch Rug

Design by Tammy Hildebrand

Gauge

3 V-sts = 4 inches; 4 corner shell rnds = 5 inches

Check gauge to save time.

Pattern Notes

Weave in loose ends as work progresses.

Ch-3 counts as first dc throughout.

Join rnds with a sl st unless otherwise stated.

Work with 2 strands of same-color yarn held tog throughout.

Rnd 1 establishes RS of rug.

Pattern Stitch

V-st: [Dc, ch 1, dc] in indicated st.

Rug

Rnd 1 (RS): With MC, ch 6, join to form a ring, ch 3, 23 dc in ring, join in 3rd ch of beg ch-3. (24 dc)

Rnd 2: Attach CC in any dc, ch 4 (counts as first dc, ch-1), dc in same dc, sk next dc, [V-st in next dc, sk next dc] rep around, join in 3rd ch of beg ch-4, fasten off. (12 V-sts)

Rnd 3: Attach MC in any ch-1 sp, [ch 3, dc, ch 2, 2 dc] in same ch-1 sp, 3 dc in next V-st, [{2 dc, ch 2, 2 dc} in next V-st, 3 dc in next V-st] rep around, join in 3rd ch of beg ch-3, fasten off.

Rnd 4: Attach CC in any ch-2 sp, [ch 3, dc, ch 2, 2 dc] in same ch-2 sp, [{sk next st, V-st in next st} 3 times, {2 dc, ch 2, 2 dc} in next ch-2 sp] 5 times, [sk next st, V-st in next st] 3 times, join in 3rd ch of beg ch-3, fasten off.

Rnd 5: Attach MC in any ch-2 sp, [ch 3, dc, ch 2, 2 dc] in same sp, [3 dc in next ch-1 sp of V-st, dc in next ch-1 sp of V-st, 3 dc in next ch-1 sp of V-st, {2 dc, ch 2, 2 dc} in next ch-2 sp] 5 times, 3 dc in next ch-1 sp of V-st, dc in next ch-1 sp of V-st, 3 dc in next ch-1 sp of V-st, join in 3rd ch of beg ch-3, fasten off.

Rnd 6: Attach CC in any ch-2 sp, [ch 3, 2 dc, ch 2, 3 dc] in same sp, [sk next 2 sts, V-st in next st, {sk next st, V-st in next st} twice, {3 dc, ch 2, 3 dc} in next ch-2 sp] 5 times, sk next 2 sts, V-st in next st, [sk next st, V-st in next st] twice, join in 3rd ch of beg ch-3, fasten off.

Rnd 7: Attach MC in any ch-2 sp, [ch 3, dc, ch 2, 2 dc] in same sp, [sk next st, dc in next st, 3 dc in each ch-1 sp of each V-st, sk next st, dc in next st, {2 dc, ch 2, 2 dc} in next ch-2 sp] 5 times, sk next st, dc in next st, 3 dc in each ch-1 sp of each V-st, sk next st, dc in next st, join in 3rd ch of beg ch-3, fasten off.

Rnd 8: Attach CC in any ch-2 sp, [ch 3, 2 dc, ch 2, 3 dc] in same sp, [sk next 2 sts, V-st in next st, V-st in center st of each 3-st group, V-st in next st, {3 dc, ch 2, 3 dc} in next ch-2 sp] 5 times, sk next 2 sts, V-st in next st, V-st in center st of each 3-st group, V-st in next st, join in 3rd ch of beg ch-3, fasten off.

When the winter wind blows, you'll really appreciate the size of this hexagon–shaped area rug!

Rnds 9–16: Rep Rnds 7 and 8 alternately.

Rnd 17: With MC, rep Rnd 8.

Fringe

Knot 6 (10-inch-long) strands of MC in sp between each 3-st group and in each ch-2 sp.

Knot 6 (10-inch-long) strands of alternating CC in center st of each 3-st group. Trim fringe evenly. ✂

Hint

From Shirley Patterson

Need an idea to help get rid of those extra scraps of yarn? Go crazy with tassels! Use any color combination of yarns and threads to make short, medium or long tassels. Add pizzazz to your next project!

Granny Square Rug

Design by Michele Wilcox

Skill Level: Beginner

Size: 18 x 24 inches

Materials

- Elmore-Pisgah Peaches & Crème worsted weight cotton yarn: 2 balls each black #2, light green #55 and verde green #53, small amount each peacock #19, persimmon #33, deep purple #49, shrimp #21, red #95 delft blue #28 and yellow #10

- Size K/10½ crochet hook or size needed to obtain gauge

- Tapestry needle

Gauge

Rnd 1 = 2 inches in diameter; 4 sc = 1½ inches

Check gauge to save time.

Pattern Notes

Weave in loose ends as work progresses.

Ch-3 counts as first dc throughout.

Join rnds with a sl st unless otherwise stated.

Square

Note: Make 2 flowers each with peacock, persimmon, deep purple, shrimp, red and delft blue.

Rnd 1 (RS): With yellow, ch 5, join to form a ring, ch 3, 11 dc in ring, join in 3rd ch of beg ch-3, fasten off. (12 dc)

Rnd 2: Attach flower color with a sl st in any dc, [ch 2, dc in same st as sl st, 3 tr in next dc, {dc, ch 2, sl st} in next dc, sl st in next dc] rep around, fasten off. (4 petals)

Rnd 3: Attach light green with sl st between any 2 petals, [ch 4, sl st between next 2 petals] rep around.

Rnd 4: Sl st into ch-4 sp, [ch 3, 2 dc, ch 2, 3 dc] in same ch-4 sp, ch 1, [{3 dc, ch 2, 3 dc} in next ch-4 sp, ch 1] rep around, join in 3rd ch of beg ch-3, fasten off.

Rnd 5: Attach black in any corner ch-2 sp, [ch 3, 2 dc, ch 2, 3 dc] in same corner ch-2 sp, ch 1, 3 dc in next ch-1 sp, ch 1, [{3 dc, ch 2, 3 dc} in next corner ch-2 sp, ch 1, 3 dc in next ch-1 sp, ch 1] rep around, join in 3rd ch of beg ch-3, fasten off.

Rnd 6: Attach verde green in any corner ch-2 sp, ch 1, [{sc, ch 2, sc} in corner ch-2 sp, sc in each dc and each ch-1 sp across edge] rep around, join in beg sc, fasten off. (52 sc; 4 ch-2 sps)

Using photo as a guide, or as desired, working through both lps with RS tog, sew squares tog in 3 rows of 4 squares each.

If you like stitching granny squares, this is the rug for you. With 12 squares to stitch, you'll be able to select colors to match your decor or make each a different combination of colors for a fun look!

Edging

Rnd 1 (RS): Attach verde green in any sc, ch 1, sc evenly sp around, working [sc, ch 2, sc] in each corner ch-2 sp, join in beg sc, fasten off.

Rnd 2 (RS): Attach light green in any sc, ch 1, sc in each sc around, working [sc, ch 2, sc] in each corner ch-2 sp, join in beg sc, fasten off. ✄

Striped Throw Rug

Design by Diane Poellot

Skill Level: Beginner

Size: 18 x 33 inches, excluding fringe

Materials

- Worsted weight yarn: 7 oz black, 3 oz assorted scrap colors
- Size 8 afghan crochet hook or size needed to obtain gauge
- Tapestry needle

Gauge

4 sts = 1 inch; 3 rows = 1 inch
Check gauge to save time.

Pattern Note

Leave a 6-inch length of yarn at beg and ending of each row.

Rug

Row 1 (RS): With black, ch 110, draw up a lp in 2nd ch from hook, retaining all lps on hook, draw up a lp in each rem ch across, fasten off, attach scrap color, yo, draw through first lp on hook, [yo, draw through 2 lps on hook] rep across until 1 lp rem, fasten off.

Rows 2–48 (RS): With black, retaining all lps on hook, draw up a lp in each vertical bar across, fasten off, attach scrap color, yo, draw through first lp on hook, [yo, draw through 2 lps on hook] rep across until 1 lp rem, fasten off.

Row 49: With black, inserting hook in same manner as afghan st, sl st in each st across, fasten off.

Pull fringe through center of each end st. Trim ends evenly. ✂

This striped throw rug is reminiscent of rugs from a couple of decades past! With so many colors, you might just empty your scrap basket!

Scrap Fashions

From fashion favorites to quick
and easy accessories, you will find
a multitude of delightful projects
to keep you busy and make good
use of the leftovers in your scrap
basket. Freshen your wardrobe
with a spicy vest or plan for fall
weather with back-to-school
ideas for the kids!

Dawn to Dusk Sweater

Design by Jewdy Lambert

Gauge

4 dc = 1 inch; 4 dc rows = 1 inch
Check gauge to save time.

Pattern Notes

Weave in loose ends as work progresses.

Join rnds with a sl st unless otherwise stated.

Ch-3 counts as first dc throughout.

Sweater requires any 4 shades each of brown and grape, and 2 shades of moss.

Any yarn textures will do from smooth, tweed, mohair, etc. The more variety the better.

Number of ounces used will vary and you may substitute small amounts of various colors instead of colors used.

To shorten or to lengthen sweater, remember 2 rows = 1 inch, adjust as desired, simply omit or add rows. Any sleeve rnds may be omitted as desired for shorter length.

Fasten off yarn when no longer in use.

Pattern Stitch

Rib st: On RS rows, fpdc around dc directly below, sk st directly behind post st. On WS rows, bpdc around dc directly below, sk st directly behind post st. All rib sts will be on RS of sweater.

Front

Make 2

Row 1 (RS): Beg at bottom with ribbing, with MC, ch 32 (34, 36) dc in 3rd ch from hook, dc in each rem ch across, turn. (31, 33, 35 dc)

Row 2 (WS): Ch 1, rib st around dc directly below, [sc in next st, rib st around dc directly below] rep across, turn.

Row 3: With B, ch 1, sc in each sc, rib st around each dc directly below, turn.

Row 4: With MC, ch 1, sc in each sc, rib st around each dc, turn.

Row 5: With C, rep Row 3.

Rows 6 & 7: With MC, rep Row 3.

Row 8: With B, rep Row 3.

Row 9: With C, rep Row 3.

Row 10: With MC, rep Row 3.

Body

Row 1 (RS): With MC, dc in each st across, turn.

Row 2: With E, ch 3, dc in each st across, turn.

Row 3: With H, rep Row 2.

Notes: Rows 4–6 represent a closed diamond. Using diagram as a guide, do not be concerned if closed diamond rep does not work evenly across. Maintain color pattern of Row 4 on all 3 rows.

Row 4: With H, ch 3, dc in next 2 sts, [with E dc in next st, with H, dc in each of next 3 sts] rep across, turn.

No one will ever know this gorgeous sweater was stitched from your scrap basket. The beautiful colors and wonderful design will make this sweater a wardrobe favorite!

Rows 5 & 6: Continuing in dc sts, complete closed diamond rows.

Row 7: Rep Row 3.

Row 8: Rep Row 2.

Row 9: Attach J, ch 1, sc in same st, with B, sc in each of next 2 sts, [with J, sc in next st, with B, sc in each of next 2 sts] rep across, turn.

Row 10: With 1 strand each C and E held tog, ch 3, dc in each st across, turn.

Rows 11 & 12: Ch 3, dc in each st across, turn.

Row 13: Rep Row 9.

Row 14: Attach MC, ch 3, dc in each st across, turn.

Notes: Rows 15–17 represent open diamond. Using diagram as a guide, do not be concerned if open diamond rep does not work evenly across. Maintain color pattern of Row 15 on all 3 rows.

Row 15: With MC, ch 3, dc in
Continued on page 78

Raindrops on Windowpanes Pullover

Design by Ann E. Smith

Skill Level: Intermediate

Size

Adult small (medium, large and extra-large)

Bust: 42 (45, 48, 51) inches

Length: 24 (25, 26, 27) inches

Instructions are for smallest size, with larger sizes in parentheses.

Materials

- Lion Brand Jiffy 2-ply brushed acrylic yarn (2½ oz per ball multicolor and heather; 3 oz per ball solids): 6 (7, 8, 9) balls Detroit multicolor #315 (MC), 1 (2, 2, 2) balls each heather blue #111 (A) and lilac #144 (B), 1 (1, 1, 2) balls each dusty blue #108 (C), pastel blue #105 (D) and light pink #101 (E)
- Size K/10½ crochet hook or size needed to obtain gauge
- Safety pins or placement markers
- Tapestry needle

Gauge

15 sts = 6 inches; 18 rows = 6 inches
Check gauge to save time.

Pattern Notes

Weave in loose ends as work progresses.

When changing color at the end of a row, draw up a lp in last sc with current color; complete the sc with next color. Cut and join yarns for each strip, working over the tails as work progresses.

Pattern Stitch

Puff st: [Yo, insert hook in indicated st, yo, draw up a lp] 3 times in same st, yo, draw through 6 lps on hook, yo, draw through 2 lps on hook.

Body Pattern

Note: A multiple of 4 sts plus 3; a rep of 8 rows.

Row 1 (WS): With MC, ch 1, sc in first sc, [puff st in next sc, sc in each of next 3 sc] rep across to last 2 sts, puff st in last sc, changing to CC, turn.

Row 2: With CC, ch 1, sc in next st, puff st in next st, sc in next st, [fpdc over fpdc, sc in next st, puff st in next st, sc in next st] rep across, turn.

Row 3: With CC, ch 1, sc in each st across, changing to MC in last st, turn.

Row 4: With MC, ch 1, sc in first 3 sc, [fpdc over fpdc, sc in next 3 scs rep across, turn.

Rows 5–8: Rep Rows 1–4.

Back

Foundation (RS): Beg at the lower edge and above border, with MC, ch 56 (60, 64, 68), sc in 2nd ch from hook, sc in next 2 chs, [dc in next ch, sc in next 3 chs] rep across, turn. (55, 59, 63, 67 sts)

Row 1: Rep Row 1 of body pattern, changing to A in last st.

Row 2: With A, ch 1, sc in next st, puff st in next st, sc in next st, [fpdc over dc post of directly below, sk the sc behind fpdc, sc in next st,

Stitch this beautiful pullover in springy pastels to add a little warmth to your cold-weather wardrobe!

puff st in next st, sc in next st] rep across, turn.

Rows 3 & 4: Rep Rows 3 and 4 of body pattern.

Rows 5–8: With color A as CC, rep Body Pattern Rows 1–4.

Stripes

Rep Body Pattern Rows 1–8 using [B, C, D, E, A] for CC stripes; rep between [ ] for pattern.

Work even in pattern to 23 (24, 25, 26) inches from beg, ending with a WS row.

First shoulder & neck shaping

Work in established pattern across first 19 (21, 23, 25) sts, turn. Work even on these sts to 24 (25, 26, 27) inches from beg, ending with a RS row, fasten off.

Second shoulder & neck shaping

With RS facing, sk center 17 sts, attach yarn with sl st in next st, ch 1, work in established pattern on rem 19 (21, 23, 25) sts to same length as first shoulder.

Front

Work the same as for back until front measures 22½ (23½, 24½, 25½) inches from beg, ending with a WS row.

First shoulder

Work in established pattern across first 21 (23, 25, 27) sts, turn. Dec 1 st at neckline edge every other row twice. Work even on 19 (21, 23, 25) sts to same length as back, ending with a RS row, fasten off.

Second shoulder

With RS facing, sk center 13 sts, attach yarn with a sl st in next st, ch 1, work in established pattern on the 21 (23, 25, 27) sts, turn. Complete as for first shoulder.

Sleeve

Make 2

Beg at lower edge with MC, ch 24 (24, 28, 28), work foundation and Rows 1–4 as for back. (23, 23, 27, 27 sts)

In same stripe pattern as for back and including new sts into pattern as they accumulate, inc 1 st each edge now, then every 6th row 4 times and every 4th row 5 (6, 5, 6) times.

To include new sts into pattern on Rows 12 and 32 work as follows: ch 1, sc in first sc, dc in next sc, work in pattern to last 2 sts, dc in next sc, sc in last sc, turn.

Rows 14 & 34: Ch 1, sc in first sc, fpdc over dc 2 rows below, work pattern across to last 2 sts, fpdc over dc 2 rows below, sc in last sc, turn.

Work even on the 43 (45, 47, 49) sts to 17 inches from beg, ending with a RS row, fasten off.

Finishing

Sew shoulder seams. Place markers 9 (9½, 10, 10½) inches each side of shoulder seam. Set in sleeve between markers. Sew sleeve and side seams.

Sleeve Edging

With RS facing, attach MC with a sl st in rem foundation ch closest to seam and below a fpdc, [{ch 8, sl st in same ch}, sl st in each of next 4 chs] rep around, sl st to join, fasten off.

Lower Edging

Rep the same as sleeve edging.

Neckline

Rnd 1: With RS facing, attach MC with a sl st near seam, ch 1, sc in same sp as joining, work 49 sc evenly sp around neckline, sl st to join in beg sc. (50 sc)

Rnds 2 & 3: Ch 1, sc in each sc around, sl st to join in beg sc.

Rnd 4: Ch 1, sc in each sc around, sl st to join in front lp of beg sc.

Rnd 5: Sl st in front lp of next sc, [{ch 8, sl st in same front lp} sl st in front lp of each of next 5 sc] rep around, ending with ch 8, sl st in same front lp, sl st in front lp of each of next 4 sc.

Rnd 6: Sl st into rem back lp of Rnd 4, ch 1, sc in same st, sc in each rem lp around, sl st to join in beg sc.

Rnd 7: Working through both lps, sl st in each sc around, fasten off. ✂

Pretty Pastels Sweater

Design by Melissa Leapman

Perfect for summer outings, this beautiful sweater uses a variety of pastels for a light and springy look!

Gauge

19 sts = 4 inches; 10 rows = 4 inches

Check gauge to save time.

Pattern Notes

Weave in loose ends as work progresses.

Ch-2 counts as first hdc throughout.

Pastel Pattern

Foundation Row (WS): Sc in 2nd ch from hook, [ch 1, sk next 2 chs, 3 dc in next ch, ch 1, sk next 2 chs, sc in next ch] rep across, change to MC, turn.

Row 1 (RS): Ch 3 (counts as first dc throughout), dc in first sc, [ch 1, sk next dc, sc in next dc, ch 1, [dc, ch 1, dc] in next sc] rep across, ending with ch 1, 2 dc in last sc, change color, turn.

Row 2: Ch 1, sc in first dc, [ch 1, 3 dc in next sc, ch 1, sk next ch-1 sp, sc in next ch-1 sp] rep across, ending with ch 1, 3 dc in next sc, ch 1, sc in top of beg ch-3, change to MC, turn.

Rep Rows 1 and 2 in color sequence for pattern.

For color sequence, work 1 row each [A, MC, B, MC, C, MC, D, MC, E, and MC] rep for pattern.

Textured Hdc Pattern

Ch 2, sk first st, [hdc through back lp of next st, hdc through front lp of next st] rep across, ending row with hdc through back lp of next st, hdc in top of ch-2, turn.

Back

With hook size G and A, ch 86 (98, 110, 122), work even in pastel pattern until piece measures approximately 10 (11, 12, 12) inches from beg, ending after Row 2 of pattern, change to MC, turn.

With RS facing, ch 3, sk first sc, dc in next ch-1 sp, *sc in next 3 dc,

dc in next ch-1 sp, dc in next sc **, dc in next ch-1 sp, rep from * across, ending last rep at **, turn. (85, 97, 109, 121 sts)

Continue even with MC in textured hdc pattern until piece measures approximately 14 (14½, 15, 15) inches from beg, ending after a WS row.

Armhole shaping

Sl st into first 7 (9, 9, 13) sts, ch 2, sk next st, continue in pattern across row until 6 (8, 8, 12) sts rem, turn. (73, 81, 93, 97 sts)

Continue even, until piece measures approximately 22 (23, 23½, 24) inches, ending after a WS row.

First neckline shaping

With RS facing, work across first 22 (26, 32, 34) sts, turn. Dec 1 st at neck edge every row twice, then continue even on this side until piece measures approximately 23 (24, 24½, 25) inches from beg, fasten off.

Second neckline shaping

With RS facing, sk next 29 sts, attach yarn with a sl st in next st, ch 2, complete as for first neckline shaping.

Lower edging

With hook size F, attach MC with a sl st to first ch of foundation ch, ch 1, working across foundation ch, sc in same ch as beg ch-1, [sk next 2 chs, {ch 1, dc} 4 times in next ch, ch 1, sk next 2 chs, sc in next ch] rep across, fasten off.

Front

Work as for back until piece measures approximately 19½ (20½, 21, 21½) inches from beg, ending after a WS row.

First neckline shaping

With RS facing, work across first

25 (29, 35, 37) sts, turn. Dec 1 st at neckline edge every row 4 times, then every other row once. Continue even on this side until piece measures approximately 23 (24, 24½, 25) inches from beg, fasten off.

Second neckline shaping

With RS facing, sk next 23 sts, attach yarn with sl st in next st, ch 2, continue same as first neckline shaping.

Lower edging

Rep lower edging as for back.

Sleeve

Make 2

Foundation Row (RS): With hook size G and MC, ch 60 (68, 74, 80), hdc in 3rd ch from hook, hdc in each rem ch across, turn. (59, 63, 73, 79 sts)

Beg textured hdc pattern and inc 1 st each side every row 13 (12, 9, 8) times. (85, 91, 91, 95 sts)

Continue even until sleeve measures approximately 7½ (7½, 6¼, 6¼) inches from beg, fasten off.

Lower edging

Rep lower edging as for back.

Finishing

Sew shoulder seams. Set in sleeves and sew sleeve and side seams.

Neck Band

Rnd 1: With RS facing and with hook size F, attach MC with sl st to left shoulder seam, ch 1, work 90 sc evenly sp around neckline, sl st to join in beg sc.

Rnd 2: Ch 1, sc in same st as beg ch-1, *sk next 2 sc, [ch 1, dc] 4 times in next sc, ch 1, sk next 2 sc **, sc in next sc, rep from * around, ending last rep at **, sl st to join in beg sc, fasten off. ✄

Spicy Vest

Design by Melissa Leapman

Skill Level: Intermediate

Size

Bust: 39¾ (46, 53½) inches

Materials

- Patons Decor worsted weight yarn (100g/210 yds per skein): 2 (2, 3) skeins claret #1657 (A), 2 skeins each orange #1713 (B), maize #1710 (C), Christmas red #1605 (D) and sublime #1716 (E)

- Size H/8 crochet hook or size needed to obtain gauge

- Size G/6 crochet hook

- 7 (⅝-inch) decorative buttons

- Tapestry needle

Gauge

14 sts = 4 inches; 13 rows = 4 inches

Check gauge to save time.

Pattern Notes

Weave in loose ends as work progresses.

Ch-3 counts as first dc throughout.

Work 2 rows each color [A, B, C, D and E] rep color sequence.

Textured Pattern

Foundation Row (RS): Dc in 4th ch from hook, dc in each rem ch across, turn.

Row 1 (WS): Ch 1, sc in each dc across, change color, turn.

Row 2: Ch 1, sc in first 3 sts, [fpdc around dc directly below, sk sc directly behind fpdc, sc in next sc, fpdc around dc directly below, sk sc directly behind fpdc, sc in each of next 3 sc] rep across, turn.

Row 3: Ch 1, sc in each st across, change color, turn.

Row 4: Ch 3, dc in each sc across, turn.

Row 5: Ch 1, sc in each dc across, change color, turn.

Row 6: Ch 1, sc in first 2 sts, [fpdc around dc directly below, sk sc behind fpdc, sc in each of next 3 sts, fpdc around dc directly below, sk sc directly behind fpdc, sc in next st] rep across, ending with sc in last st, turn.

Row 7: Rep Row 3, change color.

Row 8: Rep Row 4.

Rep Rows 1–8 in color sequence for pattern.

Back

With hook size H and A, ch 71 (83, 95), work even in textured pattern on 69 (81, 93) sts until piece measures approximately 16 inches from beg, ending after Row 3 of pattern.

Armhole shaping

Sk first 5 (7, 9) sts, attach yarn with sl st to next st, ch 3, continue in pattern across row until 5 (7, 9) sts rem, turn. (59, 67, 75 sts)

Dec 1 st each side every row 2 (3, 5) times, then every other row 3 (4, 4) times. (49, 53, 57 sts)

Continue even until back measures approximately 24¼ (24¾, 25½) inches from beg, ending after a WS row.

First neckline shaping

Work across first 15 (16, 18) sts, turn. Dec 1 st at neck edge every row twice, then continue even on this side until piece measures 25½ (26, 26½) inches from beg, fasten off.

Second Neckline Shaping

With RS facing, sk next 19 (21, 21) sts, attach yarn with sl st in next st, complete as for first neckline shaping.

Left Front

With hook size H and A, ch 35 (41, 47), work even in textured pattern on 33 (39, 45) sts until piece measures approximately 16 inches from beg, ending after Row 3 of pattern.

Nothing adds versatility to a wardrobe like a vest and this spicy vest is sure to be a favorite. Dress up a pair of blue jeans or a skirt for a more polished look!

Armhole shaping

Sk first 5 (7, 9) sts, attach yarn with sl st in next st, ch 3, work to end of row. Dec 1 st at armhole edge every row 2 (3, 5) times, then every other row 3 (4, 4) times and *at the same time,* when piece measures 17 (17½, 18) inches, shape neckline by dec 1 st at neckline edge every other row 10 (11, 11) times. (13, 14, 16 sts)

Continue even until front measures the same as back to shoulder, fasten off.

Right Front

Work the same as left front, reversing all shaping.

Assembly

Sew shoulder and side seams.

Vest Edging

Row 1 (RS): With hook size G, attach A to lower right front edge, ch 1, sc evenly sp up right front,

around neckline and down left front, working 2 sc at each front corner of neckline and dec a sc at beg of each back neck shaping.

Note: Place 7 markers evenly sp up right front for buttonhole placement, making sure that first and last are ¼-inch from lower edge and neck edge.

Row 2: Ch 1, sc in each sc around,

making inc sts at neckline edge and dec a sc at beg of each back neck shaping, turn.

Row 3: Ch 1, rep Row 2 working 7 buttonholes on right front with ch 2, sk next 2 sts.

Row 4: Rep Row 2, working 2 sc in each ch-2 sp of each buttonhole.

Row 5: Rep Row 2, fasten off. Sew buttons opposite buttonholes.

Armhole Trim

Rnd 1 (RS): With hook size G, attach A, ch 1, sc evenly sp around, sl st to join in beg sc, turn.

Rnds 2–4: Ch 1, sc around, working sc dec sts as needed at curves to maintain shape, sl st to join in beg sc. At the end of Rnd 4, fasten off. ✂

Granny Square Shawl

Design by Ann E. Smith

Skill Level: Beginner

Size: 15 x 65 inches, including fringe

Materials

- Patons Look at Me sport weight yarn (1¾ oz per ball): 5 balls navy #6371 (MC), 1 ball each (CC) happy days variegated #6376, fun 'n games variegated #6377, jewel tones variegated #6379, lilac #6358, peacock #6360 and green apple #6362

- Size F/5 crochet hook or size needed to obtain gauge

- Tapestry needle

Gauge

Motif = 4½ inches square
Check gauge to save time.

Pattern Notes

Weave in loose ends as work progresses.

Ch-3 counts as first dc throughout.

Join rnds with a sl st unless otherwise stated.

Use assembly diagram as a guide for color of each motif.

Motif

Make 39

Rnd 1 (RS): With CC, ch 4, 2 dc in 4th ch from hook, [ch 3, 3 dc] 3 times in same 4th ch from hook, ch 3, join in 4th ch of beg ch-4, fasten off.

Rnd 2 (RS): Attach MC in any ch-3 sp, ch 3, [2 dc, ch 3, 3 dc] in same ch-3 sp, ch 1, [{3 dc, ch 3, 3 dc} in next ch-3 sp, ch 1] rep around, join in 3rd ch of beg ch-3, fasten off.

Rnd 3 (RS): Attach CC in any ch-3 sp, ch 3, [2 dc, ch 3, 3 dc] in same ch-3 sp, ch 1, 3 dc in next ch-1 sp, ch 1, [{3 dc, ch 3, 3 dc} in next ch-3 sp, ch 1, 3 dc in next ch-1 sp, ch 1] rep around, join in 3rd ch of beg ch-3, fasten off.

Rnd 4 (RS): Attach MC in first dc to left of any corner ch-3 sp, ch 1, sc in same dc as joining, sc in next 10 sts across edge to next corner ch-3 sp, 3 sc in corner ch-3 sp, [sc in next 11 sts across edge, 3 sc in corner ch-3 sp] rep around, join in beg sc. (56 sc)

Rnd 5 (RS): Ch 1, sc in each sc around, working 3 sc in each center corner sc, join in beg sc. (64 sc)

Rnd 6 (RS): Rep Rnd 5, fasten off. (72 sc)

Finishing

Using assembly diagram as a guide for placement, with RS facing and working through back lps only, sl st motifs tog.

COLOR KEY	
A Happy days variegated	
B Fun 'n games variegated	
C Jewel tones variegated	
D Lilac	
E Peacock	
F Green apple	

Trim

Rnd 1 (RS): Working in back lps only, attach MC in first sc in corner to work across long edge, *ch 1, sc in back of each st across long edge to corner, working across short edge, sl st in back lp of first sc, [ch 25, sl st in back lp of next sc] rep across to corner, rep from * around, join, fasten off. ✄

Wrap this delightful shawl around your shoulders as you watch television or read a book. A great way to use up excess yarn, you can make motifs in any number of color combinations!

B	C	F
F	D	B
C	A	E
E	F	A
A	B	D
D	E	C
B	C	F
F	D	B
C	A	E
E	F	A
A	B	D
D	E	C
B	C	F

Assembly Diagram

Balloon Appliqués

Design by Kathryn Clark

Skill Level: Beginner

Size: 1¼ x 2 inches

Materials

- Crochet cotton size 10: 10 yds each green, red and blue, small amounts dark green, dark red and navy

- Size 7 steel crochet hook or size needed to obtain gauge

- Fiberfill

- Sewing needle and matching thread

Dress up your child's favorite pair of overalls with a cute balloon bouquet. So quick and easy to make, you can even dress up a shirt to match!

Gauge

8 dc = 4 inches

Check gauge to save time.

Pattern Notes

Weave in loose ends as work progresses.

Make a balloon from each green, red and blue (lighter shades) and use darker shades for Rnd 3.

Join rnds with a sl st unless otherwise stated.

Balloon

Make 4

Rnd 1 (RS): With lighter shade, ch 8, 2 dc in 4th ch from hook, 2 dc in next ch, dc in next ch, 2 dc in next ch, 3 dc in last ch, working on opposite side of foundation ch, 2 dc in next ch, dc in next ch, 2 dc in next ch, join in top of beg ch. (16 sts)

Rnd 2: Ch 4 (counts as first tr), 2 tr in same st as beg ch, 2 tr in next st, 3 tr in next st, 2 tr in each of next 2 sts, dc in next st, 2 dc in each of next 2 sts, 3 dc in next st, 2 dc in next st, 3 dc in next st, 2 dc in each of next 2 sts, dc in next st, 2 tr in each of next 2 sts, join in 4th ch of beg ch-4, fasten off. (34 sts)

Rnd 3: Attach darker shade in first st of previous rnd, ch 1, sc in same st as beg ch-1, sc in each of next 20 sts, ch 4, 3 hdc in 3rd ch from hook, ch 3, sl st in last ch of ch-4, sc in each of next 13 sts, join in beg sc, fasten off.

Finishing

Use photo as a guide for placement on overalls. With sewing needle and matching thread, sew balloons to overalls using blind st, inserting a scrap of fiberfill before closing to make the balloon stand out. With double strand of sewing thread, embroider a small bow at base of each balloon using lazy daisy sts; embroider the string using split st. ✂

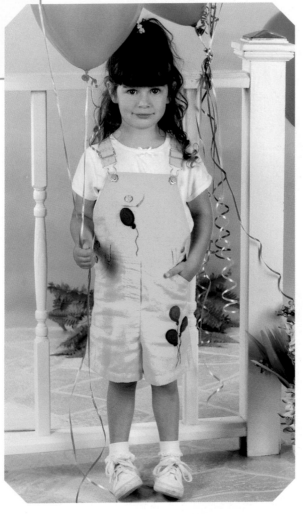

Block Party
T-Shirt
Pattern is
on page 62

Denim
Skirt Trim
Pattern is
on page 63

Block Party T-Shirt

Design by Margaret Nobles

Skill Level: Beginner

Size

Large block: 2 inches square

Small block: 1½ inches square

Materials

- Crochet cotton size 10: small amount each orange, gold, turquoise, purple and white

- Size 8 steel crochet hook or size needed to obtain gauge

- White T-shirt

- Fusible web

- Sewing needle and thread

- Tapestry needle

Gauge

8 sc = 1 inch

Check gauge to save time.

Pattern Notes

Weave in loose ends as work progresses.

Join rnds with a sl st unless otherwise stated.

Make blocks from all colors as desired except white.

Large Block

Make 4

Row 1: Ch 16, sc in 2nd ch from hook, sc in each rem ch across, turn. (15 sc)

Rows 2–15: Ch 1, sc in each sc across, turn.

Rnd 16 (RS): Ch 1, sc evenly sp around outer edge, working 3 sc in each corner st, join in beg sc, fasten off.

Small Block

Make 4

Row 1: Ch 11, sc in 2nd ch from hook, sc in each rem ch across, turn. (10 sc)

Rows 2–10: Ch 1, sc in each sc across, turn.

Rnd 11 (RS): Ch 1, sc evenly sp around outer edge, working 3 sc in each corner st, join in beg sc, fasten off.

Finishing

Thread tapestry needle with white cotton; embroider a ch-swirl design on RS of 2 blocks.

Following manufacturer's directions, apply fusible web to WS of each block and then arrange blocks in desired pattern and apply to T–shirt. For added security, st around outer edge of each block. ✄

Jazz up a T-shirt with blocks of different colors and sizes. Once the blocks are made, let your kids help lay them out to design their own shirt!

Denim Skirt Trim

Design by Tammy Hildebrand

Gauge

[Sc {2 dc, ch 1, 2 dc}] = 1 inch
Check gauge to save time.

Pattern Notes

Weave in loose ends as work progresses.

Join rnds with a sl st unless otherwise stated.

Star

Rnd 1 (RS): With natural, ch 3, join to form a ring, ch 3 (counts as first dc), 23 dc in ring, join in 3rd ch of beg ch-3, fasten off. (24 dc)

Rnd 2: Attach grape in any dc, ch 1, sc in same dc as beg ch-1, *dc in next st, [tr, ch 3, sc in 3rd ch from hook, tr] in next st, dc in next st **, sc in next st, rep from * around, ending last rep at **, join in beg sc, fasten off.

Sew bead to center of Rnd 1 and

The trendy trim on this denim skirt is just what you need to send your little girl off to school happy and in style!

sew star to skirt through center of Rnd 1.

Pocket Trim

Note: For a complete point, ch 6; for each additional point add 4 chs to length desired.

Row 1: With natural, ch desired length, sc in 2nd ch from hook, [sk next ch, {2 dc, ch 1, 2 dc} in next ch, sk next ch, sc in next ch] rep across, fasten off.

Row 2: Attach grape in first sc, ch 1, sc in same st as beg ch-1, [sc in next st, sk next st, {2 dc, ch 3, sc in 3rd ch from hook, 2 dc} in next ch-1 sp, sk next st, sc in each of next 2 sts] rep across, fasten off.

With sewing needle and thread, stitch trim to pocket edge.

Hem Trim

Note: For a complete point, ch 9; for each additional point, add 6 chs to length desired.

Row 1: With natural, ch desired number of chs, dc in 4th ch from hook, dc in each rem ch across, turn.

Row 2: Ch 1, sc in first st, [sk next 2 sts, 5 dc in next st, sk next 2 sts, sc in next st] rep across, turn.

Row 3: Ch 1, sc in first st, [dc in each of next 2 sts, {dc, ch 1, dc} in next st, dc in each of next 2 sts, sc in next st] rep across, fasten off.

Row 4: Attach grape with sc in first st, [sk next st, {dc, ch 1, dc} in next st, {2 dc, ch 3, sc in 3rd ch from hook, 2 dc} in next ch-1 sp, sk next st, {dc, ch 1, dc} in next st, sk next st, sc in next st] rep across, fasten off.

With sewing needle and thread, sew to bottom of skirt. ✂

Hooded Jacket

Design by Ann E. Smith

Skill Level: Intermediate

Size: Child's 4 (6 and 8)

Chest: 33¾ (36, 38) inches

Length: 17½ (19½, 22) inches

Instructions are for smallest size, with larger sizes in parentheses.

Materials

- Coats & Clark Red Heart Sport sport weight yarn (2½ oz per skein): 3 (4, 4) skeins paddy green #687 (MC), small amount each jockey red #904, yellow #230 and skipper blue #846

- Size G/6 crochet hook or size needed to obtain gauge

- Size F/5 crochet hook

- 4 (1-inch) wooden barrel buttons

- Straight pins

- Safety pins or placement markers

- Tapestry needle

Gauge

15 sts = 4 inches; 14 rows = 4 inches
Check gauge to save time.

Pattern Notes

Weave in loose ends as work progresses.

Ch-3 counts as first dc throughout.

Back

Row 1 (RS): Beg at lower edge with hook size G and MC, ch 64 (68, 72), sc in 2nd ch from hook, sc in each rem ch across, turn. (63, 67, 71 sc)

Row 2: Ch 3, dc in each sc across, turn.

Row 3: Ch 3, [fpdc around next dc, bpdc around next dc] rep across, ending with fpdc around next dc, dc in last dc, turn.

Body

Row 1 (WS): Ch 1, sc in each st across, turn.

Row 2: Ch 1, hdc in first sc, hdc in each of next 4 sc, *fpdc over next fpdc 2 rows below and sk sc behind fpdc, hdc in each of next 9 sc, fpdc over next fpdc 2 rows below and sk sc behind fpdc *, hdc in each of next 31 (35, 39) sc, rep from * to *, hdc in each of next 5 sc, turn.

Rep Rows 1 and 2 until back measures 17½ (19½, 22) inches from beg, ending with a RS row, fasten off.

Right Front

Row 1 (RS): Beg at lower edge with hook size G and MC, ch 30 (32, 34), sc in 2nd ch from hook, sc in each rem ch across, turn. (29, 31, 33 sc)

Rows 2 & 3: Rep Rows 2 and 3 of back.

Body

Row 1 (WS): Ch 1, sc in each st across, turn.

Row 2: Ch 1, hdc in first sc, hdc in each of next 12 (14, 16) sc, fpdc over next fpdc 2 rows below, sk the sc behind fpdc, hdc in each of next 9 sc, fpdc over next fpdc 2 rows below, sk the sc behind fpdc, hdc in each of next 5 sc, turn.

Rep Rows 1 and 2 until front measures 15½ (17½, 20) inches from beginning, ending with a RS row.

Neck shaping

Ch 1, sc in each st across to last 5 (6, 7) sts, turn.

Perfect for boy or girl, this hooded jacket is just right for heading back to school when the weather is beginning to turn cooler. Stitch the argyle diamonds in the primary colors shown, or select your child's school colors to show their school spirit!

Dec row: Ch 1, sk first sc, continue in established pattern across, turn. Rep dec row every other row, twice more. Work even on rem 21 (22, 23) shoulder sts to same length as back, ending with a RS row.

Left Front

Rows 1–3: Rep of right front.

Body

Row 1 (WS): Ch 1, sc in each st across, turn.

Row 2: Ch 1, hdc in first sc, hdc in each of next 4 sc, fpdc over next fpdc 2 rows below, sk the sc behind fpdc, hdc in each of next 9 sc, fpdc over next fpdc 2 rows below, sk the sc behind fpdc, hdc in each of next 13 (15, 17) sc, turn.

Rep Rows 1 and 2 until front measures 15½ (17½, 20) inches from beg, ending with a RS row, fasten off.

Neck shaping

With RS facing, sk first 5 (6, 7) sts,

attach yarn with a sl st in next st, ch 1, sc in same st as joining, continue in established pattern to end.

Dec row: Ch 1, hdc in each st across and sk last sc, turn. Rep dec row every other row, twice more. Work even on rem 21 (22, 23) shoulder sts to same length as back, ending with a RS row, fasten off.

Sleeve

Make 2

Row 1 (RS): Beg at lower edge with hook size G and MC, ch 27 (31, 35), sc in 2nd ch from hook, sc in each rem ch across, turn. (26, 30, 34 sc)

Row 2: Ch 1, sc in each sc across, turn.

Rep Row 2 until piece measures 3 inches from beg, ending with a RS row.

Body

Row 1 (WS): Ch 1, sc in each st across, turn.

Row 2 (RS): Ch 1, hdc in each sc across, turn.

Row 3: Ch 1, sc in first st, 2 sc in next st, sc in each st across to last 2 sts, 2 sc in next st, sc in last st, turn.

Row 4: Ch 1, hdc in each st across, turn.

[Rep Rows 3 and 4] 8 (5, 3) times, then inc 1 st each edge as established every 4th row 1 (4, 6) times. Work even on 46 (50, 54) sts until piece measures 11 (12, 13) inches from beg, fasten off.

Hood

Row 1: Beg at front side with hook size G and MC, ch 83 (85, 91), sc in 2nd ch from hook, sc in each rem ch across, turn. (82, 84, 90 sts)

Row 2 (RS): Ch 1, hdc in each sc across, turn.

Row 3: Ch 1, sc in each hdc across, turn.

Rep Rows 2 and 3 until piece measures 9 inches from beg, fasten off.

Argyle Diamonds

Note: Make 14 from red, yellow and blue.

Row 1: With hook size F, ch 9, sc in 2nd ch from hook, sc in each rem ch across, turn. (8 sc)

Rows 2–7: Ch 1, sc in each sc across, turn. At the end of Row 7, leaving a length of yarn, fasten off.

Finishing

Sew shoulder seams. Place markers

6½ (7, 7½) inches at each side from shoulder seams. Set in sleeve between markers. Sew underarm and side seams. Easing in fullness to fit, pin hood to WS of jacket and around the neckline. With hook size G and MC, sl st in place. Sew top edges tog to close hood.

Alternating colors, pin argyle diamonds to the areas between post sts on each front; sew in place with rem lengths of yarn. With double strand of yarn, blue on yellow, yellow on red and red on blue diamonds, make a big cross-st over center of diamond, then secure with a straight st

Continued on page 79

Dozens of Dots Sweaters

Design by Ann E. Smith

Skill Level: Beginner

Size: Child's 4 (6 and 8)

Chest: 30 (32, 34) inches

Length: 14 (16, 18) inches

Instructions are for smallest size, with larger sizes in parentheses.

Materials

- Lion Brand Wool-Ease Sportweight 3-ply sport weight yarn (5 oz/435 yds per ball): 2 (2, 3) balls white frost #501 (MC), 2½ oz green #132, small amount each purple #144, turquoise #148 and fuchsia #146

- Size H/8 crochet hook or size needed to obtain gauge

- Straight pins

- Tapestry needle

Gauge

15 sc = 4 inches; 9 sc rows = 2 inches
Check gauge to save time.

Pattern Notes

Weave in loose ends as work progresses.

Pattern Stitch

Puff st: With WS facing, [yo, insert hook in st, yo, draw up a lp] 4 times in same st, yo, draw through 8 lps on hook, yo, draw through 2 lps on hook.

Back

Row 1 (RS): With MC, ch 57 (61, 65), sc in 2nd ch from hook, sc in each rem ch across, turn. (56, 60, 64 sc)

Like bubbles in the breeze, the colorful dots seem to float across this cute sweater!

Row 2: Ch 1, sc in each sc across, turn.

Rep Row 2 until piece measures 14 (16, 18) inches from beg, fasten off.

Front

Work the same as back until piece measures 12 (14, 16) inches from beg , ending with a WS row.

First neckline shaping

Row 1 (RS): Ch 1, sc in each of next 22 (22, 23) sc, turn.

Row 2: Ch 1, sc in first sc, dec 1 sc over next 2 sc, sc in each rem sc across, turn.

Row 3: Ch 1, sc in each sc across, turn.

[Rep Rows 2 and 3] twice. (19, 19, 20 sc)

Rep Row 2 until front measures the same as back, fasten off.

Second neckline shaping

Row 1 (RS): Sk next 12 (16, 18) sc, attach MC in next sc, ch 1, sc in same sc as beg ch-1, sc in each rem sc across, turn. (22, 22, 23 sc)

Row 2: Ch 1, sc in each sc across to last 3 sc, dec 1 sc over next 2 sc, sc in next sc, turn.

Row 3: Ch 1, sc in each sc across, turn.

[Rep Rows 2 and 3] twice. (19, 19, 20 sc)

Rep Row 2 until front measures the same as back, fasten off.

Sleeve

Make 2

Row 1 (RS): Beg at lower edge, with MC, ch 31 (33, 35), sc in 2nd ch from hook, sc in each rem ch across, turn. (30, 32, 34 sc)

Row 2: Ch 1, sc in each sc across, turn.

Continue to rep Row 2, inc 1 st each edge every 4th row 3 (4, 3) times and then every 6th row 4 (4, 6) times. (44, 48, 52 sc)

Continue to rep Row 2 until sleeve measures 9 (10, 11½) inches from beg, fasten off.

Dots

Note: Make 8 each green, purple, turquoise and fuchsia, or as desired.

Do not join rnds unless otherwise indicated.

Rnd 1: Ch 2, 5 sc in 2nd ch from hook. (5 sc)

Rnd 2: [2 sc in next sc] rep around. (10 sc)

Rnd 3: [Sc in next sc, 2 sc in next sc] rep around, sl st in next st, leaving a length of yarn, fasten off. (15 sc)

Finishing

Sew shoulder seams. Place markers 6 (6½, 7) inches each side of shoulder seam. Set in sleeve between markers. Pin dots onto sweater pieces in a random manner. Using rem lengths, sew dots to sweater. Sew sleeve and side seam.

Neckline Trim

Rnd 1 (RS): Attach MC at shoulder seam, ch 1, work 48 (54, 58) hdc evenly sp around neckline opening, sl st to join in top of first hdc, turn.

Rnd 2 (WS): Ch 1, sc in same st as beg ch-1, puff st in next hdc, [sc in next hdc, puff st in next hdc] rep around, sl st to join in beg sc, fasten off, turn.

Rnd 3 (RS): Attach green with a sl st in same sc as joining, ch 1, hdc in same st as joining, hdc in each puff st and each sc around, join in top of first hdc.

Rnds 4 & 5: Ch 1, sc in each st around, sl st to join in beg sc.

Rnd 6: Ch 1, reverse sc in each st around, sl st to join in beg sc, fasten off.

Bottom Trim

Rnd 1 (RS): Attach green with sl st in side seam, ch 1, hdc in same st, working in opposite side of foundation ch, hdc in each ch around, ending with an even number of sts, sl st to join in beg hdc, fasten off, turn.

Rnd 2 (WS): Attach MC, ch 1, sc in same st as beg ch-1, puff st in next st, [sc in next st, puff st in next st] rep around, sl st to join in beg sc, fasten off, turn.

Rnd 3 (RS): Attach green, ch 1, hdc in same st as beg ch-1, hdc in each st around, sl st to join in beg hdc.

Rnd 4 (RS): Ch 1, reverse sc in each st around, sl st to join in beg sc, fasten off.

Sleeve Trim

Rnd 1 (RS): Attach green in sleeve seam, ch 1, sc in same ch as beg ch-1, sc in each rem ch around, sl st to join in beg sc. (30, 32, 34 sc)

Rnd 2: Ch 1, sc around, dec 6 (8, 10) sc sts evenly sp around, sl st to join in beg sc. (24 sc)

Rnds 3–10: Ch 1, sc in each sc around, sl st to join in beg sc. At the end of Rnd 10, fasten off.

Rnd 11 (RS): Attach white, ch 1, sc in same st as beg ch-1, puff st in next sc, [sc in next sc, puff st in next sc] rep around, sl st to join in beg sc, fasten off. ✂

Girls Scrap Poncho

Design by Tammy Hildebrand

Skill Level: Beginner

Size: Girl's small 7–8 (medium 10–12 and large 14–16)

Instructions are given for smallest size, with larger sizes given in parentheses.

Materials

- Worsted weight yarn: 4 (6, 8) oz off-white (MC), 3 (4, 5) oz various scraps (CC)
- Size J/10 crochet hook or size needed to obtain gauge
- Tapestry needle

Gauge

3 dc = 1 inch; 3 rows = 2 inches
Check gauge to save time.

Pattern Notes

Weave in loose ends as work progresses.

Ch-3 counts as first dc throughout.

Join rnds with a sl st unless otherwise stated.

Pattern Stitches

Cross-st: Sk next st, dc in next st, dc in sk st.

Beg cross-st: Ch 3, dc in previous st.

Poncho

Rnd 1 (RS): Starting at neckline, with MC, ch 56 (68, 80), dc in 4th ch from hook, dc in each of next 6 (8, 10) chs, [dc, ch 2, dc] in next ch, [dc in each of next 8 (10, 12) chs, {dc, ch 2, dc} in next ch] 5 times, join in top of beg ch. (6 ch-2 points)

Rnd 2: Beg cross-st, [cross-st over each of next 2 sts across to next ch-2 sp, {2 dc, ch 2, 2 dc} in next ch-2 sp] 6 times, join in 3rd ch of beg ch-3, fasten off.

Rnd 3: Attach CC in any ch-2 sp, ch 1, [sc, ch 2, sc] in same ch-2 sp, working in sps before each cross-st, [sc, ch 3] in each sp, sc in sp before next 2 sts, [{sc, ch 2, sc} in next ch-2 sp, {sc, ch 3} in sp before each cross-st across, sc in sp before next 2 sts] rep around, join in beg sc, fasten off.

Rnd 4: Attach MC in any ch-2 sp, ch 3, [dc, ch 2, 2 dc] in same ch-2 sp, 2 dc in each ch-3 sp across edge, [{2 dc, ch 2, 2 dc} in next ch-2 sp, 2 dc in each ch-3 sp across] rep around, join in 3rd ch of beg ch-3.

[Rep Rnds 2–4] 8 (10, 12) times.

[Rep Rnds 2 and 3] once.

With ponchos back in fashion, here's a great way to add warmth to your daughter's wardrobe and use up remnants from previous projects!

Bottom Trim

Rnd 1: Attach MC in any ch-2 sp, ch 3, 6 dc in same ch-2 sp, [sc in next ch-3 sp, {5 dc in next ch-3 sp, sc in next ch-3 sp} rep across to next ch-2 sp, 7 dc in next ch-2 sp] 5 times, sc in next ch-3 sp, [5 dc in next ch-3 sp, sc in next ch-3 sp] rep across, join in 3rd ch of beg ch-3, fasten off.

Neckline Trim

Rnd 1: Attach MC in opposite side of foundation ch, ch 1, sc in same ch, ch 1, [sc in next ch, ch 1] rep around, join in beg sc, fasten off. ✄

Pumpkin Hat

Design by Michele Wilcox

Skill Level: Beginner

Size: Child's 6–12

Materials

- Coats & Clark Red Heart TLC 3-ply light worsted weight yarn: 5 oz copper #5289, small amount each mushroom #5339 and kiwi #5657
- Size G/6 crochet hook or size needed to obtain gauge
- Tapestry needle

Gauge

7 sc rows = 1½ inches; 4 hdc = 1 inch; 3 hdc rows = 1 inch
Check gauge to save time.

Pattern Notes

Weave in loose ends as work progresses.

Join rnds with a sl st unless otherwise stated.

Ribbing

Row 1: With copper yarn, ch 19, sc in 2nd ch from hook, sc in each rem ch across, turn. (18 sc)

Rows 2–86: Ch 1, working in back lps only, sc in each st across, turn.

Hat

Row 1: Working across long edge of ribbing in ends of rows, ch 1, 86 sc across edge, turn.

Cute as a ... well, pumpkin—and warm, too. Your child will look adorable in this hat all winter long!

Row 2: Ch 1, [sc in each of next 8 sts, sc dec over next 2 sts] 8 times, sc in each of next 6 sc, turn. (78 sc)

Rows 3–17: Ch 1, hdc in each st across, turn. (78 hdc)

Row 18: Ch 1, [hdc in each of next 5 sts, hdc dec over next 2 sts] 11 times, hdc in next st, turn. (67 hdc)

Row 19: Ch 1, [hdc in each of next 4 sts, hdc dec over next 2 sts] 11 times, hdc in next st, turn. (56 hdc)

Row 20: Ch 1, [hdc in each of next 3 sts, hdc dec over next 2 sts] 11 times, turn. (45 hdc)

Row 21: Ch 1, [hdc in each of next 2 sts, hdc dec over next 2 sts] 11 times, hdc in next st, turn. (34 hdc)

Row 22: Ch 1, [hdc in next st, hdc dec over next 2 sts] 11 times, hdc in next st, turn. (23 hdc)

Row 23: Ch 1, [hdc dec over next 2 sts] 11 times, hdc in next st, fasten off. (12 hdc)

Weave a length of copper yarn through rem sts of Row 23 and pull to gather; secure. Sew seam of hat and ribbing and turn ribbing upward.

Stem

Rnd 1: With mushroom, ch 2, 6 sc in 2nd ch from hook, join in beg sc. (6 sc)

Continued on page 80

Thirty-Minute Cloche

Design by Katherine Eng

Skill Level: Beginner

Size: Adult

Materials

- Lion Brand Homespun bulky weight yarn (6 oz per skein): 2½ oz Tudor #315
- Size H/8 crochet hook or size needed to obtain gauge
- Tapestry needle

Gauge

Rnds 1 and 2 = 2 inches
Check gauge to save time.

Pattern Notes

Weave in loose ends as work progresses.

Join rnds with a sl st unless otherwise stated.

Cloche

Rnd 1: Ch 4, sl st to join to form a ring, ch 1, 8 sc in ring, join in beg sc. (8 sc)

Rnd 2: Ch 1, 2 sc in each sc around, join in beg sc. (16 sc)

Rnds 3 & 4: Ch 1, sc in first sc, ch 1, [sc in next sc, ch 1] rep around, join in beg sc.

Rnd 5: Ch 1, 2 sc in first sc, ch 1, [2 sc in next sc, ch 1] rep around, join in beg sc. (36 sc)

Rnds 6 & 7: Ch 1, sc in each of first 2 sc, ch 1, [sc in each of next 2 sc, ch 1] rep around, join in beg sc.

Rnds 8 & 9: Ch 1, sc in each of first 2 sc, ch 2, [sc in each of next 2 sc, ch 2] rep around, join in beg sc.

Rnds 10–20: Ch 1, sc in each of first 2 sc, ch 3, [sc in each of next 2

Crochet this stylish cloche from start to finish in under an hour. Since it doesn't take much yarn, it's a great way to use up your leftovers!

sc, ch 3] rep around, join in beg sc.

Rnd 21: Ch 1, sc in each of first 2 sc, [sc, ch 3, sc] in next ch-3 sp, [sc in each of next 2 sc, {sc, ch 3, sc} in next ch-3 sp] rep around, join in beg sc, fasten off. ✄

Teen Totes & Topper

Designs by Kathleen Garen

Skill Level: Intermediate

Size

Topper: One size fits all

Drawstring Tote: 6¼ inches in diameter x 7 inches

Shoulder Tote: 6¼ x 10 inches including fringe, excluding shoulder strap

Materials

- Worsted weight yarn: 1 skein each royal blue, bright lime green and turquoise
- Size I/9 crochet hook or size needed to obtain gauge
- 96 silver pony beads
- Tapestry needle

Gauge

3 cl sts = 2 inches; 2 rnds = 1½ inches

Check gauge to save time.

Pattern Notes

Weave in loose ends as work progresses.

Join rnds with a sl st unless otherwise stated.

Pattern Stitch

2-dc cl: [Yo hook, insert hook in indicated sp, yo, draw up a lp, yo, draw through 2 lps on hook] twice, yo, draw through all 3 lps on hook.

Topper

Center Top

Note: Make 1 each royal blue and turquoise.

Rnd 1 (RS): Ch 5, sl st to join to form a ring, ch 1, sc in ring, ch 1, dc in ring, ch 2, [2-dc cl, ch 2] 7 times in ring, join in top of first dc. (8 ch-2 sps)

Hat

Rnd 2: Holding the center tops tog with turquoise facing and working through both thicknesses, attach royal blue in any ch-2 sp, ch 1, sc in same ch-2 sp, ch 1, dc in next sp, ch 1, [2-dc cl in same sp, ch 1, 2-dc cl in same and next sp, ch 1] rep around, join in top of first dc. (16 sps)

Rnd 3: Sl st into next ch-1 sp, ch 1, sc in same sp, ch 1, dc in next sp, *[ch 1, dc, ch 1] in same sp, 2-dc cl in same and next ch sp, ch 1 **, 2-dc cl in same and next ch sp, rep from * around, ending last rep at **, join in top of first dc. (24 ch-1 sps)

Rnd 4: Sl st into next ch-1 sp, ch 1, sc in same sp, ch 1, dc in next sp, ch 1, [2-dc cl in same and next sp, ch 1] rep around, join in top of beg dc.

Rnd 5: Sl st into ch-1 sp, ch 1, sc in same ch sp, ch 1, dc in next sp, *ch 1, dc in same ch sp, ch 1, [2-dc cl in same and next ch sp, ch 1] twice **, 2-dc cl in same and next sp, rep from * around, ending last rep at **, dc in same ch sp, ch 1, join in top of first dc. (33 ch-1 sps)

Rnd 6: Rep Rnd 4, fasten off.

Rnd 7: Attach turquoise in any ch-1 sp, ch 1, sc in same sp, ch 1, sp dc in next ch sp, ch 1, [2-dc cl in same and next ch sp, ch 1] rep around, join in top of first dc, fasten off.

Rnd 8: With royal blue, rep Rnd 7.

Rnd 9: With bright lime green, rep Rnd 7.

Rnd 10: With royal blue, rep Rnd 7, do not fasten off.

Rnd 11: Ch 1, work 2 sc in each ch-1 sp around, join in beg sc. (66 sc)

Rnd 12: Ch 3 (counts as first dc), dc in same sc as beg ch-3, 2 dc in each rem sc around, do not join, turn.

Your fashion-conscious teen will love this hat and tote set. Select the shoulder tote or drawstring tote, or make both to match the hat in her favorite colors!

Rnd 13: Draw up a lp, remove hook, insert hook from back side into first dc, draw a lp through to join, sl st in each rem dc around, join, fasten off.

Sew 33 pony beads between sts of Rnd 8 with matching yarn.

Bow

Sl 2 pony beads into royal blue yarn, leaving a small length of yarn at beg, ch 20, sl first bead up next to ch, ch 1, sl st in each ch back to beg, ch 20, sl 2nd pony bead up next to ch, ch 1, sl st in each ch back to beg of 2nd portion of ch, leaving a length of yarn, fasten off.

Tie rem beg and ending lengths of yarn to ch on Rnd 10 of topper. Tie ch lengths into a bow.

Drawstring Tote

Rnd 1: With royal blue, ch 5, sl st

to join to form a ring, ch 1, sc, ch 1, dc in ring, ch 2, [2-dc cl in ring, ch 2] 7 times, join in top of first dc, fasten off. (8 ch-2 sps)

Rnd 2: Attach bright lime green in any ch-2 sp, ch 1, sc in same sp, ch 1, dc in next ch sp, ch 1, 2-dc cl in same sp, ch 1, [2-dc cl over same and next ch sp, ch 1, 2-dc cl in same sp, ch 1] rep around, join in top of first dc. (16 ch sps)

Rnd 3: With royal blue, rep Rnd 3 of topper, fasten off. (24 ch sps)

Rnd 4: Attach turquoise in any ch sp, ch 1, sc in same sp, ch 1, dc in next ch sp, *ch 1, dc in same sp, ch 1, [2-dc cl over same and next ch sp tog, ch 1] twice **, 2-dc cl over same and next ch sp, rep from * around, ending last rep at **, join, fasten off. (32 ch sps)

Rnd 5: Attach royal blue in any ch sp, ch 1, sc in same sp, ch 1, dc in next ch sp, ch 1, [2-dc cl over same and next ch sp, ch 1] rep around, join in top of first dc, fasten off. (32 sps)

Rnds 6–16: Rep Rnd 5 in the following color sequence: bright lime green, royal blue, turquoise, royal blue, bright lime green, royal blue, turquoise, royal blue, bright lime green, royal blue and turquoise.

Rnd 17: Attach royal blue in any ch sp, ch 2 (counts as first hdc), hdc in same sp, 2 hdc in each ch sp around, do not join, turn. (64 hdc)

Rnd 18: Draw up a lp, remove hook, insert hook from back side through first hdc of rnd, pick up

dropped lp and draw through, sl st in each st around, join, fasten off.

With royal blue yarn, sew 32 pony beads between sts of Rnd 11.

Drawstring

Make 2

With royal blue, ch 100, sl st in 2nd ch from hook, sl st in each rem ch across, fasten off.

Weave first drawstring through ch sps of Rnd 15; weave 2nd drawstring in same manner starting at opposite side from previous drawstring.

Place 2 pony beads on each end of drawstrings. Tie ends tog in a simple

knot 2 inches from end; trim ends as desired.

Shoulder Tote

Side

Make 2

Rnd 1: With royal blue, ch 8, hdc in 3rd ch from hook, [ch 1, sk next ch, hdc in next ch] twice, ch 1, sl st in first ch of beg ch-8 to join, working in end sp just made by joining, ch 1, [sc, ch 1, dc] in same sp, ch-2, 2-dc cl in same sp, ch 1 (corner made), [2-dc cl over same and next ch sp, ch 1] 3 times,

Continued on page 81

Reversible Tote Bag

Design by Darla Fanton

You'll find as many uses for this tote as it has colors. Crocheted with a double-ended hook, the reversible design gives you the opportunity to practice your technique while using up scraps from previous projects!

Gauge

5 sts = 1 inch; 9 rows = 1 inch
Check gauge to save time.

Pattern Notes

Weave in loose ends as work progresses.

Fasten off scrap colors at the end of each 2-row section; carry black along edge of work.

Join rnds with a sl st unless otherwise stated.

Front

Row 1: With double-ended hook and black, ch 202, working through back lps only, insert hook in 2nd ch from hook, yo, draw through, *to draw up a lp, insert hook in back lp of next ch, yo, draw through, leaving all lps on hook, rep from * across foundation ch. Slide all sts to opposite end of hook, turn. (202 lps on hook)

Row 2: To work lps off hook, place desired scrap color on hook with sl knot, working from left to right draw sl knot through first lp, *yo, draw through 2 lps (1 lp of each color), rep from * across until 1 lp rem on hook, do not turn.

Row 3: With same scrap color and working right to left, ch 1, sk first vertical bar, [draw up a lp under next vertical bar] 66 times, draw up a lp under next 3 vertical bars at once (double dec made), [draw up a lp under next vertical bar] 62 times, draw up a lp under next 3 vertical bars at once, [draw up a lp under next vertical bar] 67 times, slide all sts to opposite end of hook, turn. (198 lps on hook)

Row 4: Pick up black, yo and draw through 1 lp, *yo and draw through 2 lps (1 lp of each color), rep from * across until 1 lp rem on hook, do not turn.

Row 5: With black and working right to left, ch 1, sk first vertical bar, [draw up a lp under next vertical bar] 65 times, draw up a lp under next 3 vertical

bars at once, [draw up a lp under next vertical bar] 60 times, draw up a lp under next 3 vertical bars at once, [draw up a lp under next vertical bar] 66 times, slide all sts to opposite end of hook, turn. (194 lps on hook)

Rows 6–65: Following established pattern, rep Rows 2–5 noting that on each succeeding odd numbered row you will pick up 1 less st before the first double dec, 2 less sts before the 2nd double dec and 1 less st after the 2nd double dec.

***Note:** On Row 65 there will be 0 sts picked up between the 2 double decreases.*

Row 66: Rep Row 2, leaving a 16-inch length of yarn, fasten off black

With tapestry needle and rem yarn end, working through front lps of the horizontal sts, join center seam.

Gusset

Row 1: With predominantly colored side facing and using black,

Continued on page 80

Holiday Pins

Designs by Lori Zeller

Skill Level: Beginner

Size

Heart: 2 inches

Shamrock: 1½ inches

Chick in egg: 2 inches

Star: 1¾ inches

Materials

- Crochet cotton size 10: 30 yds white, 20 yds each mauve, green and yellow, scrap of orange

- Size 5 steel crochet hook or size needed to obtain gauge

- Black dimensional fabric paint

- 4 (1-inch) pin backs

- ⅛-inch-wide satin ribbon: 2 (5-inch) pieces white, 6 inches each navy and peach

- Red star-shaped button

- White heart-shaped button

- Hot-glue gun

- Tapestry needle

Gauge

5 dc = ½ inch; 2 rnds = ½ inch

Check gauge to save time.

Pattern Notes

Weave in loose ends as work progresses.

Join rnds with a sl st unless otherwise stated.

Heart

Back

Rnd 1 (RS): With mauve, ch 3, 15 dc in 3rd ch from hook, join in top of first dc. (15 dc)

Rnd 2: Ch 1, sc in same st as joining, [hdc, dc] in next st, 3 tr in next st, [2 tr, dc] in next st, 2 dc in next st, dc in each of next 2 sts, [2 dc, ch 1, 2 dc] in next st (center bottom of heart), dc in each of next 2 sts, 2 dc in next st, [dc, 2 tr] in next st, 3 tr in next st, [dc, hdc] in next st, sc in next st, join in beg sc. (30 sts; 1 ch-1 sp)

Rnd 3: Ch 1, sc in same st as joining, [hdc, dc] in next st, 2 dc in each of next 5 sts, dc in each of next 8 sts, [2 dc, ch 1, 2 dc] in next ch-1 sp, dc in each of next 8 sts, 2 dc in each of next 5 sts, [dc, hdc] in next st, sc in next st, join in beg sc, fasten off. (46 sts; 1 ch-1 sp)

Front

Rnds 1–3: Rep Rnds 1–3 of back.

Edging

Rnd 4: Holding front and back tog and working through both thicknesses, attach white in ch-1 sp at bottom of heart, ch 1, [sc, ch 2, sc] in ch-1 sp, sc in each of next 12 sts, 2 sc in each of next 7 sts, sc in each of next 8 sts, 2 sc in each of next 7 sts, sc in each of next 12 sts, join in beg sc, fasten off. (62 sts; 1 ch-1 sp)

Quickly and easily, you can stitch one or all of these pins for yourself or to give as gifts!

Finishing

Tie white ribbon into a small bow and glue to center front of mauve heart. Glue white heart-shaped button to center of bow. Glue pin back to center back of mauve heart.

Shamrock

Back

Rnd 1 (RS): With green, ch 3, 16 dc in 3rd ch from hook, join in top of first dc. (16 dc)

Rnd 2: Ch 1, [sc, hdc] in same st as joining, [dc, tr] in next st, 3 tr in next st, [tr, dc] in next st, [hdc, sc] in next st, [{sc, hdc} in next st, {dc, tr} in next st, 3 tr in next st, {tr, dc} in next st, {hdc, sc} in next st] twice, ch 3, sc in 2nd ch from hook, sc in next ch, sc in last st, join in beg sc, fasten off.

Front

Rnds 1 & 2: Rep Rnds 1 and 2 of back. At the end of Rnd 2, do not fasten off.

Edging

Rnd 3: Holding front and back tog and working through both thicknesses, sl st in first st, sc in each of next 2 sts, 2 sc in each of next 5 sts, sc in each of next 2 sts, sl st in next st, [sl st in next st, sc in each of next 2 sts, 2 sc in each of next 5 sts, sc in each of next 2 sts, sl st in next st] twice, leaving a length of cotton, fasten off.

With rem length, sew stem sections tog.

Finishing

Tie white ribbon in a small bow and glue to front of shamrock. Glue pin back to center back of shamrock.

Chick in Egg

Egg Back

Rnd 1: With white, ch 3, 14 dc in 3rd ch from hook, join in top of first dc. (14 dc)

Rnd 2: Ch 1, [sc, hdc] in same st as joining, 2 dc in each of next 10 sts, [hdc, sc] in next st, 2 sc in each of next 2 sts, join in beg sc, fasten off. (28 sts)

Egg Front

Rnds 1 & 2: Rep Rnds 1 and 2 of egg back. At the end of Rnd 2, do not fasten off.

Edging

Rnd 3: Ch 1, working on egg front only, [sc, dc] in same st as joining, [dc, sc] in next st, sc in next st, holding front and back tog and working through both thicknesses, [2 sc in next st, sc in next st] 9 times, 2 sc in next st, working on egg front only, [{sc, dc} in next st, {dc, sc} in next st] 3 times, join in beg sc, leaving a length of cotton, fasten off.

Chick Front

Row 1: With yellow, ch 10, dc in 3rd ch from hook, dc in each of next 5 chs, sc in next ch, 10 dc in last ch (head), working on opposite side of foundation ch, sc in next ch, dc in each of next 6 chs, fasten off.

Chick Back

Row 1: Rep Row 1 of chick front, do not fasten off.

Edging

Row 2: Holding both pieces tog and working through both thicknesses, ch 1, sc in each of next 6 sts, sl st in next st, sc in next st, 2 sc in each of next 8 sts, sc in next st, sl st in next st, sc in each of next 6 sts, fasten off.

Beak

Attach orange in 10th st back from end of last row, ch 1, [sc, ch 1, sc] in same st, fasten off.

Finishing

Sew chick in egg so head sticks up above egg. Paint a small black dot for eye. Tie peach ribbon into a small bow and glue to front of egg. Glue pin back to center back of egg.

Star

Back

Rnd 1: With white, ch 2, 10 sc in 2nd ch from hook, join in beg sc. (10 sc)

Rnd 2: Ch 2 (does not count as a st), work 2 dc in each sc around, join in top of first dc. (20 dc)

Rnd 3: Ch 1, [{sc, dc} in next st, {dc, tr} in next st, {tr, dc} in next st, {dc, sc} in next st] 5 times, join in beg sc.

Rnd 4: [Sl st in next st, sc in each of next 2 sts, 2 sc in next st, ch 2, 2 sc in next st, sc in each of next 2 sts, sl st in next st] 5 times, fasten off.

Front

Rnds 1–4: Rep Rnds 1–4 of back. At the end of Rnd 4, do not fasten off.

Edging

Rnd 5: Holding front and back tog and working through both thicknesses, [sl st in next st, sc in each of next 4 sts, {sc, ch 2, sc} in ch-2 sp, sc in each of next 4 sc, sl st in next st] rep around, fasten off.

Finishing

Fold navy ribbon into a lp and glue to back of star-shaped button where ribbon crosses. Glue ribbon and button to front of star so that button is at center of the star. Glue pin back to center back. ✂

each of next 2 sts, with F, dc in next st, [with MC, dc in each of next 3 sts, with F, dc in next st] rep across, turn.

Rows 16 & 17: Continuing in dc sts, complete open diamond.

Rows 18–21: Rep Rows 14–17.

Row 22: Rep Row 14.

Row 23: Attach E, ch 3, dc in each st across, turn.

Row 24: Attach H, ch 3, dc in next 4 sts, with D, dc in next st, [with H, dc in each of next 5 sts, with D, dc in next st] rep across, turn.

Row 25: Maintaining color pattern of Row 24, work 3 dc with H centered over 5 dc of previous row and 3 dc with D centered above the single dc of previous row, rep pattern across, turn.

Row 26 Maintaining color pattern of previous row, work 1 dc with H centered over 3 dc of previous row and 5 dc with D centered above 3 dc of previous row, rep pattern across, turn.

Rows 27–29: Rep Rows 24–26 reversing colors.

Row 30: With E, leaving 4 (5, 6) sts at neckline edge for neck shaping, ch 3, dc across row, turn.

Row 31: Rep Row 9.

Row 32: With F, ch 2, dc in next 2 sts, with B, dc in next st, [with F, dc in each of next 3 sts, with B, dc in next st] rep across, turn.

Rows 33–36: Maintaining color pattern of previous row of 3 dc sts with F and 1 dc with B, work the dc st with B on the diagonal away from neckline, turn. At the end of Row 36, fasten off.

Back

Row 1: Beg at bottom with ribbing, with MC, ch 67 (69, 71), dc in 3rd ch from hook, dc in each rem st across, turn. (66, 68, 70 dc)

Rows 2–10: Rep Rows 2–10 of front ribbing in same pattern and color changes.

Body

Rows 1–29: Rep pattern sts and color changes the same as for front.

Rows 30–36: Working on all sts of back, do not dec any sts, work pattern and color the same as Rows 30–36 for front.

Sew shoulder and side seams of front and back tog.

Neckline Trim

Row 1 (WS): Attach B in side edge of bottom ribbing on left front, ch 1, work evenly sp up left front, working 2 sc over each dc post, sc evenly sp around neckline, sc evenly sp down right front, turn.

Row 2 (RS): Attach C, ch 1, sc evenly sp up right front, around neckline and down left front, turn.

Row 3 (WS): Attach MC, ch 1, sc evenly sp up left front, around neckline and down right front, turn.

Buttonhole edge

Row 4 (RS): Ch 1, sc in each sc up right front only, turn.

Row 5: Ch 1, sc in each sc down right front, turn.

Row 6: Count number of sts, leaving 2 sc at beg and end of row, ch 1, sc across, working 6 buttonholes of ch 1, sk 1 sc evenly sp across, turn.

Row 7: Ch 1, sc in each sc and sc in each ch-1 sp on right front, turn.

Rows 8 & 9: Ch 1, sc in each sc on right front, turn. At the end of Row 9, fasten off.

Button edge

Row 4 (RS): Attach MC at neckline edge to work down left front only, ch 1, sc in each sc down left front, turn.

Rows 5–9: Ch 1, sc in each sc of left front, turn. At the end of Row 9, fasten off.

Sew buttons opposite buttonholes.

Sleeve

Make 2

Rnd 1 (WS): Attach A at underarm, ch 3, work 69 (73, 75) dc sts around armhole opening, join in 3rd ch of beg ch-3, turn. (60, 73, 75 dc)

Rnd 2: With MC, ch 3, dc in each st around, join in 3rd ch of beg ch-3, turn.

Note: Do not be concerned if pattern does not work out evenly.

Rnd 3: With A, ch 3, dc in next 5 sts, with B, dc in each of next 2 sts, [with A, dc in each of next 6 sts, with B, dc in each of next 2 sts] rep around, join in 3rd ch of beg st, turn.

Rnd 4: Attach I, ch 1, sc in each st around, join in beg sc, turn.

Note: Beg with Rnd 5, dec 1 dc at

joining seam on each rnd until otherwise indicated.

Rnd 5: Rep Row 2.

Rnd 6: With A, ch 3, dc in each of next 5 sts, with F, dc in next st, [with A, dc in each of next 6 sts, with F, dc in next st] rep around, join in 3rd ch of beg ch-3, turn.

Rnd 7: Rep Rnd 2.

Rnd 8: Attach H, ch-3, dc in each of next 2 sts, with MC, dc in each of next 2 sts, [with H, dc in each of next 3 sts, with MC, dc in each of next 2 sts] rep around, join in 3rd ch of beg ch-3, turn.

Rnd 9: Beg with a ch-3, with H work 5 dc and with MC work 3 dc in any pattern sequence around, join in top of beg ch-3, turn.

Rnd 10: Rep Rnd 8.

Rnd 11: Rep Rnd 2.

Rnd 12: With E, ch 3, dc in each st around, join in 3rd ch of beg ch-3, turn.

Rnd 13: Rep Rnd 2.

Rnd 14: With MC, ch 3, dc in next 2 sts, with F, dc in next st, [with MC, dc in each of next 3 sts, with F, dc in next st] rep around, join in 3rd ch of beg ch-3, turn.

Rnd 15: With MC, ch 3, with F, dc in next dc, [with MC, dc in next dc, with F, dc in next dc] rep around, join in 3rd ch of beg ch-3, turn.

Rnd 16: Rep Rnd 14.

Rnds 17–20: Rep Rnds 13–16.

Rnd 21: Rep Rnd 2.

Rnd 22: Attach B, ch 1, sc in first st, [draw up a lp of J, sc in next st, with B, sc in next st] rep around.

Rnds 23 & 24: Attach H, ch 3, dc in each st around, join in 3rd ch of beg ch-3.

Rnd 25: Rep Rnd 12.

Rnds 26 & 27: Rep Rnds 23 and 24.

Note: On the following 2 rnds, dec as needed so that at the end of Rnd 29 you will have a total of 30 (32, 34) sts on sleeve.

Rnd 28: Attach G, ch 1, sc around, dec as needed, join in beg sc, turn.

Rnd 29: Attach MC, ch 1, sc around, dec as needed, join in beg sc, turn. (30, 32, 34 sc)

Cuff

Rnd 30 (RS): With MC, ch 3, dc in each st around, join in 3rd ch of beg ch-3, turn.

Rnd 31 (WS): Attach C, ch 1, [sc in first st, bpdc around next st] rep around, join in beg sc, turn.

Rnd 32 (RS): Attach B, ch 1, sc in same sc, fpdc around dc, [sc in next sc, fpdc around next dc] rep around, join in beg sc, turn.

Rnd 33 (WS): Attach MC, ch 1, sc in same sc, bpdc around next dc, [sc in next st, bpdc around next st] rep around, join in beg sc, turn.

Rnd 34: With C, rep Rnd 32.

Rnd 35: With B, rep Rnd 33.

Rnd 36: With MC, rep Rnd 32, fasten off. ✄

COLOR KEY
OPEN DIAMOND
T MC
T F

TTTTTTTTTTT Row 17
TTTTTTTTTTT Row 16
TTTTTTTTTTT Row 15

Open Diamond

COLOR KEY
CLOSED DIAMOND
T H
T E

TTTTTTTTTTT Row 6
TTTTTTTTTTT Row 5
TTTTTTTTTTT Row 4

Closed Diamond

STITCH KEY
TT Dc sts

Hooded Jacket

Continued from page 65

through center.

Body & Hood Trim

Row 1 (RS): With hook size G, attach MC with sl st in lower corner of right front, ch 1, sc in same sp as joining, work 54 (60, 68) sc evenly sp up front to hook, 54 (56, 60) sc evenly sp around hood, 55 (61, 69) sc evenly sp to corner of left front edge, turn.

Row 2: Ch 1, sl st in back lp of each sc around, turn.

Row 3: Ch 3, dc in each rem lp around, turn.

Row 4: Ch 1, sc in each dc around, turn.

Row 5: Sl st through both lps of each sc around, fasten off.

Sew buttons to left band, skipping 3½ (5, 7) inches at lower edge, then spacing them 10 sts apart. For buttonholes, slightly spread sp between 2 dc on right band to form an opening. Turn sleeve cuff upward. ✄

Pumpkin Hat

Continued from page 70

Rnd 2: Ch 1, sc in each sc around, join in beg sc.

Rnd 3: Ch 1, [sc in next sc, 2 sc in next sc] 3 times, join in beg sc. (9 sc)

Rnds 4–6: Rep Rnd 2. At the end of Rnd 6, leaving a length of yarn, fasten off.

Sew stem to center top of hat.

Curl

Row 1: With kiwi, ch 21, 3 sc in 2nd ch from hook, 3 sc in each rem ch across, leaving a length of yarn, fasten off.

Sew curl to base of stem.

Leaf

Rnd 1: With kiwi, ch 7, sc in 2nd ch from hook, hdc in each of next 2 chs, dc in each of next 2 chs, 5 dc in last ch, working on opposite side of foundation ch, dc in each of next 2 chs, hdc in each of next 2 chs, sc in next ch, join in beg sc. (15 sts)

Rnd 2: Ch 1, 2 sc in same sc as joining, ch 2, sl st in 2nd ch from hook, [hdc in each of next 2 sts, ch 2, sl st in 2nd ch from hook] 3 times, hdc in next st, ch 2, sl st in 2nd ch from hook, hdc in same st as last hdc, [hdc in each of next 2 sts, ch 2, sl st in 2nd ch from hook] 3 times, 2 sc in last sc, join in beg sc, leaving a length of yarn, fasten off.

Sew leaf to base of stem. ✄

Reversible Tote Bag

Continued from page 75

working in the opposite side of foundation ch, pick up 202 sts, slide all sts to opposite end of hook, turn. (202 lps on hook)

Row 2: Rep Row 2 of front.

Row 3: With scrap color, working right to left, ch 1, sk first vertical bar, *draw up a lp under next vertical bar, rep from * across, slide all sts to opposite end of hook, turn. (202 lps on hook)

Row 4: Rep Row 4 of front.

Row 5: With black, rep Row 3 of gusset.

Rows 6–37: Rep Rows 2–5, ending after a Row 5.

Back

Rep Rows 2–66 of front.

Top Band

Rnd 1: With predominantly black side facing and using standard hook, join black at top edge 3 inches in from right edge with a sc, sc evenly sp around, join in beg sc.

Rnd 2: Ch 1, sc in each st around, join in beg sc.

Rnds 3–7: Rep Rnd 2.

Rnd 8: Ch 2 (counts as first hdc), hdc in each st around, join in 2nd ch of beg ch-2.

Rnds 9–15: Rep Rnd 2. At the end of Rnd 15, fasten off.

Fold band in half toward colored side. With tapestry needle and black, whipstitch top edge of band to Rnd 1 of band, tucking in yarn ends to conceal them as work progresses.

Handle

Make 4

Row 1: With black and standard hook, ch 6, sc in 2nd ch from hook, sc in each rem ch across, turn. (5 sc)

Row 2: Ch 1, sc in each sc across, turn.

Rep Row 2 until handle reaches desired length.

Note: Handles on model are 28 inches in length.

Finishing

Center the end of a handle over top band of back on predominantly black side where rnds of band were joined. Center a 2nd handle over top band on opposite side to match and using tapestry needle and black, join tog working through all 4 thicknesses. Center a button over handle on each side and attach with a cross-stitch. Rep for rem ends of handle on back, centering them in 3 inches from left side. With black yarn continue to join the 2 handles between the band. Rep for rem 2 handles and front. ✄

Teen Totes & Topper

Continued from page 73

ending in the sp at opposite end of ch, in this end sp work [2-dc cl, ch 2, 2-dc cl, ch 1, 2-dc cl, ch 2, 2-dc cl], ch 1, [2-dc cl over same and next ch sp, ch 1] 3 times, ending in first end sp, work [2-dc cl, ch 2, 2-dc cl], ch 1, join in top of first dc, fasten off. (14 ch sps)

Rnd 2: Attach bright lime green in any ch-1 sp on long side, ch 1, sc in same sp, ch 1, dc in next sp, ch 1, *2-dc cl over this sp and next sp, ch 1*, rep * to * across until working into the ch-2 corner sp, in corner sp work 2-dc cl, ch 2, 2-dc cl, ch 1, 2-dc cl over same sp and next ch sp, rep * to * to next corner, rep corner, continue to rep in same manner around, join in top of first dc, fasten off. (22 ch sps)

Rnd 3: Attach royal blue in any ch-1 sp along side edge, rep Rnd 2. (30 ch sps)

Rnd 4: Attach turquoise in any ch-1 sp along side edge, rep Rnd 2. (38 ch sps)

Sew 4 pony beads with matching yarn to center of each sp on beg of Rnd 1.

Trim

Row 1: On first side, starting in top right corner, attach royal blue, ch 1, 2 sc in same ch sp, 2 sc in each ch sp across edge, ending with 2 sc in top left corner (top opening edge), fasten off.

Rnd 2: On 2nd side, starting in top right corner, attach royal blue, ch 1, 2 sc in same ch sp, 2 sc in each ch sp across edge, ending with 2 sc in top left corner (top opening edge), holding both sides tog, matching ch sps and working through both thicknesses, work 2 more sc sts in top left corner, work 2 sc in each ch sp to bottom corner, work 4 sc in corner, 2 sc in each sp across bottom, 4 sc in next corner, 2 sc in each sp up

opposite edge, 2 sc in same corner as beg, sl st in first st of beg of 2nd side, fasten off.

Shoulder Strap

With royal blue, ch 100 (or as desired), sl st to join through both thicknesses of 2nd st, turn, draw up a lp, remove hook, insert hook in other side of next st, pick up dropped lp, sl st in each ch across, sl st in opposite side of top edge, fasten off.

Side Tie

Make 2

Leaving a length of yarn at beg, sl 2 pony beads onto royal blue yarn, ch 9, sl 1 bead close to hook, ch 1, sl st in each rem ch, ch 11, sl 2nd

bead close to ch, ch 1, sl st in each rem ch across, leaving a length of yarn, fasten off. Secure rem ends to side of strap at joining of tote.

Fringe

Sl 9 pony beads onto royal blue yarn, attach yarn with sc in corner bottom st, ch 3, sl 1 bead up next to hook, ch 1, sl st in each of 3 chs, ch 1, sk 1 st on tote, sc in next st, [ch 4, sl 1 bead up next to hook, ch 1, sl st in each of 4 chs, ch 1, sk next st on tote, sc in next st] rep across, with next fringe having 5 chs, then 6 chs, then 7 chs, then the next 4 fringes will have 6 chs, 5 chs, 4 chs and 3 chs, sc in next corner st, fasten off. ✀

Artistic Scraps

The smallest scraps can be turned into a work of art that's simply elegant. Frame a favorite picture with tiny flowers, or create your own picture by framing a doily or crocheting a lovely greeting card!

Tulipmania Table Topper

Design by Dot Drake

Skill Level: Intermediate

Size: 34 x 37 inches

Materials

- Crochet cotton size 10: 1300 yds white (MC), 915 yds various scrap colors (CC)
- Size 8 steel crochet hook or size needed to obtain gauge
- Tapestry needle

Gauge

Rnds 1 and 2 = 1¾ inches; motif = 4¾ inches

Check gauge to save time.

Pattern Notes

Weave in loose ends as work progresses.

Join rnds with a sl st unless otherwise stated.

Ch-3 counts as first dc throughout.

Each motif requires approximately 18 yds MC and 15 yds CC. Border requires approximately 200 yds MC. Make and join a total of 61 motifs.

First Motif

Rnd 1 (RS): With MC, ch 5, join to form a ring, join in beg sc. (12 sc)

Rnd 2: [Ch 12, sl st in same sc, working over edge of first ch of ch-12, work 22 sc over lp, sl st in next 2 sc] 6 times, fasten off. (6 lps)

Rnd 3: With CC, *ch 10, draw lp through first ch, in lp just made work 8 sc over first half of lp, sc in 11th sc next 22 sc of Rnd 2 of lp, 8 sc over rem of same lp, ch 22, draw lp through 13th ch of ch-22, work 8 sc over first half of ch-8 lp, sc in next sc on same lp of Rnd 2,

8 sc over 2nd half of same lp, rep from * around, join to joining of first lp.

Rnd 4: [{5 sc, ch 3, 5 sc, ch 5, 5 sc, ch 3, 5 sc} over ch-12 sp, sc between next 2 sc lps] rep around, join in beg sc, fasten off.

Rnd 5: Attach MC in ch-5 sp, [ch 3, 2 dc, ch 3, 3 dc] in same ch-5 sp, *[ch 5, dc in next ch-3 sp] twice, ch 5 **, [3 dc, ch 3, 3 dc] in next ch-5 sp (for corner shell), rep from * around, ending last rep at **, join in 3rd ch of beg ch-3, fasten off. (6 corner shells)

Second Motif

Rnds 1–4: Rep Rnds 1–4 of first motif.

Rnd 5: Attach MC in ch-5 sp, [ch 3, 2 dc, ch 3, 3 dc] in same ch-5 sp, [ch 5, dc in next ch-3 sp] twice, ch 5, †3 dc in ch-5 sp of working motif, ch 1, sc in corner ch-3 sp of previous motif, ch 1, 3 dc in same ch-5 sp of working motif (for corner joining), [ch 2, sc in next ch-5 sp on previous motif, ch 2, dc in next ch-3 sp of working motif] twice, ch 2, sc in next ch-5 sp on previous motif, ch 2, rep from † to, *[ch 5, dc in next ch-3 sp] twice, ch 5 **, [3 dc, ch 3, 3 dc] in next ch-5 sp, rep from * around, ending last rep at **, join in 3rd ch of beg ch-3, fasten off.

Remaining Motifs

Continue to make motifs joining to previous motifs in hexagon shape. Make and join 9 motifs for the center strip, then working out from each outer edge from center strip in rows with 1 less motif each row

until at outer edge on each side only 5 motifs are joined in row. When more then 1 motif is joined at a corner junction, sc in same sp.

Border

Rnd 1 (RS): Attach MC in ch-3 corner sp before a joining of motifs, ch 1, sc in ch-5 sp, [ch 7, sc in next ch sp] twice, *ch 7 dc in next ch sp before joining of

Set the table for a summer tea party with this beautiful table topper. A vase of fresh flowers would make the perfect centerpiece!

motifs, ch 7, tr in joining of 2 motifs, ch 7, dc in next ch sp after join of motifs [ch 7, sc in next ch sp] rep until 1 ch sp before joining of 2 motifs, rep from * around, join in beg sc.

Rnd 2: Ch 10 (counts as first dc, ch 7), [ch 7, dc in next ch sp] rep around, ending with ch 3, tr in 3rd ch of beg ch-10 to position hook in center of last ch sp.

Rnd 3: Ch 1, sc in same sp as beg ch-1, ch 11, draw lp through 7th ch from hook, in ring just formed work [4 sc, ch 3] 3 times, 4 sc in same ring, ch 4, *sc in next ch sp of Rnd 2, ch 11, draw lp through 7th ch from hook, in ring just formed work 4 sc, ch 1, sc in adjacent ch-3 sp, ch 1 **, [4 sc in ring, ch 3] twice, 4 sc in same ring, ch 4, rep from * around, ending last rep at **, 4 sc in ring, ch 3, 4 sc in ring, ch 1, sc in first ch-3 sp of rnd, ch 1, 4 sc in ring, ch 4, join in beg sc, fasten off. ✂

Dappled Blossoms Table Runner

Design by Carol Alexander

Skill Level: Intermediate

Size: 16 x 41 inches

Materials

- Crochet cotton size 10: 150 yds variegated pastels, 450 yds white, 65 yds each violet, delft blue, soft yellow, 60 yds each medium rose, spruce, medium peach

- Size 7 steel crochet hook or size needed to obtain gauge

- 75 (5mm) white pearl beads

- Bead needle

- Tapestry needle

- Starch

Gauge

Rnd 1 of motif = 1¼ inches in diameter; motif = 2½ inches

Check gauge to save time.

Pattern Notes

Weave in loose ends as work progresses.

Join rnds with a sl st unless otherwise stated.

Pattern Stitches

Extended dc (edc): Yo, insert hook in indicated st, yo, draw up a lp, yo, draw through 1 lp on hook, [yo, draw through 2 lps on hook] twice.

V-st: [Dc, ch 3, dc] in indicated st.

Joining V-st: Dc in indicated st on working motif, ch 1, sl st in ch-3 sp of corresponding V-st on previous motif, ch 1, dc in same sp as previous dc on working motif.

Beg tr cl: Ch 3 (counts as first tr), *yo hook twice, insert hook in indicated st, yo, draw up a lp, [yo, draw through 2 lps on hook] twice, rep from * once, yo, draw through all 3 lps on hook.

Tr cl: *Yo hook twice, insert hook in indicated st, yo, draw up a lp, [yo, draw through 2 lps on hook] twice, rep from * twice, yo, draw through all 4 lps on hook.

Dc picot (dcp): Ch 5, dc in 5th ch from hook.

Picot (p): Ch 3, sl st in 3rd ch from hook.

Picot shell (pshell): [2 dc, p, 2 dc] in indicated st.

First Motif

Rnd 1 (RS): With variegated pastels, ch 5, join to form a ring, ch 1, [2 sc in ring, ch 3, dc in top of last sc, ch 3, sl st in top of same sc] 8 times, join in beg sc, fasten off. (8 flower petals)

Rnd 2: Attach white in free sc of Rnd 1 between any 2 flower petals, ch 11 (counts as edc, ch-7), *edc in free sc of Rnd 1 between next 2 petals, ch 4 **, edc in free sc of Rnd 1 between next 2 petals, ch 7, rep from * 7 times, ending last rep at **, join in 4th ch of beg ch-11, fasten off. (8 edc; 4 ch-7 sps; 4 ch-4 sps)

Rnd 3: Attach delft blue cotton in any ch-7 sp, ch 1, *[sc, hdc, 3 dc, ch 3, 3 dc, hdc sc] in ch-7 sp, [sc, ch 1, 2 dc, ch 1, 2 dc, ch 1, sc] in next ch-4 sp, rep from * 3 times, join in beg sc, fasten off.

Flower Center

With delft blue, ch 5, sl st in beg ch (first petal made), [ch 4, sl st

Stitch this exquisite table runner to brighten an entry hall or dining room. Wherever it is displayed it is sure to draw many favorable comments!

in same ch] 7 times, fasten off. (8 petals) Holding flower center evenly behind pearl bead, sew bead and center securely to flower as shown.

Rnd 4: Attach white in corner ch-3 sp, ch 1, *[3 sc, ch 3, 3 sc] in corner ch-3 sp, ch 1, V-st between next 2 sc, ch 1, [sc, ch 1, sc] in ch-1 sp between next 2 dc, ch 1, V-st between next 2 sc, ch 1, rep from * 3 times, join in beg sc, fasten off.

Remaining Motifs

Note: Make 13 motifs each with Rnd 3 worked in violet and soft yellow. Make 12 motifs each with Rnd 3 worked in delft blue, spruce, medium peach and medium rose. Join according to placement chart.

Following placement chart, rep Rnds 1–3 of first motif and flower center, using appropriate color

for Rnd 3 and same color for flower center.

Rnd 4 (Joining rnd): Attach white in corner ch-3 sp, ch 1, in same sp work 3 sc, ch 1, sl st in corresponding corner ch-3 sp on previous motif, ch 1, 3 sc in same ch-3 sp on working motif, ch 1, joining V-st between next 2 sc, ch 1, in ch-1 sp between next 2 dc work (sc, sl st in corresponding ch-1 sp on previous motif, sc) ch 1, joining V-st between next 2 sc, ch 1, in next corner ch-3 sp work (3 sc, ch 1, sl st in corresponding corner ch-3 sp on previous motif, ch 1, 3 sc), complete rem of rnd same as for first motif.

Following placement chart, make and join 73 more motifs in same manner as 2nd motif. When joining a corner to previously joined corners, work joining sl st into center of previous joining.

Border

Rnd 1: Attach white in corner ch-3 sp at right end of long side of runner, ch 1, *[sc, ch 2, sc] in corner sp, ch 3, sc in last sc of corner group, [ch 3, sc in next V-st, ch 3, sc in ch-1 sp between next 2 sc, ch 3, sc in next V-st, ch 3, sc in first sc of next corner group, ch 3, sc in corner joining, ch 3, sc in last sc of next corner group] 15 times, †ch 3, sc in next V-st, ch 3, sc in ch-1 sp between next 2 sc, ch 3, sc in next V-st, ch 3, sc in first sc of next corner group, ch 3, [sc, ch 2, sc] in corner sp ch 3, sc in last sc of corner group, [ch 3, sc in next V-st, ch 3, sc in ch-1 sp between next 2 sc, ch 3, sc in next V-st, ch 3, sc in first sc of next corner group, ch 3, sc in corner joining, ch 3, sc in last sc of next corner group] 5 times, rep from † to † once, rep from * once, join in beg sc.

Rnd 2: Sl st in corner sp, ch 2, 2 hdc in same sp, *3 hdc in each ch-3 sp across to next corner **, 3 hdc in corner sp, rep from * 3 times, ending last rep at **, join in 2nd ch of beg ch-2.

Notes: While working Rnd 3, adjust spacing of sts needed between [ ], keeping sts consistent between opposite sides.

Total number of ch-3 sps on each side must be an odd number.

Rnd 3: Sl st in next corner st, ch 1, *sc in corner st, sc in each of next 6 sts, [ch 3, sk next 3 sts, sc in each of next 8 sts] rep across, ending in 10 sts from next corner st, ch 3, sk next 3 sts, sc in each of next 6 sts, rep from * 3 times, join in beg sc.

Rnd 4: Sl st in corner ch-4 sp, beg tr cl in same sp, [dcp, tr cl] 6 times in same corner sp, *ch 2, sc in 4th sc of next 6-sc group, [ch 2, pshell in next ch-3 sp, ch 2, sc in 5th sc of next 8-sc group, ch 2, tr cl in next ch-3 sp, {dcp, tr cl} 4 times in same sp, ch 2, sc in 5th sc of next 8-sc group] rep across, ending in 5th sc of last 8-sc group before corner, ch 2, pshell in next ch-3 sp, ch 2, sc in 4th sc of next 6-sc group, ch 2 **, tr cl in next corner sp, [dcp, tr cl] 6 times in same corner sp, rep from * 3 times, ending last rep at **, join in top of beg tr cl.

Rnd 5: *Sl st in next dcp, [ch 2, p, ch 2, sl st in next dcp] 5 times, [ch 4, {sc, ch 3, sc} in p of next pshell, ch 4, sl st in next dcp, {ch 2, p, ch 2, sl st in next dcp} 3 times] rep across, ending just before last p shell before corner, ch 4, [sc, ch 3, sc] in p of next p shell, ch 4, rep from * 3 times, join in beg sl st, fasten off.

Starch and block runner. ✂

R	Y	B	P	V	S	R	Y	B	P	V	S	R	Y	B
P	V	S	R	Y	B	P	V	S	R	Y	B	P	V	S
Y	B	P	V	S	R	Y	B	P	V	S	R	Y	B	P
V	S	R	Y	B	P	V	S	R	Y	B	P	V	S	R
B	Y	P	P	R	S	B	Y	V	P	S	R	Y	B	V

Placement Chart

COLOR KEY
R Medium rose
B Delft blue
Y Soft yellow
V Violet
S Spruce
P Medium peach

Cross-Stitch Bookmark

Design by Sandy Scoville

Skill Level: Beginner

Size: 1⅞ x 7 inches, excluding tassel

Materials

- Crochet cotton size 10: 30 yds white, 20 yds each pink, light green, yellow, aqua and peach
- Size 6 steel crochet hook or size needed to obtain gauge
- Tapestry needle

Gauge

9 dc = 1 inch

Check gauge to save time.

Pattern Notes

Weave in loose ends as work progresses.

Ch-3 counts as first dc throughout.

Join rnds with a sl st unless otherwise stated.

To join new color, work last st until 2 lps rem on hook, yo with new color and draw through rem 2 lps on hook.

Pattern Stitch

Cross-st: Sk next 2 sts, dc in next st, ch 1, crossing in front of last dc, dc in 2nd skipped st.

Bookmark

Row 1 (WS): With white, ch 18, dc in 4th ch from hook, work 4 cross-sts across ch, dc in each of next 2 chs, turn. (2 dc; 4 cross-sts, 2 dc)

Row 2: Ch 3, dc in next dc, work 4 cross-sts, dc in each of next 2 dc, turn.

Row 3: Rep Row 2, fasten off, turn.

Row 4: Attach pink, ch 3, dc in each dc and each ch-1 sp across, turn. (16 dc)

Row 5: Ch 3, dc in each dc across, fasten off, turn.

Row 6: Attach white, ch 3, dc in next dc, work 4 cross-sts, dc in each of next 2 dc, turn.

Rows 7 & 8: Rep Rows 2 and 3.

Row 9: Attach light green, rep Row 4.

Row 10: Rep Row 5.

Rows 11–13: Rep Rows 6–8.

Row 14: Attach yellow, rep Row 4.

Row 15: Rep Row 5.

Rows 16–18: Rep Rows 6–8.

Row 19: Attach aqua, rep Row 4.

Row 20: Rep Row 5.

Rows 21–23: Rep Rows 6–8.

Row 24: Attach peach, rep Row 4.

Row 25: Rep Row 5.

Rows 26–28: Rep Rows 6–8. At the end of Row 28, do not fasten off.

Rnd 29: Ch 1, working around outer edge, [sc in next st, ch 3] rep evenly sp around, join, fasten off.

Tassel

Cut 10 strands white and 2 strands each rem color each 6 inches in length. Fold strands in half, insert hook between 2nd and 3rd cross-sts of Row 1, draw strands through at fold, to form a lp on hook, draw cut ends through lp on hook. Pull gently to secure. Trim ends evenly. ✄

A quick and easy project, this bookmark is a great way to use scraps of any color!

Americana Bookmarks

Designs by Lori Zeller

Skill Level: Beginner

Size

Granny's Daughter: 1¼ x 6¼ inches

Delicate Diamonds: 2 x 6 inches

Materials

- Crochet cotton size 10: 25 yds each navy and cream, 20 yds burgundy

- Size 5 steel crochet hook or size needed to obtain gauge

- Tapestry needle

- Tapestry needle

Gauge

Granny square = ¾ inch; diamond motif = 1¼ inches corner to corner
Check gauge to save time.

Pattern Notes

Weave in loose ends as work progresses.

Ch-3 counts as first dc throughout.

Join rnds with a sl st unless otherwise stated.

Granny's Daughter

Square

Make 5 navy and 4 burgundy

Rnd 1 (RS): Ch 5, join to form a ring, ch 3, 2 dc in ring, ch 3, [3 dc in ring, ch 3] 3 times, join in 3rd ch of ch-3, fasten off.

Edging

Rnd 1: Attach cream with a sc in ch-3 sp of navy square, ch 3, sc in same sp, [ch 3, sk next dc, sc in next dc, ch 3, insert hook in next ch-3 sp, yo, draw up a lp, insert

hook in any ch-3 sp of a burgundy square, yo, draw up a lp, yo, draw through all 3 lps on hook, ch 3, sk next dc, sc in next dc, ch 3, insert hook in next ch-3 sp, yo, draw up a lp, insert hook in any ch-3 sp of a navy square, yo, draw up a lp, yo, draw through all 3 lps on hook] 4 times, [ch 3, sk next dc, sc in next dc, ch 3, {sc, ch 3, sc} in next ch-3 sp] twice, [ch 3, sk next dc, sc in next dc, {insert hook in next ch-3 sp, yo, draw up a lp} twice, yo, draw through all 3 lps on hook] 8 times, ch 3, sk next dc, sc in next dc, ch 3, sc in next ch-3 sp, ch 3, sk next dc, sc in next dc, ch 3, join in beg sc. (44 ch-3 sps)

Rnd 2: Sl st in first ch-3 sp, ch 1, [sc, ch 3, sc] in same ch-3 sp, *[ch 3, sc in next ch-3 sp] 18 times, ch 3, [sc, ch 3, sc] in next ch-3 sp, [ch 3, sc in next ch-3 sp] twice, ch 3 **, [sc, ch 3, sc] in next ch-3 sp, rep from * around, ending last rep at **, join in beg sc.

Rnd 3: Sl st in next ch-3 sp, ch 1, sc in same sp, *ch 3, dc in 3rd ch from hook, sc in same ch-3 sp as last sc, [ch 3, sc in 3rd ch from hook, sc in next ch-3 sp] 20 times, ch 3, dc in 3rd ch from hook, sc in same ch-3 sp as last sc, [ch 3, dc in 3rd ch from hook, sc in next ch-3 sp] 4 times, rep from * around, join in beg sc, fasten off.

Delicate Diamonds

First Motif

Rnd 1: With navy, ch 4, join to form a ring, ch 1, [sc in ring, ch 5] 4 times, join in beg sc.

Rnd 2: Sl st in first ch-5 sp, ch 3, 4 dc in same sp, ch 4, [5 dc in next

ch-5 sp, ch 4] 3 times, join in 3rd ch of ch-3.

Rnd 3: Ch 1, sc in same st as joining, *[ch 3, sk next dc, sc in next dc] twice, ch 3, [sc, ch 3, sc] in next ch-4 sp, ch 3 **, sc in next dc, rep from * around, ending last rep at **, join in beg sc, fasten off.

Second Motif

Rnds 1 & 2: With burgundy, rep Rnds 1 and 2 of first motif.

Stitch a little bit of Americana for the book lover in your life!

Rnd 3: Ch 1, sc in same st as joining, *[ch 3, sk next dc, sc in next dc] twice, ch 3 **, [sc, ch 3, sc] in next ch-4 sp, ch 3, sc in next dc, rep from * 3 times, ending last rep at **, ch 3, sc in next ch-4 sp, ch 1, sl st in ch-3 sp at corner point of previous motif, ch 1, sc in same ch-4 sp, ch 3, join in beg sc, fasten off.

Third Motif

Rnds 1 & 2: With navy, rep Rnds 1 and 2 of first motif.

Rnd 3: Rep Rnd 3 of 2nd motif, joining 3rd motif to opposite corner point.

Edging

Rnd 1: Attach cream in corner ch-3 sp point, ch 4 (counts as first dc, ch-1), [dc in ch-3 sp, ch 1] 5 times in same corner ch-3 sp, sk next ch-3 sp, sc in next ch-3 sp, *[ch 3, sc in next ch-3 sp] twice, ch 1, [sc, ch 3, sc] in next ch-3 sp, ch 1, sc in next ch-1 sp, [ch 3, sc in next ch-3 sp] twice, ch 3, sk next ch-3 sp on navy motif and next ch-3 sp on burgundy motif, sc in next ch-3 sp, [ch 3, sc in next ch-3 sp] twice,

ch 1, [sc, ch 3, sc] in next ch-3 sp, ch 1, sc in next ch-1 sp, [sc, ch 3, sc] in next ch-3 sp] twice, ch 3, sk next ch-3 sp on burgundy motif and next ch-3 sp on navy motif, sc in next ch-3 sp, [ch 3, sc in next ch-3 sp] twice, ch 1, [sc, ch 3, sc] in next ch-3 sp, ch 1, sc in next ch-1 sp, [ch 3, sc in next ch-3 sp] twice, ch 1 **, [dc in next ch-3 sp,

ch 1] 6 times, sk next ch-3 sp, sc in next ch-3 sp, rep from * around, ending last rep at **, join in 3rd ch of ch-4.

Rnd 2: Sl st into first ch-1 sp, ch 1, sc in same sp, [ch 3, dc in 3rd ch from hook, sc in next ch-1 sp] 4 times, ch 3, dc in 3rd ch from hook, sk next ch-1 sp, *[sc in next ch-3 sp, ch 3, dc in 3rd ch from

hook] twice, sc in next ch-3 sp, ch 3, dc in 3rd ch from hook, sc in same ch-3 sp as last sc, [ch 3, dc in 3rd ch from hook, sc in next ch-1 sp] twice, ch 3, dc in 3rd ch from hook, sk next ch sp *, rep from * to * twice, sc in next ch-1 sp, rep from 8 to *, join in beg sc, fasten off. ✄

Pansies & Heart Cards

Designs by Jennifer Moir

Skill Level: Beginner

Size

Pansies card: 5¾ x 6¾ inches

Heart card: 3¾ x 4¼ inches

Materials

- Crochet cotton size 20: Scrap amount each white, cream, lilac, gold, camel, medium blue, green

- Size 9 steel crochet hook or size needed to obtain gauge

- Craft glue

- Scissors

- Tape measure

- 2 sheets heavy purple paper

- 2 sheets heavy white paper

- 10 inches each ⅛-inch-wide ribbon: white, pink

- Fabric stiffener

- Tapestry needle

Gauge

5 tr rows = 1½ inches

Check gauge to save time.

Pattern Notes

Weave in loose ends as work progresses.

Join rnds with a sl st unless otherwise stated.

Pansies Card

Vase

Row 1: Beg at bottom of vase, with cream, ch 19, 2 tr in 5th ch from hook, 2 tr in next ch, tr in each of next 11 chs, 2 tr in next ch, 3 tr in last ch, turn. (21 tr)

Row 2: Ch 4 (counts as first tr throughout), 4 tr in same st as ch-4, [sk next 4 tr, 5 tr in next tr] rep across, turn. (5 groups of 5-tr)

Row 3: Sl st into center tr of first 5-tr group, ch 4, 4 tr in same st, [ch 1, 5 tr in center tr of next 5-tr group] rep across, turn.

Rows 4–6: Sl st into center tr of 5-tr group, ch 4, 4 tr in same st, [ch 2, 5 tr in center tr of next 5-tr group] rep across, turn.

Rows 7 & 8: Sl st into center tr of 5-tr group, ch 4, 4 tr in same st, [ch 3, 5 tr in center tr of next 5-tr group] rep across, turn.

Row 9: Sl st into center tr of 5-tr group, ch 4, 6 tr in same st, [ch 3, 7 tr in center tr of next 5-tr group] rep across, turn.

Row 10: Ch 1, sc in first tr, sk 2 tr, 5 tr in next tr, [{sc, ch 4, sc} in next ch-3 sp, 5 tr in center tr of next 7-tr group] rep across, ending with sc in top of ch-4, turn.

Row 11: Ch 4, 3 tr in same sc as ch-4, sc in center tr of next 5-tr group, [4 tr in next ch-4 sp, sc in center tr of next 5-tr group] rep across, ending with 4 tr in last sc, fasten off.

Base

Row 1: Working in opposite side of foundation ch, sk first ch, attach cream in next ch, ch 1, sc in same ch, sc in each of next 13 chs, turn. (14 sc)

Row 2: Ch 4, tr in next sc, [ch 4, sk next 2 sc, tr in each of next 2 sc] rep across, turn.

Row 3: Ch 1, sc in sp between next 2 tr, [5 sc in next ch-4 sp, sc in sp between next 2 tr] rep across, turn. (19 sc)

Row 4: Ch 4, 5 tr in same sc as ch-4, [sk next 2 sc, sc in next sc, sk next 2 sc, 6 tr in next sc] rep across, fasten off.

Crochet one of these cheery greetings to brighten a friend's day or to frame and display!

Pansy

Note: Make 1 each gold, lilac, camel and medium blue.

Rnd 1: Ch 7, join to form a ring, ch 3 (counts as first dc throughout), 2 dc in ring, ch 7, [3 dc in ring, ch 7] 4 times, join in 3rd ch of ch-3. (15 dc; 5 ch-7 sps)

Rnd 2: Sl st into center dc of 3-dc group, ch 1, sc in same dc, [12 dc in next ch-7 sp, sc in center dc of 3-dc group] 3 times, ch 4, [dtr, ch 1] 10 times in next ch-7 sp, [tr, ch 1, dc] in same ch-7 sp, sc in center dc of next 3-dc group, [dc, ch 1, tr] in next ch-7 sp, [ch 1, dtr] 10 times in same ch-7 sp, ch 4, join in beg sc, fasten off.

Triple Leaf

Make 2

Row 1: With green, ch 13, 6 tr in 5th ch from hook, turn. (7 tr)

Row 2: Ch 3, [dc dec over next 2 sts] twice, dc in next st, do not work in last st, turn. (4 dc)

Row 3: Ch 1, sk first st, sc dec over next 2 sts, do not work in last st, ch 3, sc in 3rd ch from hook,

working down side of leaf, ch 1, sl st in top of st at end of Row 2, ch 2, sl st in top of st at end of Row 1, ch 4, sl st in same ch as beg 6-tr, sl st in next ch on foundation ch (first leaf completed).

Row 4: Ch 6, 6 tr in 5th ch from hook, turn. (7 tr)

Rows 5 & 6: Rep Rows 2 and 3 to complete 2nd leaf.

Row 7: Ch 6, 6 tr in 5th ch from hook, turn. (7 tr)

Rows 8 & 9: Rep Rows 2 and 3 to complete 3rd leaf, sc in each rem ch of beg foundation ch, fasten off.

Finishing

Saturate all crocheted piece with fabric stiffener and allow to dry completely. Cut purple paper to measure 5 x 6 inches. Cut white paper to measure 6¾ x 11½ inches;

fold in half to measure 5¾ x 6¾ inches. Glue purple paper centered on white card.

Glue vase to front of card. Arrange and glue leaves and pansies to card.

Heart Card

Heart

Row 1: Starting at bottom of heart, with white ch 6, dc in 6th ch from hook, turn.

Row 2: Ch 6, sc in next ch lp, ch 3, dc in 3rd ch of ch-6, turn.

Row 3: Ch 6, sc in next ch lp, ch 4, sc in next ch lp, ch 3, dc in 3rd ch of ch-6, turn.

Row 4: Ch 6, sc in next ch lp, [ch 4, sc in next ch lp] twice, ch 3, dc in 3rd ch of ch-6, turn.

Rows 5–13: Ch 6, sc in next ch lp, [ch 4, sc in next ch lp] rep across,

ending with ch 3, dc in 3rd ch of ch-6, turn. (13 lps)

Row 14: Ch 4, sc in next ch lp, [ch 4, sc in next ch lp] rep across, ending with ch 1, dc in 3rd ch of ch-6, turn.

Row 15: Ch 1, sc in dc, ch 4, sk ch-1 sp, [sc in next ch lp, ch 4] rep across, ending with sc in 3rd ch of ch-4, turn.

Row 16: Ch 4, sc in next ch lp, [ch 4, sc in next ch lp] rep across, ending with ch 1, dc in sc at end of row, turn.

Rows 17 & 18: Rep Rows 15 and 16.

Row 19: Ch 1, sc in top of dc, ch 4, sk ch-1 sp, [sc in next ch lp, ch 4] rep across, ending with sc in next lp, ch 1, dc in 3rd ch of ch-4, turn. (10 lps)

Continued on page 108

Irish Roses Photo Frame

Design by Nazanin Fard

Skill Level: Beginner

Size: 6 x 7½ inches

Materials

- DMC Cebelia crochet cotton size 20: 100 yds white
- Size 7 steel crochet hook or size needed to obtain gauge
- 6 x 7½-inch Pres-On classic oval photo frame
- 7 x 8½-inch 55 percent cotton, 45-percent rayon eggshell fabric
- 9½ x 12½ inches white CPE easy felt
- 6½ x 8-inch batting
- 25 inches ¼-inch-wide white ruffled lace
- 12 inches 3mm stringed pearls
- 2 (5mm) pearl beads
- Fabri-tac glue
- Bead needle

Gauge

Rose = 1¼ inches in diameter; 10 sc = 1 inch

Check gauge to save time.

Pattern Notes

Weave in loose ends as work progresses.

Join rnds with a sl st unless otherwise stated.

Rose

Make 2

Rnd 1 (RS): Ch 5, join to form a ring, ch 3 (counts as first dc), 11 dc in ring, join in 3rd ch of ch-3. (12 dc)

Rnd 2: [Ch 3, sk next dc, sl st in next dc] rep around. (6 ch-3 sps)

Rnd 3: Sl st into ch-3 sp, ch 1, [sc, hdc, 3 dc, hdc, sc] in each ch-3 sp around, join in beg sc. (6 petals)

Rnd 4: Working behind petals, sl st into next skipped dc of Rnd 1, [ch 5, sl st in next skipped dc of Rnd 1] rep around. (6 ch-5 sps)

Rnd 5: Sl st into ch-5 sp, ch 1, [sc, hdc, 5 dc, hdc, sc] in each ch-5 sp around, join in beg sc, fasten off. Sew a pearl bead to center of rose.

Leaf

Make 2

Row 1: Ch 15, sc in 3rd ch from hook, sc in each of next 11 chs, 3 sc in last ch, working on opposite side of foundation ch, sc in each of next 11 chs, turn. (26 sc)

Rows 2–5: Ch 1, sk first sc, sc in each sc across to center sc of 3-sc group, 3 sc in center sc, sc in each sc across to last 3 sc, turn. At the end of Row 5, fasten off.

Curly Tail

Make 4

Row 1: Ch 18, 2 dc in 3rd ch from hook, 3 dc in each rem ch across, fasten off.

Display your favorite photo framed in beautiful Irish crocheted roses, and finished with a string of pearls and ruffled lace!

Finishing

Remove paper from top part of photo frame. Place batting on front and cut edges to size. Place fabric on the batting and follow manufacturer instructions to cover right side. Glue string of pearls to inside edge of frame. Glue ruffled lace to outer edge of frame. Cover back and stand with white felt. Place photo at center of frame back, making sure it is placed in line with front opening. Secure front to back. Glue roses, leaves and curly tails as desired. ✂

Floral Heart Picture

Design by Dot Drake

Gauge

Heart = 8¼ x 8¼ inches; large flower = 3½ inches in diameter
Check gauge to save time.

Pattern Notes

Weave in loose ends as work progresses.

Join rnds with a sl st unless otherwise stated.

Heart

Large flower

Rnd 1 (RS): With white, ch 7, join to form a ring, sl st in each ch around.

Rnd 2: Ch 1, 25 sc over ring, join in beg sc. (25 sc)

Rnd 3: Working in front lps only, ch 1, sc in same st, ch 3, sk next st, [sc in next st, ch 3, sk next st] rep around, join in back lp of last sc.

Rnd 4: Working in rem back lps of Rnd 2, ch 1, sc in same st, ch 4, sk next 4 sc, [sc in next st, ch 4, sk next 4 sts] rep around, join in beg sc, fasten off. (5 lps)

Rnd 5: Attach pink in any ch-4 sp, ch 1, [sc, hdc, dc, 5 tr, dc, hdc, sc] in each ch-4 sp around, join in beg sc. (5 petals)

Rnd 6: Ch 2, working in back of Rnd 5, [sl st at base of center tr of next petal, ch 5] rep around, join in beg sl st. (5 lps)

Rnd 7: [{2 sc, ch 12, 2 sc} in ch-5 sp, ch 1] rep around, join in beg sc.

Rnd 8: Sl st in ch-12 sp, [{3 sc, 2 hdc, 3 dc, 5 tr, 3 dc, 2 hdc, 3 sc} in ch-12 sp, sl st across 2nd sc of 2, ch 1, sc in next sc] rep around, join in beg sc, fasten off.

Rnd 9: Attach white in first sc worked over ch-12 lp ch 1 and beg in same sc, [sc in each of next 2 sc worked over ch-12 lp, {ch 5, sl st in 5th ch from hook (for p), sc in each of next 3 sts} 3 times, sc in same sc as last sc, sc in each of next 2 sts, {ch 5, sl st in 5th ch from hook (for p), sc in each of next 3 sts} twice, ch 5, sl st in 5th ch from hook (for p), sc in each of next 2 sc] rep around, join in beg sc, fasten off.

Leaf

Make 2

Row 1: With aqua, ch 9, sc in 2nd ch from hook, sc in each of next 6 chs, 3 sc in last ch, working on opposite side of foundation ch, sc in next 5 chs, turn.

Row 2: Working in back lps only, ch 1, sc in each of next 6 sts, 3 sc in next st, sc in each of next 6 sts, turn.

Row 3: Working in back lps only, ch 1, sc in each of next 7 sts, 3 sc in next st, sc in each of next 5 sts, turn.

Row 4: Working in back lps only, ch 1, sc in each of next 6 sts, 3 sc in next st, sc in each of next 6 sts, turn. [Rep Rows 3 and 4] 3 times, then rep Row 3 and join with sl st to 2 p on large flower as shown and 1 p on next petal with dc. Attach 2nd leaf to opposite side of large flower to 3 p.

A beautiful way to display your crochet skills, this unique floral heart is also a great way to use up your leftovers!

Ring

Wind aqua around tip of little finger 8 times, sl off finger and insert hook through center, draw up a lp, ch 1, 2 sc in ring, [ch 2, 3 sc in ring] 6 times, dc in 2nd p from end on 1 petal, 3 sc in ring, dc in 2nd p on next petal, sc in ring, join in beg sc, fasten off.

Small Flower

Make 2

Rnds 1 & 2: Rep Rnds 1 and 2 of large flower.

Rnd 3: Working in front lps only, ch 1, sc in same st, ch 4, sk next 4 sts, [sc in next st, ch 4, sk next 4 sts] rep around, join in beg sc, fasten off.

Rnd 4: Attach yellow in ch-4 sp, ch 1, [sc, hdc, 5 dc, hdc, sc] in each ch-4 sp around, join in back of beg sc. (5 petals)

Rnd 5: [Ch 5, sc behind and between next 2 petals] rep around.

Rnd 6: Ch 1, [sc, hdc, 7 dc, had, sc] in each ch-5 sp around, join in beg sc, fasten off.

Rnd 7: Attach white in first sc of petal, ch 1, [sc in next 5 sts, ch 3,

sl st in 3rd ch from hook, sc in next st, ch 5, sl st in 5th ch from hook, sc in same place as last sc, sc in next st, ch 3, sl st in 3rd ch from hook, sc in next 4 sc] twice, sc in each of next 5 sts of next petal, ch 3, sl st in 3rd ch from hook, sc in next st, ch 2, sc in tip of leaf, ch 2, sc in same st on petal as last sc, sc in next st, ch 3, sl st in 3rd ch from hook, sc in next 5 sts, ch 3, sl st in 3rd ch from hook, sc in next st, ch 2, dc in next free p on flower, ch 2, sc in same st as last sc on small flower, sc in next st, ch 3, sl st in 3rd ch from hook, sc in next 4 sts, sc in next 5 sts, ch 3, sl st in 3rd ch from hook, sc in next st, ch 2, dc in p on side of ring, ch 2, sc in same st as last sc on small flower, sc in next st, ch 3,

sl st in 3rd ch from hook, sc in next 4 sts, join, fasten off.
Join 2nd small flower to opposite edge in reverse order of joining.

Border

Rnd 1: Attach white with sc in ch-3 p on small flower following joining with ring on right flower, [ch 5, tr in 5th ch from hook] twice, [sc in next ch-3 p on flower, ch 5, tr in 5th ch from hook] twice, [ch 5, tr in 5th ch from hook, sc in next ch-3 p] twice, [ch 5, tr in 5th ch from hook] twice, dc in tip of leaf, [ch 5 tr in 5th ch from hook, sk 3 rows of leaf, sc in next row] 3 times, ch 5, tr in 5th ch from hook, dc in same p on large flower as leaf joining, [ch 5, tr in 5th ch from hook, sc in next p on large

flower] twice, [ch 5, tr in 5th ch from hook] twice, sc in 3rd p on next petal, ch 5, tr in 5th ch from hook, dc in next p, ch 5, tr in 5th ch from hook, dc in same p, ch 5, tr in 5th ch from hook, sc in next p, [ch 5, tr in 5th ch from hook] twice, sc in 3rd p on next petal, ch 5, tr in 5th ch from hook, sc in next p, ch 5, tr in 5th ch from hook, dc in same p on petal as leaf was joined, [ch 5, tr in 5th ch from hook, sc in edge of leaf] 4 times, [ch 5, tr in 5th ch from hook] twice, sc in first ch-3 p of next petal, ch 5, tr in 5th ch from hook, sc in next ch-3 p, [ch 5, tr in 5th ch from hook] twice, sc in next ch-3 p on next petal, ch 5, tr in 5th ch from hook, sc in next ch-3 p,
Continued on page 108

Pansies Barrette

Design by Nazanin Fard

Crocheted pansies provide a splash of spring color to this delightful barrette— it's perfect for gift-giving!

Gauge

10 dc = 1 inch

Check gauge to save time.

Pattern Notes

Weave in loose ends as work progresses.

Join rnds with a sl st unless otherwise stated.

Size 10 ombre crochet threads can be substituted for pearl cotton threads.

Pansy

Make 5

Rnd 1: With 1 strand each cream and golden yellow held tog, ch 7, join to form a ring, ch 3 (counts as first dc throughout), 2 dc in ring, ch 7, [3 dc in ring, ch 7] 4 times, join in 3rd ch of beg ch-3, fasten off.

Rnd 2: With 1 strand each dark lilac and light lilac held tog, attach in center dc of 3-dc group, ch 1, sc in same dc as beg ch-1, [16 dc in next ch-7 sp, sc in center dc of next 3-dc group] 3 times, [sc, hdc, dc, 16 tr, dc, hdc, sc] in next ch-7 sp, sc in center dc of 3-dc group, [sc, hdc, dc, 16 tr, dc, hdc, sc] in next ch-7 sp, join in beg sc, fasten off.

Sew a pearl bead to the center of pansy.

Leaf

Make 2

Row 1: With 1 strand each spruce green and medium green held tog, ch 19, sc in 2nd ch from hook, sc in each of next 16 chs, 3 sc in last ch, working on opposite side of foundation ch, sc in next 14 chs, turn. (34 sc)

Rows 2–6: Ch 1, sk first sc, sc in each sc to center sc of 3-sc group, 3 sc in center sc, sc in each sc across until 3 sc rem, turn. At the end of Row 6, fasten off.

Finishing

Using photo as a guide, glue a leaf to each side of barrette. Arrange pansies as desired and glue to barrette. Spray pansies and leaves with stiffening spray. ✄

Beaded Coin Purse

Design by Nazanin Fard

Skill Level: Beginner

Size: 3 x 3 inches, excluding strap

Materials

- DMC Cébélia crochet cotton size 10 (284 yds per ball): 1 ball light pale yellow #745
- Size 7 steel crochet hook or size needed to obtain gauge
- 405 (3mm) gold beads
- Cream mini-swirl rose with leaves
- 1-inch hook-and-loop tape
- Sewing needle and matching thread
- Bead needle

Gauge

10 sc = 1 inch
Check gauge to save time.

Pattern Note

Weave in loose ends as work progresses.

Pattern Stitch

Bead sc: Push bead close to hook, sc in next sc.

Purse

Note: String the 405 beads onto light pale yellow cotton and push beads along cotton until pattern indicates to use a bead.

Row 1: Ch 31, sc in 2nd ch from hook, sc in each rem ch across, turn. (30 sc)

Row 2: Ch 1, sk next sc, [sc in next sc, bead sc in next sc] rep across, ending with sc in first ch, turn.

Row 3: Ch 1, sk first sc, sc in each sc across, ending with sc in first ch, turn.

Row 4: Ch 1, sk first sc, sc in each of next 2 sc, [bead sc in next sc, sc in next sc] rep across, ending with sc in next sc, sc in first ch, turn.

Row 5: Rep Row 3.

[Rep Rows 2–5] until piece measures 6½ inches. A total of 30 beaded rows.

Row 6: Ch 1, sk first sc, sc in each sc across, ending with sc in first ch, turn.

Rep Row 6 until piece measures 1 inch beyond beaded rows, fasten off.

With WS facing and beg with the 1-inch unbeaded sc section fold bottom up 2½ inches and sew side seams.

Strap

Leaving a 6-inch length at beg, [ch 3, {yo hook, insert hook in first ch of ch-3, yo, draw up a lp, yo, draw through 2 lps on hook} 3 times, yo, draw through all 4 lps on hook] rep to desired length, leaving a 6-inch length, fasten off.

Sew strap to each side of top opening of purse.

Made to be worn around the neck, this delicate coin purse showcases your beading skills.

Finishing

Sew hook-and-loop tape centered on the 1-inch unbeaded section and rem piece centered on underside flap. Sew ribbon rose on center front of flap in line with fastener that is on the underside. ✄

Floral Harvest Doily

Design by JoHanna Dzikowski

Skill Level: Beginner

Size: 17 inches

Materials

- Crochet cotton size 10: 100 yds natural, 50 yds spruce, 45 yds camel, 12 yds maize, 10 yds orchid pink
- Size B/1 crochet hook or size needed to obtain gauge
- Tapestry needle

Gauge

Motif = 6½ inches in diameter; flower = 2½ inches

Check gauge to save time.

Pattern Notes

Weave in loose ends as work progresses.

Ch-3 counts as first dc throughout.

Join rnds with a sl st unless otherwise stated.

Rnd 1 establishes RS of motif.

Center Motif

Rnd 1 (RS): With maize, ch 6, join to form a ring, ch 1, 12 sc in ring, join in front lp of beg sc. (12 sc)

Rnd 2 (RS): Working in front lps only, [ch 4, tr in same st, sl st in each of next 2 sts] 6 times. (6 petals)

Rnd 3 (RS): Sl st in rem back lp of Rnd 1, working in back lps only, ch 1, sc in same st as ch-1, ch 3, sk 1 st, [sc in next st, ch 3, sk 1 st] 5 times, join in beg sc, fasten off, turn. (6 ch-3 sps)

Rnd 4 (WS): Attach camel in ch-3 sp, ch 1, [sc, 2 dc, ch 1, 2 dc, sc] in each ch-3 sp around, join in beg sc. (6 petals)

Rnd 5 (WS): Working in same ch-3 sp of Rnd 3, sl st across into ch-3 sp between 2-dc groups, ch 1, [1 sc, ch 4, 1 sc] in ch-3 sp between dc sts of previous rnd, *[1 sc, ch 4, 1 sc] in next ch-3 sp between dc sts of previous rnd, rep from * around, join in beg sc. (6 ch-4 sps)

Rnd 6 (WS): Ch 1, [sc, 3 dc, ch 2, 3 dc, sc] in each ch-4 sp around, join in beg sc, fasten off. (6 petals)

Rnd 7 (WS): Attach spruce in ch-2 sp, ch 6 (counts as first dc, ch-3), dc in same ch-2 sp, ch 3, sc in sp between petals, ch 3, [{dc, ch 3, dc} in next ch-2 sp, ch 3, sc in sp between petals, ch 3] rep around, join in 3rd ch of beg ch-6.

Rnd 8 (WS): Sl st into ch-3 sp, ch 3, 4 dc in same ch-3 sp, *[ch 3, sc in next ch-3 sp] twice, ch 3 **, 5 dc in next ch-3 sp, rep from * around, ending last rep at **, join in 3rd ch of beg ch-3, fasten off. (6 groups 5-dc)

Rnd 9 (WS): Attach natural in center dc of 5-dc group, ch 3, 4 dc in same dc, *ch 4, sk next ch-3 sp, [dc, ch 3, dc] in next ch-3 sp, ch 4, sk next ch-3 sp **, 5 dc in center dc of 5-dc group, rep from * around, ending last rep at **, join in 3rd ch of beg ch-3.

Rnd 10 (WS): Sl st into center dc of 5-dc group, [ch 3, 2 dc, ch 3, 3 dc] in same dc, *ch 3, sc in next ch-4 sp, ch 3, [2 dc, ch 3, 2 dc] in next ch-3 sp, ch 3, sc in next ch-4 sp, ch 3 **, [3 dc, ch 3, 3 dc] in center dc of 5-dc group, rep from * around, ending last rep at **, join in 3rd ch of beg ch-3, fasten off.

Remaining Motifs

Note: Make 6 motifs. Work Rnds 1–3 of flower with orchid pink on 3 motifs and maize on 3 motifs.

Rnds 1–9: Rep Rnds 1–9 of center motif.

Rnd 10 (WS): Sl st into center dc of 5-dc group, [ch 3, 2 dc, ch 3, 3 dc] in same dc, ch 3, sc in next ch-4 sp, ch 3, [2 dc, ch 3, 2 dc] in next ch-3 sp, ch 3, sc in next ch-4

Natural earth tones are reflected in the quiet beauty of this delicate doily!

sp, ch 3, 3 dc in center dc of next 5-dc group, ch 1, sl st in ch-3 sp of previous motif, ch 1, 3 dc in same dc, ch 3, sc in next ch-4 sp on working motif, ch 3, 2 dc in next ch-3 sp, ch 1, sl st in ch-3 sp of previous motif, ch 1, 2 dc in same ch-3 sp, ch 3, sc in next ch-4 sp, ch 3, 3 dc in center dc of next 5-dc group, ch 1, sl st in ch-3 sp of previous motif, ch 1, 3 dc in same dc, *ch 3, sc in next ch-4 sp, ch 3, [2 dc, ch 3, 2 dc] in next ch-3 sp, ch 3, sc in next ch-4 sp, ch 3 **, [3 dc, ch 3, 3 dc] in center dc of next 5-dc group, rep from * around, ending last rep at **, join in 3rd ch of beg ch-3, fasten off.

Using photo as a guide for placement, continue joining motifs in same manner to previous motifs, joining last motif to previous, center and 2nd motif to close circle. ✂

Lilac Fantasy Doily

Design by Dot Drake

Skill Level: Intermediate

Size: 13 inches in diameter

Materials

- Crochet cotton size 10: 125 yds white, 50 yds each lilac and lavender, 75 yds pale green, 20 yds pale yellow, 10 yds dark yellow
- Size 8 steel crochet hook or size needed to obtain gauge
- Tapestry needle

Gauge

Flower = 2½ inches in diameter; 4 dc rows = 1 inch

Check gauge to save time.

Pattern Notes

Weave in loose ends as work progresses.

Ch-3 counts as first dc throughout.

Join rnds with a sl st unless otherwise stated.

Pattern Stitches

Popcorn (pc): Work 5 dc in ch sp, remove hook, insert hook in first dc of 5-dc group, pick up dropped lp and draw through st on hook.

Beg pc: Ch 3, 4 dc in same ch sp, remove hook, insert hook in 3rd ch of beg ch-3, pick up dropped lp and draw through st on hook.

Outer Flower

Make 6

Rnd 1 (RS): With pale yellow, ch 7, join to form a ring, ch 1, 16 sc in ring, join in beg sc. (16 sc)

Rnd 2: Ch 1, sc in same sc, ch 3, sk next sc, [sc in next sc, ch 3, sk next sc] rep around, join in beg sc, fasten off. (8 ch-3 sps)

Rnd 3: Attach white in any ch-3 sp, beg pc in same ch sp, ch 6, [pc in next ch-3 sp, ch 6] rep around, join in top of beg pc, fasten off. (8 pc)

Rnd 4: Attach lavender in any ch-6 sp, ch 1, [sc, hdc, 5 dc, hdc, sc] in each ch-6 sp around, join in beg sc. (8 petals)

Rnd 5: Sl st behind and between petals, ch 1, sc in same st, ch 6, [sc behind and between next 2 petals, ch 6] rep around, join in beg sc, fasten off.

Rnd 6: Attach lilac in any ch-6 sp, ch 1, [sc, hdc, dc, 7 tr, dc, hdc, sc] in each ch-6 sp around, join in beg sc, fasten off.

Center Flower

Rnd 1 (RS): With lavender, ch 6, join to form a ring, ch 1, 12 sc in ring, join in beg sc. (12 sc)

Rnd 2: Rep Rnd 2 of outer flower. (6 ch-3 sps)

Rnd 3: Rep Rnd 3 of outer flower. (6 pc)

Rnd 4: Attach pale yellow in ch-6 sp, ch 1, [sc, hdc, 7 dc, hdc, sc] in each ch-6 sp around, join in beg sc. (6 petals)

Rnd 5: Rep Rnd 5 of outer flower.

Rnd 6: Attach dark yellow in any ch-6 sp, ch 1, [sc, hdc, dc, 4 tr, ch 3, sl st in top of last tr, 3 tr, dc, hdc, sc] in each ch-6 sp around, join in beg sc, fasten off. (6 petals)

Rnd 7: Attach pale green in sc between 2 petals, ch 1, sc in same st as beg ch-1, [ch 30, sc in same st, ch 6, sc in ch-3 at tip of next petal, ch 13 (leaf foundation ch), sc in 2nd ch from hook, *hdc in next ch, dc in next ch, tr in each of next 2 chs, 2 tr in next ch, tr in each of next 2 chs, dc in next ch, hdc in next ch **, 3 sc in next ch, working on opposite side of ch-13, rep from * to **, join in first sc of leaf, holding an outer flower next to point of leaf, sc in 4th tr of any petal, ch 6, sc between next 2-sc between petals of center flower] rep around, join in beg sc, fasten off.

Accent your home with this beautiful doily crocheted in soft pastel shades!

Note: Row 8 is worked clockwise around doily. If you are left-handed start the row with RS facing; if you are right-handed start the row with WS facing.

After each arch is completed over each flower, continue working clockwise around doily.

Row 8: Attach white in ch-30 sp, ch 3, 6 dc in same sp, ch 3, turn, dc in next dc, ch 3, turn, dc in next dc, dc in top of ch-3, turn, dc in each of next 3 dc, [ch 5, turn, dc in each of next 4 dc] 3 times, ch 2, turn, sc in 4th tr of 2nd free petal of outer flower, *ch 2, turn, dc in next 4 dc, [ch 5, turn, dc in next 4 dc] 3 times, ch 2, sc in last ch-5 sp on same inner side, ch 2, turn, dc in each of next 4 dc, turn, ch 5, dc in each of next 4 dc, ch 2, turn, sc in 4th tr of next free petal of outer flower *, rep from * to * 3 times, ch 2, turn, dc in each of next 4 dc, [ch 5, turn, dc in each of next 4 dc] 3 times, ch 3, turn, dc in each of next 3 dc, ch 3, turn, dc in each of next 2 dc, ch 3, turn, dc in next dc, leaving a length of cotton, fasten off.

Rep Row 8 working around each outer flower and join to last ch-5 sp of arch worked over previous outer flower with ch 2, sc in ch-5 sp, ch 2. After arch over each outer flower is completed, with rem length, sew last 2 dc of each arch to opposite edge of beg 7-dc sts.

Rnd 9: Attach pale green in 2nd free ch-5 sp of any arch, ch 1, sc in same ch-5 sp, [*ch 8, sl st in 5th ch from hook, ch 5, sl st in same place, ch 4, sl st in same place, ch 3, sc in next ch-5 sp *, rep from * to * to 2nd free ch-5 sp from joining, ch 4, sc in 2nd free ch-5 sp of arch around next outer flower] rep around, join in beg sc, fasten off. ✄

Dainty Blues Doily

Design by Lori Zeller

Skill Level: Intermediate

Size: 8¼ inches in diameter

Materials

- Crochet cotton size 10: 50 yds white, 30 yds blue, 25 yds navy
- Size 5 steel crochet hook or size needed to obtain gauge
- Tapestry needle

Gauge

Rnds 1–4 = 1¾ inches in diameter
Check gauge to save time.

Pattern Notes

Weave in loose ends as work progresses.

Ch-3 counts as first dc throughout.

Join rnds with a sl st unless otherwise stated.

Pattern Stitches

V-st: [Dc, ch 1, dc] in indicated st.

Fpsc: Insert hook from front to back to front again around vertical post of indicated st, yo, draw up a lp, yo, draw through 2 lps on hook.

Double V-st: [Dc, ch 1] 3 times in indicated sp, dc in same sp.

Shell: [Dc, ch 1] 5 times in indicated sp, dc in same sp.

2-dc cl: [Yo hook, insert hook in indicated st, yo, draw up a lp, yo, draw through 2 lps on hook] twice, yo, draw through all 3 lps on hook.

Doily

Rnd 1 (RS): With white, ch 6, join to form a ring, ch 4 (counts as first dc, ch-1 throughout), [dc in ring, ch 1] 15 times, join in 3rd ch of ch-4. (16 dc; 16 ch-1 sps)

Rnd 2: Ch 1, sc in same st as joining, ch 2, fpdc around next dc, ch 2, [sc in next dc, ch 2, fpdc around next dc, ch 2] rep around, join in beg sc.

Rnd 3: Ch 1, fpsc around same sc as joining, ch 3, fpsc around next fpdc, ch 3, [fpsc around next sc, ch 3, fpsc around next fpdc, ch 3] rep around, join in beg sc.

Rnd 4: Sl st in first ch-3 sp, ch 1, [sc, ch 3, sc] in same ch-3 sp, ch 1, [{sc, ch 3, sc} in next ch-3 sp, ch 1] rep around, join in beg sc, fasten off.

Rnd 5: Working in ch-2 sps of Rnd 2 and working behind Rnds 3 and 4, attach blue in any ch-2 sp of Rnd 2, ch 4, dc in same ch-2 sp, ch 1, [V-st in next ch-2 sp, ch 1] rep around, join in 3rd ch of ch-4.

Rnd 6: Sl st into ch-1 sp, ch 1, working through ch-3 sps of Rnd 4 and ch-1 sps of V-sts of Rnd 5, sc in same ch sp as joining and first ch-3 sp of Rnd 4, ch 4, [sk next ch-1 sp, sc in next ch-3 sp and ch-1 sp of V-st, ch 4] rep around, join in beg sc, fasten off.

Rnd 7: Attach navy with sc in any unworked ch-1 sp between V-sts of Rnd 5, holding ch-4 lps in front of work, ch 5, [sc in next unworked ch-1 sp of Rnd 5, ch 5] rep around, join in beg sc.

Rnd 8: Sl st in first ch-5 sp, ch 4, V-st in same sp, [V-st, ch 1, dc] in each rem ch-5 sp around, join in 3rd ch of ch-4.

Rnd 9: Sl st in first ch sp, ch 1, sc in same sp, ch 3, sc in next ch-1 sp, ch 1, sc in ch-4 lp of Rnd 4, ch 1, [sc in next ch-1 sp of Rnd 8, ch 3, sc in next ch-1 sp, ch 1, sc in next ch-4 lp of Rnd 4, ch 1] rep around, join in beg sc.

Rnd 10: Sl st in first ch-3 sp, ch 6, dc in same sp, ch 5, [{dc, ch 3, dc} in next ch-3 sp, ch 5] rep around, join in 3rd ch of ch-6, fasten off.

Rnd 11: Attach blue in first ch sp of previous rnd, [sc, ch 4, sc] in same sp, ch 5, [{sc, ch 4, sc} in next ch-3 sp, ch 5] rep around, join in beg sc, fasten off.

This handsome doily with a hint of the nautical is a perfect complement to your summer decor!

Rnd 12: Attach white in first ch-4 sp of previous rnd, ch 4, [V-st, ch 1, dc] in same sp, ch 2, sc around ch-5 of Rnds 10 and 11 tog, ch 2, [double V-st in next ch-4 sp, ch 2, sc around ch-5 of Rnds 10 and 11 tog, ch 2] rep around, join in 3rd ch of ch-4.

Rnd 13: Sl st in first ch sp, ch 1, [sc, ch 3, sc] in same sp, [sc, ch 3, sc] in next 2 ch-1 sps, ch 7, [{sc, ch 3, sc} in each of next 3 ch-1 sps, ch 7] rep around, join in beg sc.

Rnd 14: Sl st in first ch sp, ch 2, dc in same sp, [2-dc cl, ch 3, 2-dc cl] in next ch-3 sp, 2-dc cl in next ch-3 sp, [ch 3, dc in 3rd ch from hook] twice, sk ch-7 lp, *2-dc cl in next ch-3 sp, [2-dc cl, ch 3, 2-dc cl] in next ch-3 sp, 2-dc cl in next ch-3 sp, [ch 3, dc in 3rd ch from hook] twice, sk ch-7 lp, rep from * around, join in top of first dc, fasten off.

Rnd 15: Attach blue in first ch-3 sp of previous rnd, ch 4, [dc, ch 1] 4 times in same ch-3 sp, dc in

Continued on page 109

Rose Trellis Doily

Design by Valmay Flint

Skill Level: Beginner

Size: 12½ inches in diameter

Materials

- Crochet cotton size 20: Scrap amounts of pink, green, cream, aqua, shaded greens, yellow, orange, brown, lilac, red, shaded blues, shaded browns, light pink, dark blue, bright pink, dark peach, burgundy, baby blue, light peach, light aqua, shaded lilacs, gold, teal, shaded oranges

- Size 10 steel crochet hook or size needed to obtain gauge

- Tapestry needle

Gauge

Rnds 1–7 = 2⅜ inches; rose = 1¼ inches in diameter

Check gauge to save time.

Pattern Notes

Weave in loose ends as work progresses.

Join rnds with a sl st unless otherwise stated.

Use cotton colors desired, the more colors the better.

Center Rose

Rnd 1 (RS): With pink, ch 6, join to form a ring, ch 6 (counts as first dc, ch-3), [dc in ring, ch 3] 5 times, join in 3rd ch of ch-6. (6 ch sps)

Rnd 2: Ch 1, [sc, 4 dc, sc] in each ch-3 sp around, join in beg sc. (6 petals)

Rnd 3: Working behind petals and around dc post of Rnd 1, ch 1, [sc around next dc post of Rnd 1, ch 5] rep around, join in beg sc. (6 ch sps)

Rnd 4: Ch 1, [sc, 7 dc, sc] in each ch-5 sp around, join in beg sc, fasten off.

Rnd 5: Attach green in 4th dc of petal, ch 1, sc in 4th dc of petal, ch 9, [sc in 4th dc of next petal, ch 9] rep around, join in beg sc.

Rnd 6: Ch 8 (counts as first dc, ch-5), dc in 5th ch of ch-9 sp, ch 5, [dc in next sc, ch 5, dc in 5th ch of ch-9, ch 5] rep around, join in 3rd ch of ch-8. (12 dc)

Rnd 7: Ch 3 (counts as first dc throughout), 5 dc in next ch-5 sp, [dc in next dc, 5 dc in next ch-5 sp] rep around, join in 3rd ch of ch-3, fasten off. (72 dc)

Rnd 8: Attach cream in dc, ch 1, sc in same dc, [ch 5, sk next 2 dc, sc in next dc] rep around, ending with ch 2, dc in beg sc. (24 ch sps)

Rnd 9: Ch 1, sc in same sp as ch-1, [ch 6, sc in next ch sp] rep around, ending with ch 3, dc in beg sc.

Rnd 10: Ch 1, sc in same sp as ch-1, [ch 7, sc in next ch sp] rep around, ending with ch 4, dc in beg sc.

Rnd 11: Ch 1, sc in same sp as ch-1, ch 8, [sc in next ch sp, ch 8] rep around, join in beg sc.

Rnd 12: Ch 3, 5 dc in next ch sp, [dc in next dc, 5 dc in next ch sp] rep around, join in 3rd ch of ch-3, fasten off. (144 dc)

Rnd 13: Attach aqua, rep Rnd 8. (48 ch sps)

Rnd 14: Ch 1, sc in same sp as ch-1, [ch 5, sc in next ch sp] rep around, ending with ch 2, dc in beg sc.

Rnds 15 & 16: Rep Rnd 9.

Rnds 17–19: Rep Rnds 10–12. (288 dc)

Just like planting a flower garden, this colorful doily offers a variety of colors sure to brighten any room!

Outer Rose Ring

Make 24

Note: Use a variety of colors.

First rose

Rnds 1–3: Rep Rnds 1–3 of center rose.

Rnd 4: Ch 1, in ch-5 sp work sc, 4 dc, sl st in dc of Rnd 19, 3 dc and 1 sc in same ch sp, in next ch-5 sp work 1 sc, 4 dc, sk next 5 dc of Rnd 19, sl st in next dc, 3 dc and 1 sc in same ch-5 sp (2 petals joined to doily), [sc, 7 dc, sc] in each of next 4 ch-5 sps, fasten off.

Second rose

Rnds 1–3: Rep Rnds 1–3 of center rose.

Rnd 4: Ch 1, [in next ch-5 sp work sc, 4 dc, sk next 5 dc of Rnd 19, sl st in next dc, 3 dc and sc in same ch-5 sp] twice (2 petals joined to doily), [sc, 7 dc, sc] in each of next 3 ch-5 sps, in last ch-5 sp work sc, 4 dc, sl st in center dc of adjacent petal of previous rose, 3 dc and sc in same ch-5 sp, join in beg sc, fasten off.

Continued on page 109

Pansies & Heart Cards

Continued from page 93

First lobe

Row 20: [Ch 4, sc in next ch lp] 4 times, ch 1, dc in next lp, turn.

Row 21: [Ch 4, sc in next ch-4 lp] 4 times, turn.

Row 22: [Ch 4, sc in next ch-4 lp] 3 times, ch 1, dc in next lp, turn.

Row 23: [Ch 4, sc in next ch-4 lp] twice, ch 1, dc in next lp, turn.

Row 24: [Ch 4, sc in next ch-4 lp] twice, fasten off.

Second lobe

Row 20: Attach white with sl st in end ch-4 lp of Row 19, ch 1, sc in same sp, [ch 4, sc in next ch lp] 4 times, ch 1, dc in same lp as first lobe, turn.

Row 21: [Ch 4, sc in next ch lp] 4 times, turn.

Row 22: [Ch 4, sc in next ch lp] 3 times, ch 1, dc in last lp, turn.

Row 23: [Ch 4, sc in next ch lp]

twice, ch 1, dc in last lp, turn.

Row 24: [Ch 4, sc in next lp] twice, fasten off.

Edging

Rnd 1: Attach white in center lp between lobes, ch 1, sc in same lp, ch 1, [sc in next ch lp, ch 3] rep around outer edge, working [sc, ch 3] twice, sc in center bottom point of heart, ending after last sc in last lp, ch 1, join in beg sc, fasten off.

Rnd 2: Attach lilac in center bottom ch-3 sp, ch 1, sc in same sp, [ch 4, sc in next ch-3 sp] rep around outer edge at center top between lobes, sc in ch-3 sp, sk next ch-1 sp sc in center sc between lobes, sk next ch-1 sp, sc in next ch-3 sp, ending with join in beg sc, fasten off.

Flower

Rnd 1: With lilac, ch 2, 6 sc in

2nd ch from hook, join in back lp of beg sc. (6 sc)

Rnd 2: Working in back lps only, sl st in next st, [ch 4, 3 tr in same st as sl st, sl st in next st] rep around, fasten off. (6 petals)

Finishing

Saturate heart and flower with fabric stiffener and allow to dry completely. Cut purple paper to measure 4¼ x 4½ inches. Cut white paper to measure 5 x 9 inches; fold in half to measure 4¾ x 4½ inches. Glue purple paper centered on white card.

Glue heart centered on card. Fold both lengths of ribbon into a bow and glue to center of heart, glue flower centered over ribbon bows. ✄

Floral Heart Picture

Continued from page 97

[ch 5, tr in 5th ch from hook] twice, sc in next ch-3 p, ch 5, tr in 5th ch from hook, dc in each of next 2 ch-2 sp on ring, ch 5, tr in 5th ch from hook, join in beg sc.

Rnd 2: Sl st into center of ch-5 sp, ch 1, sc in same ch sp, [ch 7, sc in next ch-5 sp] 16 times, ch 7, [dc, ch 7, dc] in center bottom ch-5 sp, [ch 7, sc in next ch-5 sp] 17 times, ch 7, sc in each of next 2 ch-5 sps, ch 7, join in beg sc.

Rnd 3: Ch 1, [7 sc in each ch-7 sp] 35 times, 5 sc in each of next 2 ch sps at center top of heart, join in beg sc, fasten off.

Rnd 4: Attach pink in sp between 2 groups of 5-sc at center top, ch 1, sc in same sp [ch 4, sk next 3 sc, sc in next sc] rep around, join in beg sc.

Rnd 5: Ch 1, 3 sc in first ch-4 sp, 2 sc in next ch-4 sp, ch 5, draw lp through 2nd sc of 3-sc in previous sp, *[3 sc, ch 3, sl st in 3rd ch from hook, 3 sc] in ch-5 sp, 2 sc in same ch-4 sp as last 2 sc, 2 sc in next ch-4 sp, ch 5, draw lp through first sc of 2-sc in previous sp, rep from * around, join in beg sc, fasten off.

Embellishments

Curl

Make 2

With white, ch 2, sc in 2nd ch from hook, turn

(always turn in the same direction), sc in single vertical bar, [turn, sc in double vertical bars] rep cording until piece measures 12 inches long, leaving a 4-inch length, fasten off. Sew each end in a small lp as shown.

Side ring

Note: Make 1 each yellow and aqua.

Wind cotton around tip of little finger 8 times, sl off, insert hook in ring, yo, draw up a lp, ch 1, 2 sc in ring, ch 3, [3 sc in ring, ch 3] 7 times, sc in ring, join in beg sc, fasten off.

Finishing

Gently press heart with steam iron. Cut construction paper to fit frame. Position heart in center of paper, glue in place. Using photo as a guide, arrange curl and side ring at each side of heart and glue in place. Insert finished piece into frame. ✄

Dainty Blues Doily

Continued from page 104

same ch-3 sp, ch 3, working behind previous rnd, sc in ch-7 lp of Rnd 13, ch 3, [shell in next ch-3 sp, ch 3, working behind previous rnd, sc in ch-7 lp of Rnd 13, ch 3] rep around, join in 3rd ch of ch-4, fasten off.

Rnd 16: Attach white with a sc in first ch-1 sp of previous rnd, [ch 3, sc in next ch-1 sp] 4 times, ch 1, sc in next ch-3 lp of Rnd 14, ch 4, sc in next ch-3 lp of Rnd 14, ch 1, [sc in next ch-1 sp of Rnd 15, {ch 3, sc in next ch-1 sp} 4 times, ch 1, sc in next ch-3 lp of Rnd 14, ch 4, sc in next ch-3 lp of Rnd 14, ch 1] rep around, join in beg sc.

Rnd 17: Sl st in first ch-3 sp, ch 1, sc in same sp, [ch 3, sc in next ch-3 sp] 3 times, ch 7, sk next ch-4 lp, [sc in next ch-3 sp, {ch 3, sc in next ch-3 sp} 3 times, ch 7, sk next ch-4 lp] rep from * around, join in beg sc.

Rnd 18: Sl st in first ch-3 sp, [ch 2, dc, ch 3, 2-dc cl] in same sp, *ch 4, sk next ch-3 sp, [2-dc cl, ch 3, 2-dc cl] in next ch-3 sp, ch 4, working behind ch-7 lp of previous rnd, sc in next ch-4 lp of Rnd 16, ch 4 **, [2-dc cl, ch 3, 2-dc cl] in next ch-3 sp, rep from * around, ending last rep at **, join in first dc, fasten off.

Rnd 19: Attach blue with sc in first ch-3 sp of previous rnd, ch 3, sc in same sp, *ch 4, working behind ch-4 lp of previous rnd, sc in unworked ch-3 sp of Rnd 17, ch 4, [sc, ch 3, sc] in next ch-3 sp of Rnd 18, ch 2, working in front of previous rnd, [sc, ch 3, sc] in unworked ch-7 lp of Rnd 17, ch 2 **, [sc, ch 3, sc] in next ch-3 sp of Rnd 18, rep from * around, ending last rep at **, join in beg sc, fasten off.

Rnd 20: Attach navy with sc in first ch-3 sp of previous rnd, ch 3, sc in same sp, *ch 4, working in front of previous rnd, sc in unworked ch-4 lp of Rnd 18, ch 4, [sc, ch 3, sc] in next ch-3 sp of Rnd 19, ch 4, sk next ch-2 sp, sc in next ch-3 sp, sk next ch-2 sp **, [sc, ch 3, sc] in next ch-3 sp, rep from * around, ending last rep at **, join in beg sc, fasten off.

Rnd 21: Attach white in first ch-3 sp of previous rnd, ch 4, [V-st, ch 1, dc] in same sp, *ch 2, working behind previous rnd, sc in next ch-4 of Rnd 19, ch 3, sc in next ch-4 sp of Rnd 19, ch 2, double V-st in next ch-3 sp of Rnd 20, ch 2, sc in next ch-4 sp, ch 3, sc in next ch-4 sp, ch 2 **, double V-st in next ch-3 sp, rep from * around, ending last rep at **, join in 3rd ch of ch-4.

Rnd 22: Sl st in first ch sp, ch 1, [sc, ch 3, sc] in same sp, [sc, ch 3, sc] in each of next 2 ch-1 sps, *ch 1, working in front of previous rnd, sc in unworked ch-4 lp of Rnd 20, ch 1, [sc, ch 3, sc] in next ch-3 sp of Rnd 21, ch 1, sc in next unworked lp of Rnd 20, [sc, ch 3, sc] in each of next 3 ch-1 sps, ch 1, sk next ch-2 sp, [sc, ch 3, sc] in next ch-3 sp, ch 1, sk next ch-2 sp **, [sc, ch 3, sc] in each of next 3 ch-1 sps, rep from * around, ending last rep at **, join in beg sc, fasten off. ✂

Rose Trellis Doily

Continued from page 106

Rep 2nd rose until 23 roses are completed. On the 24th rose to close ring, after joining to Rnd 19 of doily, join next petal to first rose, work 2 petals and join last petal to previous rose.

Border

Rnd 20: Attach shaded greens in 4th dc of first free petal on any rose, ch 1, sc in same dc as ch-1, ch 5, sc in 4th dc of next petal of same rose, ch 10, [sc in 4th dc of petal on next rose, ch 5, sc in 4th dc of next petal on same rose, ch 10] rep around, join in beg sc.

Rnd 21: Sl st into center of ch-5, ch 1, sc in same ch-5 sp, *[ch 6, sc in ch-10 sp] twice **, ch 6, sc in next ch-5 sp, rep from * around, ending last rep at **, ch 3, dc in beg sc.

Rnd 22: Ch 1, sc in same ch sp, ch 6, [sc in next ch sp, ch 6] rep around, join in beg sc, fasten off.

Rnd 23: Attach yellow, rep Rnd 10.

Rnd 24: Rep Rnd 10, fasten off.

Rnd 25: Attach orange, rep Rnd 11.

Rnd 26: Rep Rnd 11, fasten off. (72 ch sps)

Rnd 27: Attach brown, rep Rnd 12. (432 dc) ✂

Bazaar Quickies

Whether you are looking for quick bazaar crafts or delightful gift items, this chapter is packed with wonderful ideas for any occasion!

Flower Time Headband & Pin

Designs by Margaret Nobles

Skill Level: Beginner

Size

Headband: Standard size

Pin: 1½ inches in diameter

Materials

- Crochet cotton size 10: small amounts orange, purple, blue, red, yellow, green, aqua, navy
- Size 8 steel crochet hook or size needed to obtain gauge
- Wire-tooth headband
- 5 (½-inch) round mirrors
- 5 (½-inch) plastic rings
- Black felt
- 1½-inch cardboard circle
- 3mm pearl bead
- 1-inch pin back
- Craft glue
- Tapestry needle

Gauge

Flower = 1 inch
Check gauge to save time.

Pattern Notes

Weave in loose ends as work progresses.

Join rnds with a sl st unless otherwise stated.

Headband

Flower

Make 3

Rnd 1 (RS): Attach yellow to plastic ring, ch 1, 20 sc over ring, join in beg sc, fasten off. (20 sc)

Note: Work a flower with each purple, blue and red.

Rnd 2: Working in front lps only, attach flower color, ch 1, sc in same st, ch 2, [sc in next st, ch 2] rep around, join in beg sc, fasten off.

Leaf

Working in rem back lps of Rnd 1, attach green, ch 1, [sc, hdc, dc] in same st as beg ch-1, [tr, dtr, tr] in next st, [dc, hdc, sc] in next st, fasten off.

Headband

Row 1: Attach navy to headband before first wire tooth, ch 1, work 8 sc before the first wire tooth over headband, work 4 sc between each wire tooth of headband, 8 sc after last wire tooth of headband, fasten off.

Row 2: Attach orange in first sc of previous row, ch 1, sc in each of next 8 sc, [sk 1 sc, sc in next sc] rep across to last 8 sc, sc in each of last 8 sc, do not turn.

Row 3: Ch 1, work 3 reverse sc sts over headband before first wire tooth, reverse sc across working each reverse sc between each wire tooth, work 3 reverse sc over headband after last wire tooth, fasten off.

Finishing

Cut a small strip of black felt approximately 1 x 2¾ inches.

Position and glue 3 mirrors on the felt; glue a flower centered over each mirror. Allow to dry completely. Trim excess felt from outer edge of 3-flower group. Position

> What little girl wouldn't be delighted with this charming headband and pin? They're a great last-minute gift idea and a nice way to use up those little scraps!

and glue flowered strip to headband as desired.

Pin

Flower

Make 2

Rnd 1: Rep Rnd 1 of headband flower.

Rnd 2: Rep Rnd 2 of headband flower working 1 flower each purple and aqua.

Leaf

Work the same as for headband leaf, working 2 leaves on purple flower.

Butterfly

Rnd 1 (RS): With blue, [ch 10, sl st in first ch] twice, [ch 6, sl st in first ch] twice, fasten off.

Rnd 2 (RS): Attach orange in first ch of first ch-10 lp, *sk 1 ch, sc in each of next 2 chs, 2 hdc in next ch, [hdc, dc] in next ch, [dc, tr, dc] in next ch, [dc, hdc] in next ch, 2 hdc in next ch, sc in each of next 2 chs, rep from * around 2nd ch-10 lp, [sc in each of next 6 chs of next

ch-6 lp] twice, join in beg sc, fasten off.

Finishing

Cut black felt slightly larger than cardboard circle and glue to cardboard. Position and glue 2 mirrors to felt circle. Glue a flower centered over each mirror. Position and glue butterfly to pin; glue pearl bead to center of butterfly. Glue pin back centered on back. ✂

Heart Photo Frame Magnet

Design by Paula Wendland

Skill Level: Beginner

Size: 5 x 5½ inches

Materials

- Worsted weight yarn: small amount pink
- Sport weight yarn: small amount sage green
- Size G/6 crochet hook or size needed to obtain gauge
- Hot-glue gun
- 4 x 9 inches pink felt
- 5-inch square white poster board
- 20 inches ⅜-inch-wide pink ribbon
- 1-inch-diameter magnet
- Photo
- Tapestry needle

Gauge

Rnds 1 and 2 = 1 inch
Check gauge to save time.

Pattern Note

Weave in loose ends as work progresses.

Heart

Row 1 (RS): With pink, ch 37, sc in 2nd ch from hook, sc in each rem ch across, turn. (36 sc)

Row 2 (WS): Ch 1, sc in each of next 3 sc, [sk 1 sc, 6 dc in next sc, sk next sc, sc in each of next 10 sc] twice, sk 1 sc, 6 dc in next sc, sk next sc, sc in each of next 4 sc, leaving a length of yarn, fasten off, turn.

Row 3 (RS): Attach sage green in first sc, ch 1, [sc in next sc, {sc, ch 4, sc} in next sc] rep across, leaving a length of yarn, fasten off.

Sew ends of Rows tog to form heart. Sewn section is center top of heart between 6-dc lobes and rem 6 dc is center bottom point.

Starting at center top, weave ribbon between Rows 1 and 2 over 2 sts, under 2 sts, tie ends in a bow at center top.

Finishing

From heart pattern, cut 2 hearts from pink felt and 1 poster board heart. Glue felt to each side of poster board.

Cut photo to proper size and glue to front felt. Glue heart centered over front. Glue magnet to center back.

If you want to be able to switch photos, do not glue photo to felt, and when attaching crocheted heart to felt leave center top free. ✄

Heart pattern on page 131

Crochet this pretty little frame and add your favorite photo to display on the refrigerator or send to Grandma!

Little Gray Mouse

Design by Connie Folse

Skill Level: Beginner

Size: 2¼ x 3 inches, excluding tail

Materials

- Worsted weight yarn: Scrap amounts each gray, pink, black
- Size G/6 crochet hook or size needed to obtain gauge
- 12mm jingle bell
- Tapestry needle

Gauge

Rnds 1 and 2 = 1 inch in diameter

Check gauge to save time.

Pattern Notes

Weave in loose ends as work progresses.

Join rnds with a sl st unless otherwise stated.

Mouse

Make 2

Rnd 1 (RS): With gray, ch 2, 6 sc in 2nd ch from hook, join in beg sc. (6 sc)

Rnd 2: Ch 1, 2 sc in each sc around, join in beg sc. (12 sc)

Row 3: Ch 1, sc in each of next 4 sc, turn. (4 sc)

Row 4: Ch 1, sc in each of next 4 sc, turn.

Row 5: Ch 1, [dec 1 sc over next 2 sc] twice, turn. (2 sc)

Row 6: Ch 1, sc in each of next 2 sc, turn.

Row 7: Ch 1, dec 1 sc over next 2 sc, fasten off. (1 sc)

Note: Thread jingle bell onto gray yarn.

Rnd 8: Holding WS tog and working through both thicknesses,

This is one mouse you won't mind in the house. Glue a magnet to the back and hang it on the refrigerator where his jingle-bell tail can sound the alarm every time the door is opened!

attach gray in next unworked sc of Rnd 2, ch 1, sc in same sc in each of next 5 sc, ch 16 (for tail), push bell up next to hook, sl st in 2nd ch from hook, sl st in each of next 14 chs, sl st in same sc as last sc, sc in next 2 sc of Rnd 2, sc in first worked sc, sc in ends of Rows 3–7, 2 sc in sc of Row 7, sc in end of each of Rows 7–3, sc in next sc of Rnd 2, join in beg sc, fasten off. (22 sc)

Ear

Row 1: Attach pink with sl st in 19th sc of Rnd 8, ch 1, 2 sc in same st, turn. (2 sc)

Row 2: Ch 1, [sc, hdc] in first sc, [hdc, sc] in next sc, fasten off.

Row 3: Attach gray with sl st in same joining st as Row 1 of ear, sc in end of each Rows 1 and 2, 2 sc in each of next 4 sts, sc in ends of each Rows 2 and 1, sl st around post of 3rd sc of Row 3 of mouse, fasten off.

Eye

With black, embroider a French knot on Row 6 of mouse front. ✄

Kitty Dishcloth

Design by Michele Wilcox

Skill Level: Beginner

Size: 9½ x 12 inches

Materials

- Worsted weight 4-ply cotton: 2½ oz camel, small amount pink and black
- Size G/6 crochet hook or size needed to obtain gauge
- Tapestry needle

Gauge

4 sc = inch; 4 sc rows = 1 inch

Check gauge to save time.

Pattern Notes

Weave in loose ends as work progresses.

Ch-2 counts as first dc throughout.

Join rnds with a sl st unless otherwise stated.

Dishcloth

Row 1: Beg at bottom, with camel, ch 37, sc in 4th ch from hook, dc in next ch, [sc in next ch, dc in next ch] rep across, turn.

Rows 2–25: Ch 2, [sc in next sc, dc in next dc] rep across, turn. At the end of Row 25, fasten off.

First ear

Row 26: Attach pink, ch 1, sc in each of next 12 sts, turn. (12 sc)

Row 27: Ch 1, dec 1 sc over next 2 sc, sc in each rem sc across, turn. (11 sc)

Row 28: Ch 1, sc in each sc across to last 2 sc, dec 1 sc over next 2 sc, turn. (10 sc)

Rows 29–37: Rep Rows 27 and 28. (2 sc)

Row 38: Ch 1, dec 1 sc over next 2 sc, fasten off. (1 sc)

Second ear

Row 26: With finished ear to the right, sk next 11 sts of Row 25, attach pink in next st, ch 1, sc in same st, sc in each rem st across, turn. (12 sc)

Row 27: Ch 1, sc in each sc across to last 2 sc, dec 1 sc over next 2 sc, turn. (11 sc)

Row 28: Ch 1, dec 1 sc over next 2 sc, sc in each rem sc across, turn. (10 sc)

Rows 29–37: Rep Rows 27 and 28. (2 sc)

Row 38: Ch 1, dec 1 sc over next 2 sc, fasten off. (1 sc)

Border

Rnd 1: Attach camel in opposite side of foundation ch, ch 1, sc evenly sp around, working 3 sc in each corner point and each point of each ear, join in beg sc, fasten off.

Eye

Make 2

Rnd 1: With black, ch 2, 6 sc in 2nd ch from hook, join in beg sc, leaving a length of yarn, fasten off.

Nose

With black, rep Rnd 1 of eye.

Using photo as a guide, sew eyes and nose to center of dishcloth. With black embroider 3 whiskers at each side of nose. Embroider mouth centered below nose. ✂

Your kids will enjoy helping with the kitchen cleanup when you make this adorable dishcloth for them!

Tomato Pincushion

Design by Michele Wilcox

Skill Level: Beginner

Size: 3 x 4 inches

Materials

- Worsted weight yarn: 1 oz cherry red, small amount forest green
- Size F/5 crochet hook or size needed to obtain gauge
- 3-inch plastic foam ball
- Fiberfill
- Tapestry needle

Gauge

4 sc = 1 inch; 4 sc rnds = 1 inch
Check gauge to save time.

Pattern Notes

Weave in loose ends as work progresses.

Join rnds with a sl st unless otherwise stated.

Slice a small amount of top and bottom edge of plastic foam ball so that it sits flat.

Pincushion

Rnd 1 (RS): With cherry red, ch 2, 6 sc in 2nd ch from hook, join in beg sc. (6 sc)

Rnd 2: Ch 1, 2 sc in each sc around, join in beg sc. (12 sc)

Rnd 3: Ch 1, [sc in next sc, 2 sc in next sc] rep around, join in beg sc. (18 sc)

Rnd 4: Ch 1, [sc in each of next 2 sc, 2 sc in next sc] rep around, join in beg sc. (24 sc)

Rnd 5: Ch 1, [sc in each of next 3 sc, 2 sc in next sc] rep around, join in beg sc. (30 sc)

Rnd 6: Ch 1, [sc in each of next 4 sc, 2 sc in next sc] rep around, join in beg sc. (36 sc)

Rnd 7: Ch 1, [sc in each of next 5 sc, 2 sc in next sc] rep around, join in beg sc. (42 sc)

Rnd 8: Ch 1, [sc in each of next 6 sc, 2 sc in next sc] rep around, join in beg sc. (48 sc)

Rnd 9: Ch 1, [sc in each of next 7 sc, 2 sc in next sc] rep around, join in beg sc. (54 sc)

Rnds 10–13: Ch 1, sc in each sc around, join in beg sc.

Rnd 14: Ch 1, [sc in each of next 7 sc, dec 1 sc over next 2 sc] rep around, join in beg sc. (48 sc)

Rnd 15: Ch 1, [sc in each of next 6 sc, dec 1 sc over next 2 sc] rep around, join in beg sc. (42 sc)

Rnd 16: Ch 1, [sc in each of next 5 sc, dec 1 sc over next 2 sc] rep around, join in beg sc. (36 sc)

Rnd 17: Ch 1, [sc in each of next 4 sc, dec 1 sc over next 2 sc] rep around, join in beg sc. (30 sc)

This old-fashioned tomato-style pincushion is the perfect idea for the seamstress or gardener on your gift list!

Insert plastic foam ball into crocheted piece. Stuff around sides with fiberfill, do not place stuffing on top and bottom.

Rnd 18: Ch 1, [sc in each of next 3 sc, dec 1 sc over next 2 sc] rep around, join in beg sc. (24 sc)

Rnd 19: Ch 1, [sc in each of next 2

Continued on page 129

Fishbowl Place Mat

Design by Beverly Mewhorter

Gauge

4 dc = 1 inch

Check gauge to save time.

Pattern Notes

Weave in loose ends as work progresses.

Ch-3 counts as first dc throughout.

Join rnds with a sl st unless otherwise stated.

Place Mat

Rnd 1 (RS): With light blue, ch 4, 11 dc in 4th ch from hook, join in 4th ch of ch-4. (12 dc)

Rnd 2: Ch 3, dc in same st as ch-3, 2 dc in each dc around, join in 3rd ch of ch-3. (24 dc)

Rnd 3: Ch 3, dc in same st as ch-3, dc in next dc, [2 dc in next dc, dc in next dc] rep around, join in 3rd ch of ch-3. (36 dc)

Rnd 4: Ch 3, dc in same st as ch-3, dc in each of next 2 dc, [2 dc in next dc, dc in each of next 2 dc] rep around, join in 3rd ch of ch-3. (48 dc)

Rnd 5: Ch 3, dc in same st as ch-3, dc in each of next 3 dc, [2 dc in next dc, dc in each of next 3 dc] rep around, join in 3rd ch of ch-3. (60 dc)

Rnd 6: Ch 3, dc in same st as ch-3, dc in each of next 4 dc, [2 dc in next dc, dc in each of next 4 dc] rep around, join in 3rd ch of ch-3. (72 dc)

Rnd 7: Ch 3, dc in same st as ch-3, dc in each of next 5 dc, [2 dc in next dc, dc in each of next 5 dc] rep around, join in 3rd ch of ch-3. (84 dc)

Rnd 8: Ch 1, sl st in first dc, *sc in next dc, dc in next dc, 2 tr in next dc, dc in next dc, sc in next dc, sl st in next dc **, sl st in next dc, rep from * around, ending last rep at **, fasten off. (12 scallops)

Goldfish

Make 3

Row 1: With vibrant orange, ch 4, sc in 2nd ch from hook, sc in each of next 2 chs, turn. (3 sc)

Row 2: Ch 1, 2 sc in first sc, sc in next sc, 2 sc in next sc, turn. (5 sc)

Rows 3–6: Ch 1, sc in each sc across, turn.

Row 7: Ch 1, dec 1 sc over next 2 sc, sc in next sc, dec 1 sc over next 2 sc, turn. (3 sc)

Row 8: Ch 1, dec 1 sc over next 2 sc, sc in next sc, turn. (2 sc)

Row 9: Ch 1, dec 1 sc over next 2 sc, fasten off. (1 sc)

Tail

Row 10: Attach vibrant orange in opposite side of foundation ch, ch 1, sc in each of next 3 chs, turn. (3 sc)

Row 11: Ch 3, [dc, hdc, sc] in same sc as ch-3, sl st in next sc, [sc, hdc, dc, ch 3, sl st] in last sc, fasten off.

Fin

Make 3

With vibrant orange, ch 4, [dc, ch 3, sl st] in 4th ch from hook, fasten off.

Sew fin to body between Rows 5 and 6.

Finishing

Glue or sew fish evenly sp around mat.

For eye, glue black bead to Row 10.

For bubbles at front of each fish, glue 3 white sequins with pearl bead at each center. ✄

Create this cute little place mat for your fishbowl or for any variety of uses!

Set of Ornaments

Designs by Janet Rehfeldt

Crochet one or all of these pretty ornaments for a variety of occasions—they're perfect for decorating packages or giving as gifts!

Skill Level: Beginner

Size

Ballet slipper: 3½ inches

Wreath: 3¼ inches in diameter

Gift box: 2 inches square

Purse: 2 x 2 inches, excluding handle

Mary Jane shoe: 3¼ inches

Turtleneck sweater: 4½ x 3½ inches

Camellia: 4½ inches long

Tam: 2¾ inches in diameter

Beret: 2¾ inches in diameter

Materials

- Worsted weight chenille yarn: small amount of pink, red, blue, black, purple, raspberry, sage green, forest green, variegated purple
- Size 5 metallic thread: small amount silver
- Size G/6 crochet hook or size needed to obtain gauge
- Size 6 steel crochet hook
- 1 yd ⅛-inch-wide pink ribbon
- 16 inches ⅛-inch-wide green ribbon
- 4 inches ⅛-inch-wide cream ribbon
- Small spray tiny silk flowers
- 20 inches ½-inch-wide white lace with finished beading edge
- 2-inch plastic ring
- 2 (½-inch) plastic rings
- 1-inch gold ribbon bow
- Cream ribbon rose
- 1½ inch ribbon poinsettia
- Potpourri beads
- Fiberfill
- Scrap plastic canvas
- Gold metallic thread
- 8mm gray shank button
- Straight pins
- Safety pin
- Sewing needle and thread
- Craft glue
- Tapestry needle

Gauge

4 sc = 1 inch

Check gauge to save time.

Pattern Notes

Weave in loose ends as work progresses.

Join rnds with a sl st unless otherwise stated.

Ballet Slipper

Sole

Rnd 1 (RS): With pink ch 12, sc in 2nd ch from hook, sc in each of next 7 chs, hdc in next ch, dc in next ch, 4 dc in last ch, working on opposite side of foundation ch, dc in next ch, hdc in next ch, sc in each of next 7 chs, 2 sc in last ch, join in beg sc. (25 sts)

Rnd 2: Ch 1, sc in each of next 7 sts, hdc in each of next 2 sts, 2 hdc in each of next 2 sts, 2 dc in next st, 2 hdc in each of next 2 sts, hdc in each of next 2 sts, sc in each of next 8 sts, 3 sc in last st, join in beg sc, fasten off. (32 sts)

Slipper Top

Row 1: With pink, ch 33, sc in 2nd ch from hook, sc in each of next 23 chs, turn. (24 sc)

Row 2: Ch 1, sk first sc, sc in each of next 2 sts, hdc in next st, [yo, insert hook in next st, yo, draw up a lp, insert hook in next st, yo, draw up a lp, yo, draw through all 4 lps on hook] 4 times, hdc in next st, sc in each of next 3 sts, sl st in next st, turn.

Row 3: Sk first st, sl st in next st, sl st in each st to unworked ch, sc in each of next 8 chs, fasten off.

Finishing

St ends of rows of top tog to form center back of heel. Matching toe and heel sts, pin top to sole and sew top.

Thread tapestry needle with 1 yd pink ⅛-inch-wide ribbon, draw through center top back of heel with equal lengths on each side. Whipstitch along top edge on each

side of the slipper stopping where the inc sts for front of slipper begin. Crossing the two tails, thread the ribbon through the back of the heel and tie in a bow. Insert a small spray of silk flowers into toe section of slipper. For hanging lp, attach a length of metallic thread at back heel.

Wreath

Rnd 1: Attach forest green to 2-inch plastic ring, ch 1, work 22 sc over ring, join in beg sc. (22 sc)

Rnd 2: Working in back lps only, ch 1, [sc, ch 6, sc] in same st as ch-1, ch 6, [{sc, ch 6, sc} in next st, ch 6] rep around, join in beg sc.

Rnd 3: Sl st into rem front lp of Rnd 1, fold lps from Rnd 2 toward the back, working in front lps only, ch 1, holding lace behind rem front lps of Rnd 1, [insert hook in next st of rem front lp of Rnd 1 and through natural sp in lace, yo, draw up a lp, yo, draw through 2 lps on hook ch 4] rep around skipping over several holes in lace between sc sts, join in beg sc, fasten off.

Finishing

Turn lace edges under and sew tog. For hanging lp, attach a length of gold metallic thread. Fold 4-inch length of cream ribbon in half and glue to center bottom of wreath, glue gold ribbon bow over cream ribbon and glue cream ribbon rose to center.

Gift Box

Bottom

Row 1: With red, ch 7, sc in 2nd ch from hook, sc in each rem ch across, turn. (6 sc)

Rows 2–7: Ch 1, sc in each of next 6 sc, turn. At the end of Row 7, do not fasten off.

Side 1

Row 1: Ch 1, work 6 sc across side edge of rows, turn. (6 sc)

Rows 2–7: Ch 1, sc in each sc across, turn. At the end of Row 7,

fasten off.

Side 2

Row 1: Attach red in opposite side edge of bottom, ch 1, work 6 sc across edge, turn. (6 sc)

Rows 2–7: Ch 1, sc in each sc across, turn. At the end of Row 7, fasten off.

Side 3

Row 1: Attach red in opposite side of foundation ch of bottom, ch 1, sc in each of next 6 chs, turn. (6 sc)

Rows 2–7: Ch 1, sc in each sc across, turn. At the end of Row 7, fasten off.

Side 4

Row 1: Attach red in top edge of bottom square, ch 1, sc in each of next 6 sc, turn. (6 sc)

Rows 2–7: Ch 1, sc in each of next 6 sc, turn. At the end of Row 7, do not fasten off.

Top

Row 1: Ch 1, sc in each of next 6 sc, turn.

Rows 2–7: Ch 1, sc in each of next 6 sc, turn. At the end of Row 7, fasten off.

Plastic Canvas Box

Using crocheted piece as a pattern, cut 6 squares of plastic canvas. Whipstitch 5 of the squares tog to form box minus the top. Fill box with fiberfill and potpourri beads. Whipstitch top of box in place.

Finishing

Sew crocheted piece tog over plastic canvas box. Cut ⅛-inch wide green ribbon in half. Wrap each piece around box and glue at center top of box. Glue 1½-inch poinsettia to center top of box. For hanging lp, attach a length of gold metallic thread.

Purse

Row 1: With blue, ch 8, sc in 2nd ch from hook, [ch 1, sk 1 ch, sc in next ch] 3 times, turn. (4 sc; 3 ch-1 sps)

Row 2: Ch 1, sc in first sc, [sc in

next ch-1 sp, ch 1, sk next sc] twice, sc in next ch-1 sp, sc in next sc, turn. (5 sc; 2 ch-1 sps)

Row 3: Ch 1, sc in first sc, [ch 1, sk next sc, sc in next ch-1 sp] twice, ch 1, sk next sc, sc in last sc, turn. (4 sc; 3 ch-1 sps)

Rows 4–15: Rep Rows 2 and 3.

Row 16: Ch 1, dec 1 sc over first sc and next ch-1 sp, ch 1, sk next sc, sc in next ch-1 sp, ch 1, dec 1 sc over next ch-1 sp and last sc, turn.

Row 17: Sl st in first sc, sc in next ch-1 sp, ch 1, sk next sc, sc in next ch-1 sp, sl st in last sc, fasten off.

Fold Row 1 of purse up to base of Row 13 and sew sides tog.

Edging & Handle

With steel hook size 6, attach silver metallic thread to edge of Row 13, sl st around curve of purse flap to center front, ch 5, sl st in same center st (clasp lp), continue to sl st around curve to opposite edge of Row 13; ch 25 (handle), sl st at opposite side in beg st, fasten off.

Clasp

With steel hook size 6, leaving 5-inch length of silver metallic thread at beg, ch 3, join to form a ring, 4 sc in ring, leaving 5-inch length, fasten off.

Weave rem length through sc sts, draw closed into a knot. Secure clasp to front of purse in line with lp. Pass clasp through lp of edging.

Mary Jane Shoe

Sole

Rnd 1: With black, ch 10, sc in 2nd ch from hook, sc in each of next 2 chs, hdc in each of next 3 chs, dc in each of next 2 chs, 5 dc in last ch, working on opposite side of foundation ch, dc in each of next 2 chs, hdc in each of next 3 chs, sc in each of next 3 chs, join in beg sc. (21 sts)

Rnd 2: Ch 1, sc in each of next 4 sts, hdc in each of next 2 sts, 2 hdc in each of next 2 sts, 2 dc in each of next 4 sts, 2 hdc in each of next 2 sts hdc in each of next 2 sts, sc in each of next 4 sts, 3 sc in next st, join in beg sc, fasten off. (31 sts)

Shoe Top

Row 1: With black, ch 33, hdc in 2nd ch from hook, hdc in each of next 23 chs, turn. (24 hdc)

Row 2: Ch 1, sk first hdc, hdc in each of next 3 sts, [yo, insert hook in next st, yo, draw up a lp, insert hook in next st, yo, draw up a lp, yo, draw through 2 lps on hook, yo, draw through all 3 lps on hook] 4 times, hdc in each of next 4 sts, sc in each of next 8 sts, turn.

Row 3: Ch 1, sk first st, sl st in each of next 8 sts, [yo, insert hook in next st, yo, draw up a lp, insert hook in next st, yo, draw up a lp, yo, draw through all 4 lps on hook] 4 times, sl st in each rem st across to rem 8 chs from Row 1, hdc in each of next 8 chs, turn.

Row 4: Ch 1, sc in each of next 8 hdc, ch 6 (shoe strap), sc in 2nd ch from hook, sc in each of next 4 chs, sl st in next st on shoe top, fasten off.

Finishing

Sew ends of shoe top tog to form center back heel. Matching sts, pin shoe top to sole, whipstitch tog. Sew strap to opposite edge of shoe top and sew gray shank button to center of strap.

For hanging lp, attach a length of gold metallic thread to heel end of shoe.

Turtleneck Sweater

Back

Row 1: With purple, ch 10, sc in 2nd ch from hook, [ch 1, sk next ch, sc in next ch] 4 times, turn. (5 sc; 4 ch-1 sps)

Row 2 (RS): Ch 1, sc in first sc, [dc in next ch-1 sp, sc in next sc] 4 times, turn.

Row 3: Ch 1, sc in first sc, [ch 1, sk next dc, sc in next sc] 4 times, turn.

Row 4: Rep Row 2.

First Sleeve

Row 5: Ch 5, sc in 2nd ch from hook, ch 1, sk next ch, sc in next ch, ch 1, sk next ch, sc in next sc, ch 1, sk next dc, sc in next sc] 4 times, turn.

Second Sleeve

Row 6: Ch 5, sc in 2nd ch from hook, dc in next ch, sc in next ch, dc in next ch, sc in next sc, [dc in next ch-1 sp, sc in next sc] 6 times, turn.

Row 7: Ch 1, sc in first sc, [ch 1, sk next dc, sc in next sc] 8 times, turn.

Row 8: Ch 1, sc in first sc, [dc in next ch-1 sp, sc in next sc] 8 times, turn.

Neck Opening

Row 9: Ch 1, sc in first sc, [ch 1, sk next dc, sc in next sc] 3 times, ch 3, sk each of next 3 sts, sc in next sc, [ch 1, sk next dc, sc in next sc] 3 times, turn.

Row 10: Ch 1, sc in first sc, [dc in next ch-1 sp, sc in next sc] 3 times, dc in next ch, sc in next ch, dc in next ch, sc in next sc, [dc in next ch-1 sp, sc in next sc] 3 times, turn.

Rows 11 & 12: Rep Rows 7 and 8.

Row 13: Rep Row 7.

Row 14: Ch 1, sc in first sc, [dc in next ch-1 sp, sc in next sc] 6 times, turn.

Front

Row 15: Ch 1, sc in first sc, [ch 1, sk next dc, sc in next sc] 4 times, turn.

Row 16: Ch 1, sc in first sc, [dc in next ch-1 sp, sc in next sc] 4 times, turn.

Rows 17 & 18: Rep Rows 15 and 16. At the end of Row 18, fasten off.

Neckline Trim

Rnd 1: Attach purple in any st of neckline opening, ch 3, work 9 dc evenly sp around, join in 3rd ch of ch-3, fasten off. (10 dc)

Finishing

Fold sweater in half, and sew side and sleeve seams. For hanging lp, attach a length of gold metallic thread to sweater.

Camellia

Note: Make raspberry flower with forest green leaves and pink flower with sage green leaves.

Flower

Rnd 1: Attach yarn to ½-inch plastic ring, ch 1, work 15 sc over ring, join in beg sc. (15 sc)

Rnd 2: Working in front lps only, ch 5, sl st in same st as joining, [ch 5, {sl st, ch 5, sl st} in next st] rep around, ending with ch 5, sl st in same st as beg ch-5, leaving a length of yarn, fasten off.

Weave rem length of yarn through rem back lps of Rnd 1, draw closed toward center top of ring, this will gather the ch lps to center to make a fuller flower, secure, fasten off.

Double Leaf

Ch 10, *sc in 2nd ch from hook, hdc in next ch, dc in each of next 2 chs, tr in each of next 2 chs, dc in next ch, hdc in next ch, 3 sc in last ch, working on opposite side of foundation ch, hdc in next ch, dc in each of next 2 chs, tr in each of next 2 chs, dc in next ch, hdc in next ch, sc in next ch *, ch 9, rep from * to * for 2nd half of double leaf working the 3-sc to form the turn in the base of first leaf, sl st to join in beg sc, fasten off.

Finishing

Sew flower to center of double leaf. For hanging lp, attach a length of gold metallic thread as desired.

Tam

Rnd 1: With variegated purple, ch 20, using care not to twist ch, join to form a ring, ch 3 (counts as first dc throughout), dc in next ch, [2 dc in next ch, dc in each of next 3 chs] rep around to last ch, dc in last ch, join in 3rd ch of ch-3. (25 dc)

Rnd 2: Ch 3, dc in same st as joining, dc in each of next 4 dc, [2 dc in next dc, dc in each of next 4 dc] rep around, join in 3rd ch of ch-3. (30 dc)

Rnd 3: Ch 2, yo, insert hook in same st as joining, yo, draw up a

Continued on page 131

Snow People

Designs by Donna Collinsworth

Skill Level: Beginner

Size: 4½ inches tall

Materials

- Lion Brand Jiffy soft mohair-look 2-ply yarn (3 oz per skein): 2 skeins white #100, 1 skein each black #153, country green #181, heather blue #111, wine #189, Denver multicolor #307

- Size G/6 crochet hook or size needed to obtain gauge

- Small amount black and orange polymer clay

- Craft glue

- Small jingle bells

- Small buttons

- Fiberfill

- Cardboard

- Tapestry needle

Gauge

4 sc = 1 inch; 4 sc rnds = 1 inch
Check gauge to save time.

Pattern Notes

Weave in loose ends as work progresses.

Join rnds with a sl st unless otherwise stated.

Three oz white will make 5 snow people.

Dress snow people as desired.

If making stand-alone snow people decoration for a table or mantel, cut cardboard 1½-inch diameter circle and insert when indicated.

For snow people garland, thread length of yarn through hands, tie ends in a bow and secure bow with a drop of glue.

Basic Snow Doll

Head & body

Note: Stuff head and body as work progresses.

Rnd 1 (RS): With white ch 4, join to form a ring, ch 1, 8 sc in ring, join in beg sc, turn. (8 sc)

Rnd 2: Ch 1, sc in each sc around, join in beg sc, turn.

Rnd 3: Rep Rnd 2.

Rnd 4: Ch 1, [sc dec over next 2 sc, sc in each of next 2 sc] twice, join in beg sc, turn. (6 sc)

Rnd 5: Rep Rnd 2.

Rnd 6: Ch 1, [2 sc in next sc, sc in next sc] 3 times, join in beg sc, turn. (9 sc)

Rnds 7 & 8: Ch 1, [2 sc in next sc, sc in each of next 2 sc] rep around, join in beg sc, turn. (16 sc)

Rnd 9: Ch 1, [2 sc in next sc, sc in each of next 3 sc] rep around, join in beg sc, turn. (20 sc)

Rnds 10–16: Rep Rnd 2.

Rnd 17: Ch 1, [sc dec over next 2 sc, sc in each of next 3 sc] rep around, join in beg sc, turn. (16 sc)

Note: If making stand-alone decoration, insert cardboard.

Rnds 18 & 19: Ch 1, [sc dec over next 2 sc, sc in each of next 2 sc] rep around, join in beg sc, turn. (9 sc)

Rnd 20: Ch 1, sc in next sc, [sc dec over next 2 sc] 4 times, join in beg sc, leaving a length of yarn, fasten off. Sew opening closed. (5 sc)

Arm

Make 2

Rnd 1: With white, ch 6, join to form a ring, ch 1, 6 sc in ring, join in beg sc, turn. (6 sc)

Rnds 2–4: Ch 1, sc in each sc around, join in beg sc, turn.

Rnd 5: Ch 1, [sc in next sc, sc dec over next 2 sc] twice, join in beg sc, fasten off. (4 sc)

Sew to each side of body at shoulder area.

Facial features

Following directions of polymer

String these mini snow people together as a garland for your tree or mantel, or use individually as package decorations or friendly accents to your holiday table!

clay, form eyes and mouth with black, make tiny buttons and form nose with orange, form a carrot. When cool, glue to face.

Hat

Rnd 1: With black, ch 5, join to form a ring, ch 1, 10 sc in ring, join in beg sc, turn. (10 sc)

Rnds 2 & 3: Ch 1, sc in each sc around, join in beg sc, turn.

Rnd 4: Ch 2 (counts as first hdc throughout), 2 hdc in same st as ch-2, hdc in next st, sl st in each of next 2 sts, [sc, hdc] in next st, 3 hdc in next st, hdc in next st, sl st in each of next 2 sts, sc in next st, join in 2nd ch of ch-2, fasten off.

Sew or glue hat to top of head.

Stocking Cap

Rnd 1: With desired yarn, ch 12, join to form a ring, ch 1, sc in each ch around, join in beg sc, turn. (12 sc)

Rnd 2: Ch 1, sc in each sc around,

sc dec 1 sc over 2 sc near center, join in beg sc, turn. (11 sts)

Rnds 3–5: Rep Rnd 2. (8 sc)

Rnds 6–8: Ch 1, sc in each sc around, join, turn.

Rnds 9 & 10: Rep Rnd 2. (6 sc)

Rnd 11: Ch 1, [dec 1 sc over next 2 sc] 3 times, join in beg sc, fasten off. Sew a jingle bell to Rnd 11 of hat. Sew or glue hat to head.

For striped stocking cap, work Rnd 1 with MC color, then alternate CC and MC working 2 rnds of each.

Scarf

Row 1: With desired color, ch 2, sc in 2nd ch from hook, turn. (1 sc)

Rows 2–26: Ch 1, sc in sc, turn. At the end of Row 26, fasten off.

For striped scarf, work 2 rows each MC and CC alternately.

Place around neckline, overlapping as desired, and sew in place.

Vest

Row 1: Beg at bottom, with desired color, ch 30, sc in 2nd ch from hook, sc in each rem ch across, turn. (29 sc)

Row 2: Ch 1, sc in each of next 6 sc, turn. (6 sc)

Row 3: Ch 1, sc in each of next 4 sc, dec 1 sc over next 2 sc, turn. (5 sc)

Row 4: Ch 1, dec 1 sc over next 2 sc, sc in each of next 3 sc, turn. (4 sc)

Row 5: Ch 1, sc in each of next 2 sc, dec 1 sc over next 2 sc, turn. (3 sc)

Row 6: Ch 1, dec 1 sc over next 2 sc, sc in next sc, turn. (2 sc)

Row 7: Ch 1, dec 1 sc over next 2 sc, fasten off. (1 sc)

Row 8: Attach yarn in opposite end of Row 1, ch 1, sc in same sc as ch-1, sc in each of next 5 sc, turn. (6 sc)

Rows 9–13: Rep Rows 3–7.

Row 14: Sk next 4 sc of Row 1, attach yarn in next sc, ch 1, sc in same sc as ch-1, sc in each of next 8 sc, turn. (9 sc)

Rows 15–18: Ch 1, sc in each of next 9 sc, turn.

Row 19: Ch 1, sc in first sc, sl st in each of next 7 sc, sc in last sc, fasten off.

Sew 1 sc at each shoulder. Place on doll, overlapping fronts tack in place. Sew a button to front of vest.

For striped vest, work 2 rows each MC and CC, ending with 3 rows of same color on last row.

Apron

With desired color, ch 64, fasten off.

Row 1: Attach yarn in 28th ch of ch-64, ch 1, sc in same ch as ch-1, sc in each of next 9 chs, turn. (10 sc)

Continued on page 135

Jolly Snowman Ornament

Design by Sandy Abbate

Skill Level: Beginner

Size: 7½ inches

Materials

- Worsted weight yarn: 2 oz white, 1 oz black, small amount scarlet and bright orange
- Size G/6 crochet hook or size needed to obtain gauge
- 28 inches ⅛-inch-wide red ribbon
- 27 inches ⅜-inch-wide Christmas striped wire-edge ribbon
- 6-inch flat broom
- 6 inches wired evergreen garland
- 6 inches green floral wire
- Gold Merry Christmas confetti
- Gold snowflake confetti
- Fiberfill
- Tacky glue
- Tapestry needle

Gauge

5 sc = 1 inch; 4 sc rnds = 1 inch
Check gauge to save time.

Pattern Notes

Weave in loose ends as work progresses.

Do not join rnds unless otherwise stated. Use a scrap of yarn to mark rnds.

Head

Rnd 1 (RS): With white, ch 2, 6 sc in 2nd ch from hook. (6 sc)

Rnd 2: 2 sc in each sc around. (12 sc)

Rnd 3: [Sc in each of next 3 sc, 2 sc in next sc] rep around. (15 sc)

Rnd 4: Sc in each sc around.

Rnds 5–7: Rep Rnd 4.

Rnd 8: [Sc in next sc, dec 1 sc over next 2 sc] rep around. (10 sc)

Stuff head with fiberfill.

Rnd 9: [Dec 1 sc over next 2 sc] rep around. (5 sc)

Body

Upper body

Rnd 10: Rep Rnd 2. (10 sc)

Rnd 11: [Sc in next sc, 2 sc in next sc] rep around. (15 sc)

Rnd 12: [Sc in each of next 4 sc, 2 sc in next sc] rep around. (18 sc)

Rnds 13–15: Rep Rnd 4.

Rnd 16: [Sc in next sc, dec 1 sc over next 2 sc] rep around. (12 sc)

Stuff upper body with fiberfill.

Rnd 17: [Dec 1 sc over next 2 sc] rep around. (6 sc)

Lower body

Rnds 18 & 19: Rep Rnd 2. (24 sc)

Rnds 20–23: Rep Rnd 4.

Rnd 24: [Dec 1 sc over next 2 sc] rep around. (12 sc)

Stuff lower body with fiberfill.

Rnd 25: Rep Rnd 24, leaving a length of yarn, fasten off. (6 sc)

Weave rem length through sts of Rnd 25, pull to close opening, secure.

Leg

Make 2

Boot

Rnd 1: Beg at toe, with black, ch 2, 8 sc in 2nd ch from hook. (8 sc)

Rnds 2 & 3: Sc in each sc around. At the end of Rnd 3, turn.

Rows 4–6: Ch 1, sc in each of next 8 sc, turn. At the end of Row 6, leaving a length of yarn, fasten off.

This jolly little fellow is a delight to crochet and display. Make one for yourself and your friends will want one, too!

To form heel, fold Row 6 in half and sew across edge.

Rnd 7: Attach black at center back seam, ch 1, 8 sc evenly sp around opening. (8 sc)

Rnd 8: Sc in each sc around, sl st in next sc, fasten off.

Leg

Rnd 9: Working in back lps only, attach white, sc in each st around. (8 sc)

Stuff boot only with fiberfill.

Rnds 10–13: Sc in each sc around.

Rnd 14: [Dec 1 sc over next 2 sc] 4 times, sl st in next st, leaving a length of yarn, fasten off. Weave rem length through sts, pull to close opening and secure.

Arm

Make 2

Mitten

Rnd 1: With scarlet, ch 2, 8 sc in 2nd ch from hook. (8 sc)

Rnds 2 & 3: Sc in each sc around. At the end of Rnd 3, sl st in next st, fasten off.

Rnd 4: Working in back lps only, attach white, sc in each st around. (8 sc)

Rnds 5–10: Sc in each sc around. Stuff arm with fiberfill.

Rnd 11: [Dec 1 sc over next 2 sc] 4 times, sl st in next st, leaving a length of yarn, fasten off. Weave rem length through sts, pull to close opening and secure.

Hat

Rnd 1: With black, ch 2, 6 sc in 2nd ch from hook. (6 sc)

Rnd 2: 2 sc in each sc around. (12 sc)

Rnd 3: Sc in each sc around.

Rnd 4: Working in back lps only, sc in each st around.

Rnds 5 & 6: Rep Rnd 3.

Rnd 7: [Sc in next sc, 2 sc in next sc] 6 times. (18 sc)

Rnd 8: [Sc in each of next 2 sc, 2 sc in next sc] 6 times, fasten off. (24 sc)

Nose

Row 1: With bright orange, ch 5, sl st in 2nd ch from hook, sc in next ch, hdc in next ch, dc in last ch, leaving a length of yarn, fasten off.

Fold nose in half lengthwise; sew sts of Row 1 to opposite side of foundation ch.

Finishing

Working through all thicknesses, sew legs to lower body and arms to upper body.

Glue hat on head and nose to center face. With black, embroider eyes and mouth with French knots.

For hanger, attach red ribbon around neckline. Tie a 12-inch length of Christmas wire-edge ribbon around neckline in a bow.

With a length of scarlet, sew mittens tog at wrists.

Tie a length of scarlet around waistline; knot each end of yarn.

Wrap floral wire around end of crochet hook 5 times to form bowl of pipe, leaving a ½-inch stem, cut wire. Place glue on end of stem and insert into mouth behind center French knot.

Wrap evergreen garland around broom handle. Make a bow with rem length of Christmas wire-edge ribbon around base of broom handle and curl ends of ribbon.

Glue "Merry Christmas" confetti to top of bow and snowflake confetti to center of broom bristles. Glue mittens to broom handle. ✂

Country Mini Stocking

Design by Sandy Abbate

Small enough to hang on your tree, this delightful little stocking would look just as charming on your mantel or any place else you want to decorate!

Skill Level: Beginner

Size: 2¾ x 6½ inches

Materials

- Caron Victorian Gold Christmas worsted weight yarn: ½ oz each cranberry #1950, balsam #1951, lace #1952
- Size H/8 crochet hook or size needed to obtain gauge
- 7-inch circle cream tulle
- Small amount potpourri
- 18 inches ⅜-inch-wide wire-edge gold ribbon
- ¾-inch red star button
- Tapestry needle

Gauge

4 sc = 4 inch; 4 sc rnds = 1 inch
Check gauge to save time.

Pattern Notes

Weave in loose ends as work progresses.

Join rnds with a sl st unless otherwise stated.

Heel

Rnd 1 (RS): With balsam, ch 7, 3 sc in 2nd ch from hook, sc in each of next 4 chs, 3 sc in next ch, working on opposite side of foundation ch, sc in each of next 4 chs, join in beg sc. (14 sc)

Rnd 2: Ch 1, sc in same sc as joining, 3 sc in next sc, sc in each of next 6 sc, 3 sc in next sc, sc in each of next 5 sc, join in beg sc. (18 sc)

Rnd 3: Ch 1, sc in each sc around, join in beg sc, fasten off.

Foot

Rnd 1: Attach cranberry in center sc of 3-sc group, ch 1, sc in same sc, sc in each of next 9 sc, ch 10, join in beg sc. (10 sc; ch-10 sp)

Rnd 2: Ch 1, sc in each of next 10 sc, sc in each of next 10 chs, join in beg sc, fasten off. (20 sc)

Rnd 3: Attach lace with sc in same st as joining, sc in each rem sc around, join in beg sc. (20 sc)

Rnd 4: Ch 1, sc in each sc around, join in beg sc, fasten off.

Rnds 5 & 6: Attach cranberry, rep Rnds 3 and 4.

Rnds 7 & 8: Rep Rnds 3 and 4.

Toe

Rnds 9 & 10: Attach balsam, rep Rnds 3 and 4, do not fasten off. (20 sc)

Rnd 11: Ch 1, [dec 1 sc over next 2 sc] 10 times, join in beg sc. (10 sc)

Rnd 12: Rep Rnd 11, leaving a length of yarn, fasten off. (5 sc) Weave rem length through sts of Rnd 12, close opening and secure.

Leg

Rnd 1: Attach lace in side of Rnd 1 of foot, ch 1, sc in same st as beg ch-1, working across opposite side of foundation ch, sc in each of next 10 chs, sc in side of Rnd 1 of foot, sc in rem 8 sc of heel, join in beg sc. (20 sc)

Rnd 2: Ch 1, sc in each sc around, join in beg sc, fasten off.

Rnds 3 & 4: With cranberry, rep Rnds 3 and 4 of foot.

Rnds 5 & 6: Rep Rnds 3 and 4 of foot.

Rnds 7 & 8: Rep Rnds 3 and 4.

Cuff

Rnd 1: Attach balsam with sl st in same st as joining, ch 2 (does not count as a st throughout), dc in same st, dc in each rem sc around, join in first dc. (20 dc)

Rnd 2: Ch 2, dc in same st, dc in each dc around, join in first dc, turn.

Rnd 3: Ch 2, working in back lps only, dc in each dc around, join in first dc, do not turn.

Rnd 4: Rep Rnd 2, fasten off.

Rnd 5: With WS facing, attach cranberry with sl st in joining st, [ch 2, sl st in next st] rep around, fasten off. Fold cuff down at Rnd 3.

Hanger

Attach balsam with sl st in back at top of cuff, ch 13, sl st in same st, fasten off.

Finishing

Sew star button to center front of cuff. Place potpourri in center of tulle circle, gather circle around potpourri, tie with gold ribbon and make a bow and crimp ends of ribbon. Place in top of stocking. ✄

Tomato Pincushion

Continued from page 117

sc, dec 1 sc over next 2 sc] rep around, join in beg sc. (18 sc)

Rnd 20: Ch 1, [sc in next sc, dec 1 sc over next 2 sc] rep around, join in beg sc. (12 sc)

Rnd 21: Ch 1, [dec 1 sc over next 2 sc] 6 times, sl st in next st, leaving a length of yarn, fasten off. Sew opening closed.

Wedge Trim

Thread tapestry needle with a long length of forest green, knot at center top of Rnd 1, [insert needle in center bottom of Rnd 21, pull slightly to indent yarn that runs from center top to center bottom, knot to secure, bring yarn up on opposite edge, insert needle in Rnd 1, pull slightly to indent yarn that runs from center bottom to center top, knot to secure] rep until you have completed 6 wedges from top to bottom with yarn evenly sp around tomato, secure, fasten off.

Tomato Top & Bottom

Make 2

Rnd 1: With forest green, ch 2, 6 sc in 2nd ch from hook, join in beg sc. (6 sc)

Rnd 2: Ch 1, [sc, ch 2, sl st in 2nd ch from hook, sc] in each sc around, join in beg sc, fasten off.

Sew to each center top and bottom of tomato.

Strawberry

Rnd 1: With cherry red, ch 2, 6 sc in 2nd ch from hook, join in beg sc. (6 sc)

Rnd 2: Ch 1, [sc in next sc, 2 sc in next sc] 3 times, join in beg sc. (9 sc)

Rnds 3 & 4: Ch 1, sc in each sc around, join in beg sc.

Rnd 5: Ch 1, [sc in next sc, dec 1 sc over next 2 sc] 3 times, join in

beg sc, leaving a length of yarn, fasten off.

Stuff strawberry with a scrap of fiberfill and sew opening closed.

Strawberry Top

Rnd 1: With forest green, ch 2, [sc, ch 2, sl st in 2nd ch from hook] 5 times in 2nd ch of beg ch-2, ch 12, leaving a length of yarn, fasten off. Sew rem length to center top of tomato. ✄

Santa Star Ornament

Design by Ann E. Smith

This charming little Santa would make a great window decoration or tree ornament!

Skill Level: Beginner

Size: 5½ inches

Materials

- Sport weight yarn: small amount red, white, black, apricot
- Size E/4 crochet hook or size needed to obtain gauge
- 2 black E beads
- Tapestry needle

Gauge

5 sc = 1 inch; 5 sc rows = 1 inch

Check gauge to save time.

Pattern Notes

Weave in loose ends as work progresses.

Join rnds with a sl st unless otherwise stated.

Santa Back

Rnd 1 (RS): With red, ch 2, 5 sc in 2nd ch from hook, join in beg sc. (5 sc)

Rnd 2: Ch 1, 2 sc in each sc around, join in beg sc. (10 sc)

Rnd 3: Ch 1, [sc in next sc, 2 sc in next sc] rep around, join in beg sc. (15 sc)

Rnd 4: Ch 1, [sc in each of next 2 sc, 2 sc in next sc] rep around, join in beg sc. (20 sc)

Rnd 5: Ch 1, [sc in each of next 3 sc, 2 sc in next sc] rep around, join in beg sc. (25 sc)

Rnd 6: Ch 1, [sc in each of next 4 sc, 2 sc in next sc] rep around, join in beg sc. (30 sc)

First point

Row 1 (RS): Ch 1, sc in each of next 6 sc, turn. (6 sc)

Row 2: Ch 1, sc in each of next 6 sc, turn.

Row 3: Ch 1, dec 1 sc over next 2 sc, sc in each of next 2 sc, dec 1 sc over next 2 sc, turn. (4 sc)

Row 4: Ch 1, sc in each of next 4 sc, fasten off, turn.

Row 5: Attach black, ch 1, sc in each of next 4 sc, turn.

Row 6: Ch 1, sc in each of next 4 sc, turn.

Row 7: Ch 1, [dec 1 sc over next 2 sc] twice, turn. (2 sc)

Row 8: Ch 1, dec 1 sc over next 2 sc, fasten off. (1 sc)

Second–fourth points

Row 1 (RS): With finished point to the right, attach red in next sc of Rnd 6, ch 1, sc in same sc as ch-1, sc in each of next 5 sc, turn. (6 sc)

Rows 2–8: Rep Rows 2–8 of first point.

Fifth point

Row 1 (RS): With finished point to the right, attach red in next sc of Rnd 6, ch 1, sc in same sc as ch-1, sc in each of next 5 sc, turn.

Rows 2–8: Working rem of 5th point with red only, rep Rows 2–8 of first point.

Santa Front

Rnds 1–3: With apricot, rep Rnds 1–3 of back, at the end of Rnd 3, fasten off. (15 sc)

Rnd 4: Working in back lps only, attach red, rep Rnd 4 of back. (20 sc)

Rnd 5: Working in back lps only, rep Rnd 5 of back. (25 sc)

Rnd 6: Rep Rnd 6 of back. (30 sc)

Rep first–fifth points the same as for back.

Facial Features

For nose, with a double strand of apricot, [insert needle from back to front to back again over Rnd 1] 3 times, secure ends at back of front. For eyes, sew beads slightly above nose. For mouth, with red, sew a small straight st under nose.

Hair

Attach white in rem free lp of Rnd 3, [ch 1, sl st in next st] rep around, fasten off.

Hat Trim

Working on center top 7 rem free lps of Rnd 4, attach white, ch 2, sl st in same st, [sl st in next st, ch 2, sl st in same st] 5 times, fasten off.

Beard

Working in rem free lps of Rnd 4, sk next 2 sts from hat trim, attach white in next st with sl st, [ch 8, sl st in next st] 7 times, fasten off.

Finishing

Holding front and back tog, attach red, sl st evenly sp around outer edge of each red section, changing to black at outer point black sections, stuffing slightly with small amount of yarn before closing.

With RS facing, attach white in tip of 5th point, ch 3 (counts as first dc), 4 dc in same st, remove hook, insert hook in top of ch-3, pick up dropped lp, draw through st on hook, ch 1, fasten off.

For hanging lp, cut a 10-inch length of red, pass through st at center back of 5th point, knot ends tog. ✁

Set of Ornaments
Continued from page 123

lp, insert hook in next dc, yo, draw up a lp (4 lps on hook), yo, draw through 2 lps on hook, yo, draw through rem 3 lps on hook (beg puff dec), [yo, insert hook in next st, yo, draw up a lp, insert hook in next dc, yo, draw up a lp (4 lps on hook), yo, draw through 2 lps on hook, yo, draw through rem 3 lps on hook (puff dec)] rep around, join in top of beg puff dec. (15 sts)

Rnd 4: Rep Rnd 3, working last half of last puff dec in base of beg ch-2, join, leaving a length of yarn, fasten off. (8 sts)

Weave rem length through rem sts of Rnd 4, pull to close opening, secure.

Ribbing
Rnd 1: Attach variegated purple in opposite side of foundation ch, ch 1, sc in each ch around, join in beg sc. (20 sc)

Rnd 2: Ch 2, [yo, insert hook front to back to front again around vertical post of next sc, yo, draw up a lp, yo, draw through all 3 lps on hook, yo, insert hook back to front to back again around next vertical post of next sc, yo, draw up a lp, yo, draw through all 3 lps on hook] rep around, join in 2nd ch of ch-2, fasten off.

Finishing
With variegated purple make a small pompom and glue to center of Rnd 1.

For hanging lp, attach a length of gold metallic thread as desired.

Beret

Rnd 1: With raspberry, ch 16,

using care not to twist ch, join to form a ring, ch 3 (counts as first dc throughout), dc in same ch, dc in next ch, [2 dc in next ch, dc in next ch] rep around, join in 3rd ch of ch-3. (24 dc)

Rnd 2: Ch 3, dc in same st as joining, dc in each of next 2 dc, [2 dc in next dc, dc in each of next 2 dc] rep around, join in 3rd ch of ch-3.

Rnd 3: Rep Rnd 3 of tam (16 sts)

Rnd 4: Rep Rnd 4 of tam. (8 sts)

Weave rem length through sts, pull to close opening, secure.

Ribbing
Rnd 1: Attach raspberry in opposite side of foundation ch, ch 1, reverse sc in each ch around, join in beg sc, fasten off.

Top Knot
With pink, ch 4, join to form a ring, sl st in each ch around, leaving a length of yarn, fasten off. Form into a tiny ball and sew to Rnd 1 of beret.

Finishing
For hanging lp, attach a length of gold metallic thread as desired. ✁

Heart Photo Frame Magnet
Continued from page 114

Heart

Holiday Scrap Ornaments

Design by Katherine Eng

Skill Level: Beginner

Size: 3¼ inches tip to tip

Materials

- Crochet cotton size 10: Scrap amount red, burgundy, green, dark green, gold/gold metallic
- Size 7 steel crochet hook or size needed to obtain gauge
- 10 inches ¼-inch-wide green ribbon each ornament
- Tapestry needle

These pretty ornaments can easily be made in an evening or two, and the use of metallic threads offers the added holiday sparkle!

Gauge

Rnds 1 and 2 = 1 inch

Pattern Notes

Weave in loose ends as work progresses.

Use same-color cotton for Rnds 1 and 2 and a different-color cotton for each of rem 4 rnds of ornament.

Ch-3 counts as first dc throughout.

Join rnds with a sl st unless otherwise stated.

Pattern Stitch

Shell: [2 dc, ch 2, 2 dc] in indicated st.

Ornament

Make 2

Rnd 1 (RS): Ch 4, join to form a ring, ch 1, 8 sc in ring join in beg sc. (8 sc)

Rnd 2: Ch 1, sc in same sc as ch-1, shell in next sc, [sc in next sc, shell in next sc] rep around, join in beg sc, fasten off.

Rnd 3: Draw up a lp of cotton in 2nd dc of any corner shell, ch 1, sc in same dc, *shell in corner ch-2 sp, sc in next dc, shell in next sc, sk next dc **, sc in next dc, rep from * around, ending last rep at **, join in beg sc, fasten off.

Rnd 4: Draw up a lp of cotton in center ch-2 sp on any side, ch 1, sc in same ch-2 sp, *shell in next sc, sk next dc, sc in next dc, shell in corner ch-2 sp, sc in next dc, shell in next sc **, sc in next ch-2 sp, rep from * around, ending last rep at **, join in beg sc, fasten off.

Joining

Rnd 5: Place pieces tog with WS facing, draw up a lp of cotton through both lps of both sides of first sc to the left of any corner shell, ch 1, working through both thicknesses, sc in same sc, *ch 2, [sc, ch 3, sc] in next ch-2 sp, ch 2, sc in next sc, rep from * around, working ch 2 [sc, ch 3, sc] in first corner ch-2 sp, ch 50, sl st in 3rd ch of ch-50 (for hanging lp), ch 3, [sc, ch 3, sc] in same corner ch-2 sp, and working in each rem corner ch-2 sp, [sc, ch 3, sc, ch 5, sc, ch 3, sc] join in beg sc, fasten off.

Tie ribbon in a bow at base of hanger. ✂

Gold Cross Ornament

Design by Connie Folse

Skill Level: Beginner

Size: 2¼ x 3 inches

Materials

- J. & P. Coats Metallic Knit-Cro-Sheen crochet cotton size 10: 30 yds gold/gold #90G

- 2 yds gold lamé

- Size 7 steel crochet hook or size needed to obtain gauge

- 1½ x 2 inches 7-count plastic canvas

- Embroidery needle

With plastic canvas and metallic thread, you can create this beautiful ornament to hang on your tree or give as a cherished gift!

Gauge

Rnd 1, 4 sc = ½ inch
Check gauge to save time.

Pattern Notes

Weave in loose ends as work progresses.

Join rnds with a sl st unless otherwise stated.

Cross

Note: Cut plastic canvas according to graph

Rnd 1 (RS): Attach gold/gold cotton at A as indicated on graph, ch 1, work counterclockwise around plastic canvas cross, 3 sc in same square as ch-1, 3 sc in next square, sc in each of next 5 squares, [{3 sc in next square} twice, sc in each of next 9 squares] twice, [3 sc in next square] twice, sc in each of next 5 squares, join in beg sc. (52 sc)

Rnd 2: Ch 1, sc in each of next 7 sc, [sk next sc, sc in next sc] twice, sc in each of next 7 sc, [sk next sc, sc in next sc] twice, sc in each of next 15 sc, [sk next sc, sc in next sc] twice, sc in each of next 7 sc, [sk next sc, sc in next sc] twice, join in beg sc, turn. (44 sc)

Rnd 3: Ch 1, [sc in next sc, ch 5, sk each of next 2 sc, sc in next sc] 11 times, join in beg sc.

Rnd 4: Ch 1, [7 sc in next ch-5 sp] 11 times, join in beg sc, turn.

Hanger

Row 5: Sl st in each of next 4 sts, ch 6, sl st in same st, fasten off.

Embroidery

Thread embroidery needle with double length of gold lamé; following graph, embroider with straight sts through center of squares. ✄

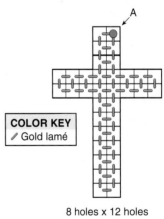

COLOR KEY
⁄ Gold lamé

8 holes x 12 holes
Cut 1

Mini Poinsettia Wreath

Design by Katherine Eng

A beautiful way to use leftovers from your holiday projects, this delicate wreath would look lovely hanging in a window!

Gauge

Small flower = 1½ inches; large flower = 1¾ inches

Check gauge to save time.

Pattern Notes

Weave in loose ends as work progresses.

Join rnds with a sl st unless otherwise stated.

Small Flower

Rnd 1 (RS): With green, ch 4, join to form a ring, ch 1, 8 sc in ring, join in beg sc, fasten off. (8 sc)

Rnd 2: Draw up a lp of red in any sc, ch 1, sc in same sc, ch 1, [sc in next sc, ch 1] rep around, join in beg sc.

Rnd 3: Sk over sc sts, *[sl st, ch 2, 3 dc, ch 2, sl st] in ch-1 sp, ch 1, rep from * around, sl st in beg sl st, fasten off.

Rnd 4: Draw up a lp of burgundy in any ch-1 sp between petals, *ch 3, [sl st, ch 2, sl st] in center dc of next petal, ch 3, sl st in next ch-1 sp, rep from * around, fasten off.

Large Flower

Rnds 1 & 2: Rep Rnds 1 and 2 of small flower.

Rnd 3: Sk over sc sts, *[sl st, ch 3, dc, tr, dc, ch 3, sl st] in ch-1 sp, ch 1, rep from * around, sl st in beg sl st, fasten off.

Rnd 4: Draw up a lp of burgundy in any ch-1 sp between petals, *ch 4, [sl st, ch 3, sl st] in center tr of next petal, ch 4, sl st in next ch-1 sp, rep from * around, fasten off.

Small Leaf

Make 2

With green ch 5, sc in 2nd ch from hook, hdc in next ch, 2 hdc in next ch, sc in last ch, fasten off.

Large Leaf

Make 2

With green, ch 7, sc in 2nd ch from hook, sc in next ch, hdc in next ch, 2 dc in next ch, hdc in next ch, sc in last ch, fasten off.

Sew flowers and leaves to wreath. Attach ribbon top of wreath and tie in a bow. ✂

Snow People

Continued from page 125

Rows 2–4: Ch 1, sc in each sc across, turn.

Row 5: Ch 1, dec 1 sc over next 2 sc, sc in each of next 6 sc, dec 1 sc over next 2 sc, fasten off. (8 sc)

Bib

Row 1: Sk 30 chs of foundation ch, attach yarn in next ch, ch 1, sc in same ch, sc in each of next 4 chs, turn. (5 sc)

Row 2: Ch 1, sc in each of next 5 sc, turn.

Row 3: Ch 1, dec 1 sc over next 2 sc, sl st in next sc, dec 1 sc over next 2 sc, fasten off.

Mrs. Snowman Hat

Rnd 1: With desired color, ch 4, join to form a ring, ch 1, 8 sc in ring, join in beg sc. (8 sc)

Rnds 2 & 3: Ch 1, sc in each sc around, join in beg sc.

Rnd 4: [Ch 3, sl st in next sc] rep around, fasten off.

Sew or glue to head. ✁

Playtime Friends

Playtime for kids of all ages, from babies to preteens, can be even more fun when creative crocheted projects are added to the mix of toys! Cuddly animals for nap time, a soft bath mitt for bath time, a colorful rug for game time and many more projects will bring hours of crocheting pleasure and playtime fun!

Beautiful Butterfly

Design by Donna Collinsworth

Gauge

2 sc = 1 inch; 3 sc rows = 1½ inches
Check gauge to save time.

Pattern Notes

Weave in loose ends as work progresses.

Join rnds with a sl st unless otherwise stated.

Body

Rnd 1: With citron, ch 4, join to form a ring, ch 1, 8 sc in ring, join in beg sc, turn. (8 sc)

Rnd 2: Ch 1, [2 sc in next sc, sc in next sc] rep around, join in beg sc, turn. (12 sc)

Rnd 3: Rep Rnd 2. (18 sc)

Rnd 4: Ch 1, sc in each sc around, join in beg sc, turn.

Rnds 5 & 6: Rep Rnd 4.

Rnd 7: Ch 1, [sc dec over next 2 sc, sc in next sc] rep around, join in beg sc, turn. (12 sc)

Rnd 8: Rep Rnd 4.

Rnd 9: Rep Rnd 2. (18 sc)

Rnds 10–12: Rep Rnd 4.

Rnd 13: Rep Rnd 7. (12 sc)

Rnd 14: Rep Rnd 4.

Rnd 15: Rep Rnd 2. (18 sc)

Rnds 16–18: Rep Rnd 4.
Stuff with fiberfill.

Rnd 19: Ch 1, [sc dec over next 2 sc, sc in each of next 4 sc] 3 times, join in beg sc, turn. (15 sc)

Rnd 20: Ch 1, [sc dec over next 2 sc, sc in each of next 2 sc] 3 times, join in beg sc, turn. (12 sc)

Rnd 21: Rep Rnd 4.

Rnd 22: Ch 1, [sc dec over next 2 sc, sc in each of next 2 sc] 3 times, join in beg sc, turn. (9 sc)
Finish stuffing with fiberfill.

Rnds 23 & 24: Rep Rnd 4.

Rnd 25: Ch 1, [sc dec over next 2 sc] 4 times, sk last sc, join in beg sc, fasten off. (4 sc)

Wing

Note: Make 4 wings in the following color combinations: Lavender center with aqua outer, aqua center with powder blue outer, powder blue center with powder blue outer, and powder pink center with lavender outer.

Center

Row 1: Ch 11, sc in 2nd ch from hook, sc in each of next 9 chs, working on opposite side of foundation ch, sc in each of next 10 chs, turn. (20 sc)

Row 2: Ch 1, sc in each of next 9 sc, 2 sc in each of next 2 sc, sc in each of next 9 sc, fasten off turn. (22 sc)

Delicate-looking, yet sturdy and durable, this pretty butterfly can hold its own when baby pulls its wings.

Outer

Row 3: Attach yarn, ch 1, sc in each of next 9 sc, 2 sc in each of next 4 sc, sc in each of next 9 sc, turn. (26 sc)

Row 4: Ch 1, sc in each of next 10 sc, 2 sc in each of next 6 sc, sc in each of next 10 sc, turn. (32 sc)

Row 5: Ch 1, sc in each of next 32 sc, fasten off.

Wing Cover

Row 1: With aqua, ch 23, sc in 2nd ch from hook, sc in each of next 8 chs, 2 sc in each of next 4 chs, sc in each of next 9 chs, turn. (26 sc)

Row 2: Ch 1, sc in each of next 10 sc, 2 sc in each of next 6 sc, sc in each of next 10 sc, turn. (32 sc)

Row 3: Ch 1, sc in each sc across, fasten off.

With matching thread, sew wing cover over wing with aqua center at matching ends.

Pocket

Row 1: With powder pink, ch 8, sc in 2nd ch from hook, sc in each

of next 4 chs, 2 sc in each of next 2 chs, attach lavender, fasten off powder pink, turn. (9 sc)

Row 2: Ch 1, sk first sc, 2 sc in each of next 3 sc, sc in each of next 5 sc, turn. (11 sc)

Row 3: Ch 1, sc in each of next 7 sc, 2 sc in each of next 4 sc, turn. (15 sc)

Row 4: Ch 1, sc in each sc across, fasten off.

With matching thread, sew pocket to wing with powder pink center, matching colors and edges. Cut an 8-inch length of yellow ribbon. Sew end of ribbon around a teething ring; sew opposite end of

ribbon to edge of same wing and place teething ring in pocket.

Rattle Cover

Row 1: With powder blue, ch 10, sc in 2nd ch from hook, sc in each rem ch across, turn. (9 sc)

Continued on page 157

Cuddle Buddies

Design by Donna Collinsworth

Gauge

2 sc = 1 inch; 3 sc rows = 1½ inches
Check gauge to save time.

Pattern Notes

Weave in loose ends as work progresses.

Join rnds with a sl st unless otherwise stated.

Bear

Body

Row 1: With aqua, ch 15, sc in 2nd ch from hook, sc in each rem ch across, turn. (14 sc)

Row 2: Ch 1, sc in each sc across, turn.

Rows 3–24: Rep Row 2.

At the end of Row 24, fasten off.

With needle and matching thread, sew long sides of body tog to form a tube. Stuff tube lightly with fiberfill. Sew opposite side of foundation ch to last row of body to form a ring.

Head

Rnd 1: With aqua, ch 4, join to form a ring, ch 1, 8 sc in ring, join in beg sc, turn. (8 sc)

Rnds 2 & 3: Ch 1, [2 sc in next sc, sc in next sc] rep around, join in beg sc. (18 sc)

Rnds 4–7: Ch 1, sc in each sc around, join in beg sc, turn.

Rnds 8 & 9: Ch 1, [sc dec over next 2 sc, sc in next sc] rep around, join in beg sc, turn. (8 sc) Stuff head with fiberfill.

Rnd 10: Ch 1, [sc dec over next 2 sc] rep around, join in beg sc, fasten off. (4 sc) Sew head to top of body.

Arm

Make 2

Rnd 1: With aqua, ch 10, join to form a ring, ch 1, sc in each ch around, join in beg sc, turn. (10 sc)

Rnds 2–6: Ch 1, sc in each sc around, join in beg sc, turn. At the end of Rnd 6, fasten off.

Hand pad

With powder blue, ch 3, join to form a ring, ch 1, 6 sc in ring, join in beg sc, fasten off. (6 sc)

With matching thread, easing in fullness, sew hand pad to end of arm. Stuff arm half full of fiberfill; fold top opening flat across and sew to side of body.

Leg

Make 2

Rnd 1: With powder blue, ch 16, join to form a ring, ch 1, sc in each ch around, join in beg sc, turn. (16 sc)

Rnds 2–8: Ch 1, sc in each sc around, join in beg sc, turn. At the end of Rnd 8, fasten off.

Foot pad

With aqua, ch 4, join to form a ring, ch 3 (counts as first dc), 8 dc in ring, join in 3rd ch of beg ch, fasten off. (9 dc)

A floppy-eared bunny and sleepy teddy are sure to become playtime favorites. Babies will love the soft bodies and be intrigued with the texture of the terry-spun yarn!

With matching thread, sew foot pad to end of leg. Stuff leg half full of fiberfill; fold top opening flat across and sew to bottom of body.

Muzzle

With powder blue, ch 4, join to form a ring, ch 1, [2 sc, 3 dc] twice in ring, join in beg sc, fasten off.

With matching thread, sew muzzle to head.

Facial Features

Using photo as a guide, embroider eyes and nose with black embroidery floss.

Ear

Make 2

With powder blue, ch 4, join to form a ring, ch 1, [sc, hdc, 3 dc, hdc, sc] in ring, do not join, fasten off.

With matching thread, sew ears to sides of head.

Continued on page 161

Baby's Bowling Set

Designs by Donna Collinsworth

Skill Level: Beginner

Size

Ball: 5 inches in diameter

Bowling pin: 7 inches tall

Materials

- Lion Brand Terry Spun yarn (120 yds per skein): 1 skein each citron #157, powder blue #105, lavender #144, powder pink #101, aqua #102
- Size J/10 crochet hook or size needed to obtain gauge
- 3 small jingle bells
- Several buttons and beads
- Small amount sand
- 4 small empty pill bottles
- Craft glue
- Fiberfill
- Tapestry needle

Gauge

2 sc = 1 inch; 3 sc rows = 1½ inches
Check gauge to save time.

Pattern Notes

Weave in loose ends as work progresses.

Join rnds with a sl st unless otherwise stated.

Experiment with different objects to place in pill bottles for different sounds.

Bowling Pin

Note: Make 1 each powder blue, aqua and lavender, working each with a citron stripe.

Rnd 1: With bowling pin color, ch 4, join to form a ring, ch 1, 8 sc in ring, join in beg sc, turn. (8 sc)

Rnd 2: Ch 1, [2 sc in next sc, sc in next sc] rep around, join in beg sc, turn. (12 sc)

Rnd 3: Ch 1, sc in each sc around, join in beg sc, turn.

Rnd 4: Rep Rnd 3, fasten off.

Rnd 5: Attach citron, ch 1, [sc dec over next 2 sc, sc in next sc] rep around, join in beg sc, turn. (8 sc)

Rnd 6: Rep Rnd 3, fasten off.

Rnd 7: Attach bowling pin color, rep Rnd 2. (12 sc)

Rnd 8: Rep Rnd 2. (18 sc)

Rnd 9: Ch 1, [2 sc in next sc, sc in each of next 2 sc] rep around, join in beg sc, turn. (24 sc)

Rnds 10–13: Rep Rnd 3.

Rnd 14: Ch 1, [sc dec over next 2 sc, sc in each of next 4 sc] rep around, join in beg sc, turn. (20 sc)

Rnd 15: Rep Rnd 3.

Rnd 16: Ch 1, [sc dec over next 2 sc, sc in each of next 2 sc] rep around, join in beg sc, turn. (15 sc)

Rnd 17: Ch 1, [sc dec over next 2 sc, sc in next sc] rep around, join in beg sc, fasten off. (10 sc)

Base

Rnd 1: With citron, ch 4, join to form a ring, ch 1, 10 sc in ring, join in beg sc, fasten off. (10 sc)

Place beads, buttons or sand in pill bottle. Apply glue to cover and place on bottle.

Stuff bowling pin with fiberfill, inserting pill bottle at center, using care to place at center and stuff with fiberfill around. Sew base to pin.

Ball

Rnd 1: With powder pink, ch 4, join to form a ring, ch 1, 8 sc in ring, join in beg sc, turn. (8 sc)

Rnds 2–4: Ch 1, [2 sc in next sc, sc in next sc] rep around, join in beg sc, turn. (27 sc)

Rnd 5: Ch 1, sc in each sc around, join in beg sc, turn.

Rnd 6: Rep Rnd 5, fasten off.

As babies learn eye-hand coordination, they love to roll a ball back and forth. Add some soft bowling pins and you'll have an avid bowler in no time!

Rnd 7: Attach aqua, rep Rnd 5, fasten off.

Rnd 8: Attach citron, rep Rnd 5, fasten off.

Rnd 9: Attach powder blue, rep Rnd 5, fasten off.

Rnd 10: Attach lavender, rep Rnd 5, fasten off.

Rnd 11: Attach powder pink, rep Rnd 5.

Rnds 12 & 13: Rep Rnd 5.

Place jingle bells in pill bottle. Apply glue to cover and place on bottle.

Stuff ball with fiberfill, inserting pill bottle at center, using care to place at center and stuff with fiberfill around.

Rnds 14–16: Ch 1, [dec 1 sc over next 2 sc, sc in next sc] rep around, join in beg sc, turn. (8 sc)

Insert stuffing to fill opening.

Rnd 17: Ch 1, [dec 1 sc over next 2 sc] 4 times, join in beg sc, fasten off. (4 sc) ✂

Patchwork Kitty

Design by Michele Wilcox

Skill Level: Beginner

Size: 9 inches tall

Materials

- Worsted weight yarn: various scrap amounts red, lime, blue, yellow and orange
- Size G/6 crochet hook or size needed to obtain gauge
- Black embroidery floss
- 18 inches decorative braid
- Fiberfill
- Tapestry needle

Gauge

4 sc = 1 inch; 4 sc rows = 1 inch
Check gauge to save time.

Pattern Note

Weave in loose ends as work progresses.

Front & Back

Make 2

Body

Row 1: With yellow, ch 26, sc in 2nd ch from hook, sc in each rem ch across, turn. (25 sc)

Row 2: Ch 1, sc in each sc across, turn.

Rows 3–15: Rep Row 2.

Row 16: Ch 1, sc in each of next 11 sc, fasten off, turn. (11 sc)

Head

Row 17: Attach red in 11th sc of previous row, ch 1, sc in same st, sc in each of next 10 sc, turn. (11 sc)

Rows 18–22: Rep Row 2.

First ear

Row 23: Ch 1, sc in each of next 3 sc, sc dec over next 2 sc, turn. (4 sc)

Row 24: Ch 1, sc dec over next 2 sc, sc in each of next 2 sc, turn. (3 sc)

Row 25: Ch 1, sc in next sc, sc dec over next 2 sc, turn. (2 sc)

Row 26: Ch 1, sc dec over next 2 sc, fasten off.

Second ear

Row 23: With first ear to the right, sk next sc of Row 22, attach red in next sc, ch 1, sc dec over same sc as beg ch-1 and next sc, sc in each of next 3 sc, turn. (4 sc)

Row 24: Ch 1, sc in each of next 2 sc, sc dec over next 2 sc, turn. (3 sc)

Row 25: Ch 1, sc dec over next 2 sc, sc in next sc, turn. (2 sc)

Row 26: Ch 1, sc dec over next 2 sc, fasten off.

Sew front and back tog with matching yarn colors, stuffing with fiberfill before closing.

Facial Features

With black embroidery floss, embroider satin-st eyes and nose and straight-sts mouth.

Tail

Make 2

Row 1: With lime, ch 6, sc in 2nd ch from hook, sc in each rem ch across, turn. (5 sc)

Rows 2–12: Ch 1, sc in each sc across, turn.

Row 13: Ch 1, sc dec over next 2 sc, sc in next sc, sc dec over next 2 sc, turn. (3 sc)

Row 14: Ch 1, draw up a lp in each sc across, yo, draw through all 4 lps on hook, fasten off.
Leaving bottom open, sew tail sections tog; stuff with fiberfill and sew to top back of body.

Front Leg

Note: Make 2 each blue and orange.

Row 1: Ch 9, sc in 2nd ch from hook, sc in each rem ch across, turn. (8 sc)

This cute kitty has more color than a calico and personality to spare. Add a delicate collar and he's ready to become part of the family!

Row 2: Ch 1, sc in each sc across, turn.

Row 3: Rep Row 2.

Row 4: Ch 1, sc dec over next 2 sc, sc in each of next 6 sc, turn. (7 sc)

Row 5: Ch 1, sc in each of next 5 sc, sc dec over next 2 sc, turn. (6 sc)

Rows 6–14: Rep Row 2. At the end of Row 14, fasten off.

Matching colors, sew leg sections tog. With toes pointing forward, sew top of leg to Row 5 of body.

Hind Leg

Note: Make 2 each blue and orange.

Rows 1–8: Rep Rows 1–8 of front leg. (6 sc)

Row 9: Ch 1, sc in each sc across, turn.

Row 10: Ch 1, 2 sc in first sc, sc in each rem sc across, turn. (7 sc)

Row 11: Ch 1, sc in each sc across to last sc, 2 sc in last sc, turn. (8 sc)

Continued on page 161

CALICO

BIRTHDAY BO

C

A

T

CH   HAPPY BIRTHDAY, MOON   Weekly Reader Books

Lucky Duck

Design by Michele Wilcox

Skill Level: Beginner

Size: 11½ inches

Materials

- Coats & Clark Red Heart TLC worsted weight yarn: 2 oz light purple #5587, small amount each fuchsia #5768, bright jade #5507, butterscotch #5263, light pink #5718, black #5012
- Size G/6 crochet hook or size needed to obtain gauge
- Fiberfill
- Tapestry needle

Gauge

5 sc = 1 inch; 5 sc rnds = 1 inch
Check gauge to save time.

Pattern Notes

Weave in loose ends as work progresses.

Do not join rnds unless otherwise stated. Use a scrap of yarn to mark rnds.

Head & Body

Rnd 1: With bright jade, ch 2, 6 sc in 2nd ch from hook. (6 sc)

Rnd 2: 2 sc in each sc around. (12 sc)

Rnd 3: [Sc in next sc, 2 sc in next sc] rep around. (18 sc)

Rnd 4: Sc in each sc around.

Rnd 5: [Sc in each of next 2 sc, 2 sc in next sc] rep around. (24 sc)

Rnd 6: [Sc in each of next 3 sc, 2 sc in next sc] rep around. (30 sc)

Rnds 7–14: Rep Rnd 4.

Rnd 15: [Sc in each of next 3 sc, sc dec over next 2 sc] rep around. (24 sc)

Rnd 16: [Sc in each of next 2 sc, sc dec over next 2 sc] rep around. (18 sc)

Rnd 17: Rep Rnd 4, changing to light pink at the end of the rnd.

Rnds 18–20: Rep Rnd 4. At the end of Rnd 20, change to light purple.

Rnd 21: Rep Rnd 4.

Rnd 22: [Sc in next sc, 2 sc in next sc] rep around. (36 sc)

Stuff head with fiberfill.

Rnd 23: Rep Rnd 4.

Rnd 24: Sc in each of next 16 sts, 2 hdc in next st, 2 dc in each of next 2 sts, 2 hdc in next st, sc in each of next 16 sts. (40 sts)

Rnd 25: Sc in each of next 18 sts, 2 hdc in next st, 2 dc in each of next 2 sts, 2 hdc in next st, sc in each of next 18 sts. (44 sts)

Rnd 26: Sc in each of next 20 sts, 2 hdc in next st, 2 dc in each of next 2 sts, 2 hdc in next st, sc in each of next 20 sts. (48 sts)

Rnd 27: Sc in each of next 22 sts, 2 hdc in next st, 2 dc in each of next 2 sts, 2 hdc in next st, sc in each of next 22 sts. (52 sts)

Rnds 28–30: Rep Rnd 4.

Rnd 31: Sc in each of next 24 sts, [sc dec over next 2 sts] twice, sc in each of next 24 sts. (50 sc)

Rnd 32: Sc in each of next 23 sts, [sc dec over next 2 sts] twice, sc in each of next 23 sts. (48 sc)

Rnd 33: Sc in each of next 22 sts, [sc dec over next 2 sts] twice, sc in each of next 22 sts. (46 sc)

Rnd 34: Sc in each of next 21 sc, [sc dec over next 2 sts] twice, sc in each of next 21 sts. (44 sc)

Rnd 35: Sc in each of next 20 sts, [sc dec over next 2 sc] twice, sc in each of next 20 sts. (42 sc)

Rnd 36: [Sc in each of next 5 sc, sc dec over next 2 sc] rep around. (36 sc)

Rnd 37: [Sc in each of next 4 sc, sc dec over next 2 sc] rep around. (30 sc)

Stuff body with fiberfill, continue stuffing as work progresses.

This darling duck will capture your fancy with his floppy wings and stubby legs.

Rnd 38: [Sc in each of next 3 sc, sc dec over next 2 sc] rep around. (24 sc)

Rnd 39: [Sc in each of next 2 sc, sc dec over next 2 sc] rep around. (18 sc)

Rnd 40: [Sc in next sc, sc dec over next 2 sc] rep around. (12 sc)

Rnd 41: [Sc dec over next 2 sc] rep around, leaving a length of yarn, fasten off.

Weave rem length through sts of Rnd 41, pull to close opening, secure, fasten off.

Eye

Make 2

With black, embroider satin-st eye centered over Rnds 8 and 9 with 2¼ inches between eyes.

Beak

Make 2

Rnd 1: With butterscotch, ch 3, 2 sc in 2nd ch from hook, 2 sc in next ch, working on opposite side of foundation ch, 2 sc in each of

Continued on page 163

Bunny Bath Mitt

Design by Cynthia See

Skill Level: Beginner

Size: 11½ inches

Materials

- Worsted weight 4-ply cotton yarn: 150 grams white, 50 grams pink ombré
- Size G/6 crochet hook or size needed to obtain gauge
- Black embroidery floss
- 24 inches ⅜-inch-wide pink ribbon
- Tapestry needle

Gauge

4 dc = 1 inch; 3 dc rnds = 1¼ inches
Check gauge to save time.

Pattern Notes

Weave in loose ends as work progresses.

Ch-3 counts as first dc throughout.

Join rnds with a sl st unless otherwise stated.

Neck

Rnd 1 (WS): With white, ch 35, join to form a ring, ch 3, dc in each ch around, join in 3rd ch of beg ch. (35 dc)

Rnd 2: Ch 3, dc in each dc around, join in 3rd ch of beg ch.

Rnds 3–6: Rep Rnd 2.

Rnd 7: Ch 5 (counts as first dc, ch-2), sk next 2 dc, [dc in next dc, ch 2, sk next 2 dc] 10 times, dc in next dc, ch 2, join in 3rd ch of beg ch-5. (12 ch-2 sps)

Head

Rnd 8: Ch 3, dc in each ch and each dc around, join in 3rd ch of beg ch. (36 dc)

Rnd 9: Ch 3, dc in next dc, 2 dc in next dc, [dc in each of next 2 dc, 2 dc in next dc] rep around, join in 3rd ch of beg ch. (48 dc)

Rnd 10: Rep Rnd 2.

Rnd 11: Ch 3, dc in each of next 20 dc, 3 dc in each of next 2 dc, dc in next dc, 3 dc in each of next 2 dc, dc in each of next 22 dc, join in 3rd ch of beg ch. (56 dc)

Rnd 12: Ch 3, dc in each of next 22 dc, 2 dc in each of next 2 dc, dc in each of next 4 dc, 2 dc in each of next 2 dc, dc in each of next 25 dc, join in 3rd ch of beg ch. (60 dc)

Rnd 13: Rep Rnd 2.

Rnd 14: Ch 3, dc in each of next 20 dc, [dc dec over next 2 dc] twice, dc in each of next 4 dc, drop white, attach pink ombré, work 6 dc in next dc, remove hook, insert hook in first dc of 6-dc group, pick up dropped lp and draw through st on hook, fasten off pink ombré (nose), pick up white, dc in each of next 4 dc, [dc dec over next 2 dc] twice, dc in each of next 22 dc, join in 3rd ch of beg ch. (55 dc; 1 pc)

Rnd 15: Ch 3, dc in each of next 20 dc, dc dec over next 2 dc, dc in each of next 3 dc, 2 dc in next dc, 2 dc in pc, 2 dc in next dc, dc in each of next 3 dc, dc dec over next 2 dc, dc in each of next 22 dc, join in 3rd ch of beg ch. (57 dc)

Rnds 16 & 17: Rep Rnd 2.

Rnd 18: Ch 3, [dc dec over next 2 dc, dc in next dc] rep around, join in 3rd ch of beg ch. (38 dc)

Rnd 19: Ch 3, [dc dec over next 2 dc, dc in next dc] rep around, ending with dc in last dc, join in 3rd ch of beg ch. (26 dc)

First Ear

Rnd 20: Ch 4, sl st in center dc at front, ch 3, dc in each of next 3 chs, dc in each dc to center front 5-dc, drop white, pick up pink ombré, dc in each dc of center front 5-dc group, drop pink ombré, pick up white, dc in each rem dc to beg ch-3, join in 3rd ch of beg ch-3. (12 white dc; 5 pink ombré dc)

Rnds 21–25: Ch 3, dc in each dc around, maintaining color changes of Rnd 20, join in 3rd ch of ch-3. (17 dc)

Rnd 26: Ch 3, [dc dec over next 2 dc, dc in next dc] 5 times, dc in next dc, join in 3rd ch of ch-3, fasten off pink ombré. (12 dc)

Rnd 27: Ch 2, dc in next dc (beg dc dec), [dc dec over next 2 dc] 5 times, join in first dc, leaving a length of yarn, fasten off. (6 dc)

Weave rem length through sts and pull to close; secure and fasten off.

Second Ear

Rnd 20: Working in rem sts of Rnd 19, attach white, rep as for Rnd 20 of first ear omitting the beg ch-4. (12 white dc; 5 pink ombré dc)

Rnds 21–27: Rep Rnds 21–27 of first ear.

Facial Features

Using photo as a guide, with black embroidery floss, embroider eyes and mouth.

Finishing

Starting at center front, weave ribbon through ch sps of Rnd 7; tie ends in a bow at center front. ✄

Make bath time extra-fun as this delightful bunny splashes
in the bubbles and washes little faces clean!

Little Critter Finger Pals

Design by Lori Zeller

Skill Level: Beginner

Size: 2–3 inches

Materials

- Pompadour baby yarn: small amount each white, yellow, peach, blue, green, pink, pastels print

- Crochet cotton size 10: 5 yds red/silver metallic

- Size C/2 crochet hook or size needed to obtain gauge

- Dimensional fabric paint: black, red and pink

- Fiberfill

- Tapestry needle

Stitch this set of six finger puppets to have on hand for a rainy day. Kids will love putting on a puppet show for Mom and Dad!

Gauge

8 sc = 1 inch; 8 sc rnds = 1 inch
Check gauge to save time.

Pattern Notes

Weave in loose ends as work progresses.

Do not join rnds unless otherwise stated. Use a scrap of yarn to mark rnds.

Basic Puppet

Rnd 1: Ch 2, 7 sc in 2nd ch from hook. (7 sc)

Rnd 2: 2 sc in each sc around. (14 sc)

Rnd 3: Sc in each sc around.

Rnds 4–6: Rep Rnd 3.

Rnd 7: [Sc dec over next 2 sc] rep around. (7 sc)

Rnd 8: Rep Rnd 3.

Rnd 9: Rep Rnd 2. (14 sc)

Rnd 10: Rep Rnd 3.

Rnd 11: Sc in each of next 4 sc, *ch 5, hdc in 2nd ch from hook, hdc in each of next 2 chs, sc in next ch * (for first arm), sc in each of next 7 sc of Rnd 10, rep from * to * (for 2nd arm), sc in each of 3 rem sc of Rnd 10.

Rnd 12: Sc in each of next 4 sc, push arm to front and sk arm sts, sc in each of next 7 sc, push arm to front and sk arm sts, sc in each of next 3 sc.

Rnds 13–18: Rep Rnd 3. At the end of Rnd 18, sl st in next st, fasten off.

Snowman

Rnds 1–18: With white, rep Rnds 1–18 of basic puppet.

Hat

Rnd 1: With red/silver metallic crochet cotton, ch 2, 7 sc in 2nd ch from hook. (7 sc)

Rnd 2: 2 sc in each sc around. (14 sc)

Rnd 3: Working in back lps only this rnd, sc in each st around.

Rnds 4–6: Sc in each sc around.

Rnd 7: Working in front lps only, [sc in next st, 2 sc in next st] rep around, sl st to join in beg sc, leaving a length of cotton, fasten off.

Finishing

Sew hat to top of head. For eyes, paint 2 black dots on face and 3 black dots on body for buttons. Paint a small red mouth below eyes.

Duck

Rnds 1–18: With yellow, rep Rnds 1–18 of basic puppet.

Beak

Rnd 1: With peach, ch 2, 6 sc in
Continued on page 162

Dragon Puppet

Design by Michele Wilcox

Gauge

5 sc = 1 inch; 5 sc rnds = 1 inch
Check gauge to save time.

Pattern Notes

Weave in loose ends as work progresses.

Do not join rnds unless otherwise stated. Use a scrap of yarn to mark rnds.

Mouth Top

Rnd 1: With fuchsia, ch 2, 6 sc in 2nd ch from hook. (6 sc)

Rnd 2: 2 sc in each sc around. (12 sc)

Rnd 3: [Sc in next sc, 2 sc in next sc] rep around. (18 sc)

Rnd 4: [Sc in each of next 2 sc, 2 sc in next sc] rep around. (24 sc)

Rnd 5: [Sc in each of next 3 sc, 2 sc in next sc] rep around. (30 sc)

Rnd 6: Sc in each sc around.

Rnd 7: [Sc in each of next 4 sc, 2 sc in next sc] rep around. (36 sc)

Rnds 8–22: Rep Rnd 6. At the end of Rnd 22, sl st in next sc, fasten off.

Mouth Bottom

Rnds 1–5: Rep Rnds 1–5 of mouth top. (30 sc)

Rnds 6–16: Sc in each sc around. At the end of Rnd 16, sl st in next st, fasten off.

With tapestry needle and length of fuchsia, sew 12 sts of Rnd 22 of mouth top to 12 sts of Rnd 16 of mouth bottom.

Head & Body

Rnd 1: Attach fuchsia to any rem sc on Rnd 22 of mouth top, ch 1, sc in each rem sc on mouth top and mouth bottom. (42 sc)

Rnds 2–29: Sc in each sc around. At the end of Rnd 29, sl st in next sc, fasten off.

Tongue

Rnds 1–3: With light pink, rep Rnds 1–3 of mouth top. (18 sc)

Rnds 4–10: Sc in each sc around. At the end of Rnd 10, sl st in next st, fasten off.

Sew Rnd 10 flat across and sew inside mouth.

Tooth

Make 2

Rnd 1: With white, ch 2, 6 sc in 2nd ch from hook. (6 sc)

Rnd 2: 2 sc in next sc, sc in each of next 5 sc. (7 sc)

Rnd 3: Sc in each sc around, sl st in next sc, fasten off.

Sew teeth inside mouth top, spacing ¼ inch apart.

Nostril

Make 2

Rnd 1: With fuchsia, ch 2, 6 sc in 2nd ch from hook. (6 sc)

Rnds 2 & 3: Sc in each sc around.

At the end of Rnd 3, sl st in next sc, fasten off.

With Rnd 3 open and facing forward, sew nostril to mouth top.

Eyeball

Make 2

Rnd 1: With white, ch 2, 6 sc in 2nd ch from hook. (6 sc)

Crochet a couple of these puppets and watch your child's imagination take over as he or she creates a kingdom with fanciful dragons and a pretty princess or a brave knight!

Rnd 2: 2 sc in each sc around. (12 sc)

Rnds 3 & 4: Sc in each sc around. Attach black animal eye to center of Rnd 1. Stuff eyeball with fiberfill; continue to stuff as work progresses.

Rnd 5: [Sc dec over next 2 sc] 6 times, sl st in next st, leaving a length of yarn, fasten off. (6 sc)

Weave rem length through sts and pull to close opening; secure.

Eyelid

Make 2

Row 1: With fuchsia, ch 2, 6 sc in 2nd ch from hook, turn. (6 sc)

Row 2: 2 sc in each sc across, turn. (12 sc)

Rnds 3–5: Sc in each sc across, turn. At the end of Row 5, leaving a length of yarn, fasten off.

Place eyelid over eyeball, sew in place, then sew to head.

Arm

Make 2

Rnd 1: With fuchsia, ch 6, join to

Continued on page 161

Little Miss Mary

Design by Vicky Tignanelli

Skill Level: Beginner

Size: Fits 9½-inch baby doll

Materials

- Sport weight yarn: 1 oz white, ½ oz lavender, small amount yellow, red, green, medium brown, black
- Size G/6 crochet hook or size needed to obtain gauge
- 8-inch yellow chenille stem
- 1⅓ yds ⅛-inch-wide dark purple ribbon
- ⅔ yd ³⁄₁₆-inch-wide dark purple picot-edge ribbon
- 18 inches ¾-inch-wide gathered lavender lace
- Small lavender silk flowers
- 1½-inch cardboard circle
- Size 4/0 snap fastener
- Cotton balls
- Hot-glue gun
- Straight pins
- Sewing needle and thread
- Tapestry and embroidery needles

Gauge

5 dc = 1 inch; 6 dc rnds = 1½ inches
Check gauge to save time.

Pattern Notes

Weave in loose ends as work progresses.

Ch-3 counts as first dc throughout.

Join rnds with a sl st unless otherwise stated.

Dress

Bodice

Row 1 (RS): With white, ch 19, sc in 2nd ch from hook, sc in each rem ch across, turn. (18 sc)

Row 2: Ch 1, 2 sc in each sc across, turn. (36 sc)

Rows 3 & 4: Ch 1, sc in each sc across, turn.

Row 5: Ch 3, dc in each of next 6 sc, ch 4, sk next 4 sc (for armhole opening), dc in each of next 14 sc, ch 4, sk next 4 sc (for armhole opening), dc in each of next 7 sc, turn. (28 dc; 2 ch-4 sps)

Row 6: Ch 1, sc in each dc and each ch across, fasten off, turn. (36 sc)

Skirt

Rnd 7 (RS): Working in back lps only, attach lavender, ch 3, 2 dc in next st, [dc in next st, 2 dc in next st] rep across, join in 3rd ch of ch-3. (54 dc)

Rnds 8–13 (RS): Ch 3, dc in each dc around, join in 3rd ch of ch-3.

Rnd 14: Ch 1, sc in each dc around, join in beg sc, fasten off.

With sewing needle and thread, sew lace to inside edge of Rnd 14 of skirt.

Apron

Row 1 (RS): Working in rem front lps of Row 6, attach white with a sl st in 14th st, ch 3, dc in same st as beg ch, 2 dc in each of next 9 sts, turn. (20 dc)

Rows 2–5: Ch 3, dc in each dc across, turn.

Row 6: Working in back lps only this row, ch 3, 2 dc in next st, [dc in next st, 2 dc in next st] rep across, turn. (30 dc)

Row 7: Ch 3, dc in each dc across, leaving a length of yarn, fasten off.

With tapestry needle and rem length, fold Rows 6 and 7 up against apron; form 3 pockets and tack with straight pins. Sew edge seam closed; weave yarn through sts to first straight pin and tack in place to form pocket; weave yarn through sts to next straight pin and tack in place to form another pocket; weave yarn through sts to opposite edge and sew side seam.

Mistress Mary, with her bonnet and basket, keeps her watering can close so her garden will grow!

Remove straight pins. Fill pockets with silk flowers

Sleeve

Make 2

Rnd 1 (RS): Attach white at underarm, ch 1, work 15 sc around armhole opening, do not join. (15 sc)

Rnds 2 & 3: Sc in each sc around, do not join. At the end of Rnd 3, sl st in next st, fasten off.

Collar

Row 1 (RS): Attach lavender in opposite side of foundation ch, ch 1, 2 sc in each ch across, turn. (36 sc)

Rows 2 & 3: Ch 1, sc in each sc across, turn. At the end of Row 3, leaving a length of yarn, fasten off.

Tack collar to bodice.

Cut a length of ⅛-inch-wide dark purple ribbon and attach to center front of collar, tie ribbon in a bow.

Waist Bow

Weave a 24-inch length of ⅛-inch

wide dark purple ribbon through Row 6 of bodice. Tie ends in a bow at back waistline.

Sew snap fastener at back neck opening.

Ballerina Slipper

Make 2

Rnd 1: With lavender, ch 7, sc in 2nd ch from hook, hdc in each of next 3 chs, dc in next ch, 6 dc in last ch, working on opposite side of foundation ch, dc in next ch, hdc in each of next 3 chs, sc in last ch, do not join. (16 sts)

Rnds 2 & 3: Hdc in each st around, do not join. At the end of Rnd 3, sl st in next st, fasten off.

Laces

Thread tapestry needle with a 12-inch length of ⅛-inch-wide dark purple ribbon; thread through both side of slipper. Running ribbon under doll's foot, cross ribbon around ankle and leg; tie in a bow at knee. Trim ends.

Sun Hat

Rnd 1: With white, ch 2, 6 sc in 2nd ch from hook, do not join rnds. (6 sc)

Rnd 2: 2 sc in each sc around. (12 sc)

Rnd 3: Rep Rnd 2. (24 sc)

Rnd 4: Sc in each sc around.

Rnd 5: [Sc in next sc, 2 sc in next sc] rep around. (36 sc)

Rnds 6–11: Rep Rnd 4. At the end of Rnd 11, sl st in next st.

Rnd 12: Ch 2 (counts as first hdc throughout), hdc in same st as beg ch, 2 hdc in each st around, join in 2nd ch of beg ch-2. (72 hdc)

Rnd 13: Ch 2, hdc in each hdc around, join in 2nd ch of beg ch-2, fasten off.

Center dark purple picot-edge ribbon on crown of hat and glue in place. Tie ends in a bow. Glue silk flowers to crown.

Flower Basket

Rnd 1: With medium brown, ch 2, 6 sc in 2nd ch from hook, do not join rnds. (6 sc)

Rnd 2: 2 sc in each sc around. (12 sc)

Rnd 3: Sc in each sc around.

Rnd 4: Rep Rnd 2. (24 sc)

Rnd 5: Rep Rnd 3.

Rnd 6: [Sc in next sc, 2 sc in next sc] 12 times. (36 sc)

Rnd 7: Rep Rnd 3.

Rnd 8: Reverse sc in each sc around, join in beg sc, fasten off.

Handle

Cut 12 lengths of medium brown yarn each 12 inches long. Holding all strands tog, make a knot 2 inches from end. Divide into 3 groups of 4 strands each and braid strands until braid measures 4 inches long. Knot all strands at end of braid. Glue handle to each side of basket. Trim yarn ends approximately ½ inch below knot. Glue silk flowers into basket.

Watering Can

Rnd 1: With yellow, ch 2, 6 sc in 2nd ch from hook, do not join rnds. (6 sc)

Rnds 2 & 3: 2 sc in each sc around. (24 sc)

Rnd 4: Sc in each sc around.

Rnd 5: [Sc in each of next 2 sc, 2 sc in next sc] 8 times. (32 sc)

Rnd 6: Rep Rnd 4.

Rnd 7: [Sc in next sc, sc dec over next 2 sc] 10 times. (22 sc)

Rnds 8–13: Rep Rnd 4.

At the end of Rnd 13, sl st in next st, fasten off.

Embroidery

Using photo as a guide, with red, white and green, use lazy daisy sts and split sts to embroider

flowers, stems and leaf on side of watering can.

Insert cardboard circle into base of watering can, stuff can with cotton balls.

Can top

Row 1: With yellow, ch 8, sc in 2nd ch from hook, sc in each rem ch across, turn. (7 sc)

Row 2: Ch 1, sc in each sc across, turn.

Row 3: Sk first sc, sc in each of next 5 sc, sl st in last sc, turn.

Row 4: Sk first sc, sc in each of next 3 sc, sl st in last sc, turn.

Row 5: Sk first sc, sc in each of next 2 sc, do not turn.

Rnd 6: Sc around outer edge of can top, join in beg sc, fasten off.

Whipstitch top to can (rounded edge should fit into left side of can.)

Side handle

Row 1: With yellow, ch 16, sc in 2nd ch from hook, sc in each rem ch across, fasten off. (15 sc)

Sew or glue handle onto left side of

can leaving a slight tail at bottom, turn tail upward.

Spout

Rnd 1: With yellow, ch 2, 3 sc in 2nd ch from hook, do not join rnds. (3 sc)

Rnd 2: 2 sc in each sc around. (6 sc)

Rnds 3 & 4: Sc in each sc around. Piece will turn inward. Pull beg yarn end tightly and weave in; turn work RS out and shape tube with blunt end of pencil.

Rnds 5–13: Sc in each sc around.

Rnd 14: 2 sc in each sc around, sl st in next sc, fasten off. (12 sc)

Fold chenille stem into fourths to measure 2 inches, insert blunt end into spout. Trim any excess with scissors.

Spout tip

Rnd 1: With yellow, ch 2, 4 sc in 2nd ch from hook. (4 sc)

Rnd 2: 2 sc in each sc around. (8 sc)

Rnd 3: 2 sc in each of next 7 sc, sl st in next sc, fasten off.

Push tip out with blunt end

of pencil.

With black, embroider tiny black sts to represent water holes on spout tip.

Whipstitch spout tip to spout. Slightly bend spout at bottom and glue to right side of can.

Top handle

Row 1: With yellow, ch 17, sc in 2nd ch from hook, sc in each rem ch across, fasten off. (16 sc)

Glue handle to can. ✄

Dryer Sheets

By Shirley Patterson

Use dryer sheets when filling a sachet—they smell really good, and used sheets are soft enough to use as stuffing. Tuck an unused sheet in along with the used sheet and the fragrance will last for a long time.

Beautiful Butterfly

Continued from page 138

Rows 2–5: Ch 1, sc in each sc across, turn.

At the end of Row 5, fasten off. Insert beads into Tic Tac container, to secure lid, apply glue and close. With WS of wing with powder blue center facing, sew rattle cover in place, inserting container before closing.

Second Teething Ring

Sew 2nd teething ring to wing with powder blue center.

Cut 2 ribbons of each color 6 inches long. With matching threads, alternating colors, sew ribbons to straight edge of same wing.

Assembly

Using photo as a guide for placement, sew wings to back of butterfly body.

Center Wing Strip

Row 1: With citron, ch 3, sc in 2nd ch from hook, sc in next ch, turn. (2 sc)

Row 2: Ch 1, sc in each of next 2 sc, turn.

Rep Row 2 until strip reaches from top to bottom of butterfly back, covering wing sections attached to body, fasten off.

Sew strip around outer edge over section that joins wings to body.

Facial Features

With sewing needle and embroidery

floss, embroider eyes with black and smiling mouth with pink. ✄

Checkerboard Rug

Design by Lori Zeller

Skill Level: Intermediate

Size: 22 x 28 inches

Materials

- Worsted weight yarn:
  7 oz black, 3 oz green,
  2 oz each blue and white,
  1 oz each dark gray,
  light yellow, dark green
- Size G/6 crochet hook or
  size needed to obtain
  gauge
- 15 x 20 inches nonskid
  backing
- Sewing needle and thread
- Tapestry needle

Gauge

4 sc = 1 inch; 4 sc rows = 1 inch
Check gauge to save time.

Pattern Notes

Weave in loose ends as work
progresses.

Join rnds with a sl st unless
otherwise stated.

Checkerboard is made in strips using
a join-as-you-go method; carry color
not in use up side of strip.

When working roadway around rug,
use scraps of yarn to mark rnds.

Pattern Stitch

Surface sl st: Holding light yellow
underneath, insert hook in st, draw
lp through to RS, [insert hook in
next st, draw lp through st and
through lp on hook] rep around.

Checkerboard

First strip

Row 1: With blue, ch 7, sc in 2nd
ch from hook, sc in each rem ch
across, turn. (6 sc)

Row 2: Ch 1, sc in each sc
across, turn.

Rows 3–5: Rep Row 2.

Row 6: Ch 1, sc in each of next
5 sc, sc in last sc, changing to
white, turn.

Rows 7–11: Rep Row 2.

Row 12: Ch 1, sc in each of next
5 sc, sc in last sc, changing to blue,
turn.

Rows 13–17: Rep Row 2.

Rows 18–41: [Rep
Rows 6–17] twice.

Row 42: Rep Row 6.

Rows 43–47: Rep
Row 2.

Row 48: Ch 1, sc
in each sc across,
fasten off.

Second strip

Row 1: Attach white at end of foundation ch of previous strip, ch 7, sc
in 2nd ch from hook, sc in each
rem ch across, sl st in end of first
row of previous strip, sl st in end of
next row of previous strip, turn.

Row 2: Sc in each sc across, turn.

Row 3: Ch 1, sc in each sc across,
sl st in end of next 2 rows of previous strip, turn.

Rows 4 & 5: Rep Rows 2 and 3.

Row 6: Sc in each of next 5 sc, sc
in last sc, changing to blue, turn.

Rows 7–11: Rep Rows 3 and 2
alternately, ending with Row 3.

Row 12: Sc in each of next 5 sc, sc
in last sc, changing to white, turn.

Rows 13–17: Rep Rows 7–11.

Rows 18–41: [Rep Rows 6–17] twice.

Rows 42–47: Rep Rows 6–11.

Row 48: Sc in each sc across,
fasten off.

Third strip

Rep 2nd strip, reversing colors.

Fourth–eighth strips

Rep strips 2 and 3 alternately ending with strip 2. Checkerboard will
have 8 squares each direction.

Checkerboard edging

Rnd 1 (RS): Attach dark gray in
last sc made of checkerboard, ch 1,
sc in each of next 48 sc, ch 2,
[working across next edge, work
48 sc across to next corner, ch 2]
3 times, join in beg sc, fasten off.

*Older kids will enjoy this rug,
perfect for keeping toes warm
or for challenging guests to
a round of checkers!*

Border Sections

First side

Row 1: Attach green to checkerboard edging with a sc in last ch-2
sp made, [dc in next sc, sc in next
sc] rep across edge, ending with dc
in next ch-2 sp, turn.

Rows 2–4: Ch 1, sc in first dc, dc
in next sc, [sc in next dc, dc in
next sc] rep across, turn.

Row 5: Ch 1, sc in each st across,
fasten off.

Second side

Rows 1–5: Working on opposite
side of checkerboard, rep first
side section.

First end

Row 1: Attach green to 2nd side
section with a sc around side of
last sc made, working in ends of
side section rows, [dc, sc] twice, dc
around end of last row before
board edging, sc in ch-2 corner sp,
[dc in next sc, sc in next sc] rep
across to ch-2 sp, dc in ch-2 sp,

working in ends of side section row on other side of checkerboard, [sc, dc] 3 times to end, turn.

Rows 2–14: Ch 1, sc in first dc, dc in next sc, [sc in next dc, dc in next sc] rep across, turn.

Row 15: Ch 1, sc in each st across, fasten off.

Second end

Rows 1–15: Working on opposite side of checkerboard, rep first end section.

Edging

Rnd 1: Attach dark gray to 2nd end with a sc if first st of last row made, [sc in each sc across, ch 2, working in side edges of rows, work 18 sc along side of end section, sc in each sc across side section and work 18 sc along side of opposite end section, ch 2] rep around, join in beg sc, fasten off.

Roadway

Row 1: Attach black to border section edging in last ch-2 sp made, ch 16, sc in 2nd ch from hook, sc in each rem ch across, sl st in first 2 sc on edging, turn.

Row 2: Sc in each sc across, turn.

Row 3: Ch 1, sc in each sc across, sl st in next 2 sc on edging, turn.

Rows 4–61: Rep Rows 2 and 3.

Row 62: Rep Row 2.

Row 63: Ch 1, sc in each sc across, sl st in ch-2 corner sp on edging, turn.

Row 64: Sc in each sc across, turn.

Row 65: Ch 16, sc in 2nd ch from hook, sc in each rem ch across, sl st in next 2 sc on Row 64, turn.

Row 66: Sc in each sc across, turn.

Row 67: Ch 1, sc in each sc across, sl st in next 2 sc on Row 64, turn.

Rows 68–80: Rep Rows 66 and 67, ending with Row 66.

Row 81: Ch 1, sc in each sc across, sl st in ch-2 corner sp and next sc on edging, turn.

Rows 82–168: Rep Rows 2 and 3, ending with Row 2.

Rows 169–171: Rep Rows 63–65.

Rows 172–186: Rep Rows 66 and 67, ending with Row 66.

Row 187: Rep Row 81.

Rows 188–250: Rep Rows 2 and 3, ending with Row 2.

Rows 251–253: Rep Rows 63–65.

Rows 254–270: Rep Rows 66 and 67, ending with Row 66.

Row 271: Rep Row 81.

Rows 272–356: Rep Rows 2 and 3, ending with Row 2.

Row 357: Rep Row 63.

Row 358: Rep Row 2.

Row 359: Sc in each sc across, working in opposite side of foundation ch of roadway, sl st in first 2 sts, turn.

Row 360: Sc in each sc across, turn.

Row 361: Ch 1, sc in each sc across, working in opposite side of foundation ch of roadway, sl st in next 2 sts, turn.

Rows 362–373: Rep Rows 360 and 361 alternately.

Row 374: Sc in each sc across.

Edging

Rnd 1: Ch 1, reverse sc around outer edge of roadway, join in beg sc, fasten off.

Checkers

Note: Make 12 each dark green and blue.

Bottom

Rnd 1: Ch 2, 8 sc in 2nd ch from hook, join in beg sc. (8 sc)

Rnd 2: Ch 1, 2 sc in each sc around, join in beg sc, fasten off. (16 sc)

Top

Rnd 1: Rep Rnd 1 of bottom.

Rnd 2: Rep Rnd 2, do not fasten off.

Rnd 3: Holding WS of top and bottom tog and working through both thicknesses, sl st in each st around, fasten off.

Finishing

With sewing needle and thread, attach nonskid backing to underside of rug. ✄

Cuddle Buddies

Continued from page 140

Bunny

With lavender, rep Bear's body, head, arm and foot pads.

With citron, rep Bear's leg and hand pads.

Muzzle

Make 2

Rnd 1: With citron, ch 4, sc in 2nd ch from hook, sc in each rem ch across, working on opposite side of foundation ch, sc in each of next 3 chs, join in beg sc, fasten off. (6 sc) With matching thread, sew muzzle to head.

Facial Features

Using photo as a guide, embroider eyes and nose with black embroidery floss.

Ear

Make 2

Row 1: With citron, ch 3, sc in 2nd ch from hook, sc in next ch, turn. (2 sc)

Rows 2–6: Ch 1, sc in each of next 2 sc, turn.

Row 7: Ch 1, [hdc, dc] in first sc, [dc, hdc] in next sc, turn. (4 sts)

Row 8: Ch 1, hdc in first st, 2 dc in each of next 2 sts, hdc in last st, fasten off. (6 sts)

With matching thread, sew Row 1 of each ear to top of head. ✄

Patchwork Kitty

Continued from page 144

Row 12: Rep Row 10. (9 sc)

Row 13: Rep Row 9.

Row 14: Ch 1, sc dec over next 2 sc, sc in each sc across to last 2 sc, sc dec over next 2 sc, turn. (7 sc)

Row 15: Rep Row 14, fasten off. (5 sc)

Matching colors, sew leg sections tog. With toes pointing forward, sew top of leg to Row 5 of body.

Place decorative braid around neckline; tie ends in a bow. ✄

Dragon Puppet

Continued from page 152

form a ring, 6 sc in ring. (6 sc)

Rnds 2–8: Sc in each sc around.

Row 9: Holding Rnd 8 flat and working through both thicknesses, ch 1, 3 sc across, turn. (3 sc)

Row 10: Ch 1, 2 sc in

each sc across, turn. (6 sc)

Row 11: [Ch 4, sc in 2nd ch from hook, sc in each of next 2 chs, sk next sc of Row 10, sl st in next sc] 3 times, fasten off. Sew arm to side of body.

Spine

Make 2

Row 1: With light purple, ch 25, sc in 2nd ch from hook, sc in each rem ch across, turn. (24 sc)

Row 2: Ch 1, [sk next 2 sc, 5 dc in next sc, sk next 2 sc, sc in next sc] 4 times, fasten off.

Sew spine sections tog, stuffing lightly with fiberfill before closing. Sew in place on back of puppet. ✄

2nd ch from hook. (6 sc)

Rnd 2: Sc in each sc around, sl st in next st, leaving a length of yarn, fasten off.

Finishing

Stuff beak lightly and sew to face. For eyes, paint 2 black dots above beak.

Elephant

Rnds 1–18: With blue, rep Rnds 1–18 of basic puppet.

Trunk

Rnd 1: With blue, ch 2, 4 sc in 2nd ch from hook. (4 sc)

Rnd 2: Sc in each sc around.

Rnd 3: Sc in each of next 3 sc, 2 sc in next sc. (5 sc)

Rnd 4: Sc in each of next 4 sc, 2 sc in next sc. (6 sc)

Rnd 5: Rep Rnd 2.

Rnd 6: [Sc in next sc, 2 sc in next sc] 3 times. (9 sc)

Rnd 7: Rep Rnd 2, sl st in next st, leaving a length of yarn, fasten off.

Ear

Make 2

Row 1: With blue, ch 4, 6 dc in 4th ch from hook, leaving a length of yarn, fasten off.

Finishing

Stuff trunk with fiberfill and sew to face. Sew ears to sides of head. For eyes, paint 2 black dots above trunk.

Rabbit

Rnds 1–18: With pastels print, rep Rnds 1–18 of basic puppet.

Ear

Make 2

Row 1: With pastels print, ch 7, sc in 2nd ch from hook, sc in each rem ch across, ch 2, sl st in last sc, working on opposite side of foundation ch, sc in each ch across, leaving a length of yarn, fasten off.

Finishing

Sew ears to top of head. For eyes, paint 2 black dots on face. For nose, paint a pink dot between eyes.

Octopus

Rnds 1–6: With green, rep Rnds 1–6 of basic puppet. (14 sc)

Rnds 7 & 8: Sc in each sc around.

Rnd 9: Sc in each of next 2 sc, [ch 10, 2 sc in 2nd ch from hook, 2 sc in each of next 8 chs, sc in next sc of Rnd 8] 4 times, sc in each of next 2 sc, [ch 10, 2 sc in 2nd ch from hook, 2 sc in each of next 8 chs, sc in next sc of Rnd 8] 4 times, sc in each of next 2 sc on Rnd 8. (8 legs)

Rnd 10: Holding legs to front of work and leaving leg sts unworked, sc in each sc around. (14 sc)

Rnds 11 & 12: Sc in each sc around. At the end of Rnd 12, sl st in next sc, fasten off.

Finishing

For eyes, paint 2 black dots on face. For mouth, paint a small red mouth below eyes.

Pig

Rnds 1–18: With pink, rep Rnds 1–18 of basic puppet.

Snout

Rnd 1: With pink, ch 2, 5 sc in 2nd ch from hook, sl st to join in beg sc. (5 sc)

Rnd 2: Working in back lps only this rnd, ch 1, sc in each sc around, sl st to join in beg sc, leaving a length of yarn, fasten off.

Ear

Make 2

With pink, ch 2, sc in 2nd ch from hook, leaving a length of yarn, fasten off.

Finishing

Sew snout to front of face and ears to top of head. For eyes, paint 2 black dots above snout. ✄

Lucky Duck

Continued from page 146

next 2 chs. (8 sc)

Rnds 2–4: Sc in each sc around.

Rnd 5: [Sc in next sc, 2 sc in next sc] rep around, sl st in next sc, fasten off.

Sew beak to front of head, slightly below and between eyes.

Wing

Make 2

Rnd 1: With fuchsia, ch 2, 6 sc in 2nd ch from hook. (6 sc)

Rnd 2: Work 2 sc in next sc, sc in each of next 5 sc. (7 sc)

Rnd 3: Sc in each of next 2 sc, 2 sc in next sc, sc in each of next 4 sc. (8 sc)

Rnd 4: Sc in each of next 4 sc, 2 sc in next sc, sc in each of next 3 sc. (9 sc)

Rnd 5: Sc in each of next 6 sc, 2 sc in next sc, 2 sc in next sc. (10 sc)

Rnd 6: Sc in each of next 8 sc, 2 sc in next sc, sc in next sc. (11 sc)

Rnd 7: Sc in each of next 10 sc, 2 sc in next sc. (12 sc)

Rnd 8: [Sc in next sc, 2 sc in next sc] rep around. (18 sc)

Rnd 9: Sc in each sc around, sl st in next sc, fasten off.

Do not stuff wing. Sew to side of body with Rnd 1 pointing upward.

Feet

Make 2

Rnd 1: With butterscotch, ch 2, 6 sc in 2nd ch from hook. (6 sc)

Rnd 2: 2 sc in each sc around. (12 sc)

Rnd 3: Sc in each sc around.

Rnd 4: Rep Rnd 3.

Rnd 5: [Sc in next sc, 2 sc in next sc] rep around. (18 sc)

Rnd 6: Rep Rnd 3.

Rnd 7: [Sc in each of next 2 sc, 2 sc in next sc] rep around. (24 sc)

Rnd 8: Rep Rnd 3, leaving a length of yarn, fasten off.

Holding Rnd 8 flat across, sew through both thicknesses to form webbed feet by [sewing between Rnds 6 and 7, and up over Rnd 8, pulling tightly to gather] twice.

Sew feet to bottom of body. ✂

Afghan Jamboree

Create warmth and comfort for those you love with this vibrant collection of afghans! Browse through this chapter to find just the right afghan to suit your decor, then find your scrap yarn basket and begin crocheting a sensation!

Floral Vines

Design by Darla Fanton

Settle down for a cozy afternoon nap under the warmth of this reversible afghan. The sample here uses 15 different scrap colors, but you can use as many or as few as you wish!

Gauge

17 sts = 4 inches; 13 rows = 2 inches

Check gauge to save time.

Pattern Notes

Weave in loose ends as work progresses.

Afghan is worked vertically, requiring the use of a flexible hook in order to accommodate the required number of sts.

When beg and ending colors, leave an 8-inch tail for fringe.

End colors after each 2-row section.

When picking up lp in horizontal st, insert hook under top lp only.

Pattern Stitch

Sl st: Insert hook in indicated st or ch-1 sp, yo and draw through st or sp and lp already on hook.

Afghan

Row 1: With green, ch 297, working from right to left and keeping lps on hook, insert hook in 2nd ch from hook, yo and draw through ch, forming a lp on hook, *[yo, sk next ch, pick up lp in next ch] twice, pick up lp in next ch, rep from * across, slide all sts to opposite end of hook, turn. (297 lps on hook)

Row 2: Place desired color on hook with a sl knot, working from left to right, draw lp knot through first lp, yo, draw through 2 lps, *ch 1, yo, draw through 4 lps, ch 1, [yo, draw through 2 lps] twice, rep from * across until there is 1 lp left on hook, do not turn.

Row 3: With scrap color, working right to left, ch 1, sk first vertical bar, pick up lp under next vertical bar, *pick up lp under next ch-1 sp, pick up lp in top of cl, pick up lp in next ch-1 sp, yo, pick up lp under next 2 vertical bars at once, rep from * across, slide all sts to opposite end of hook, turn. (297 lps on hook)

Row 4: With green, rep Row 2.

Row 5: With green, working right to left, ch 1, sk first vertical bar, pick up lp in next horizontal st, *pick up lp under next ch-1 sp, pick up lp in top of cl, pick up lp in next ch-1 sp, yo, pick up lp in

Continued on page 171

Kid's Kaleidoscope

Design by Carol Alexander

Skill Level: Beginner

Size: 43 x 61 inches

Materials

- Coats & Clark Red Heart Kids worsted weight yarn (5 oz per skein): 7 skeins white #2001, 3 skeins black #2012, small amount each periwinkle #2347 green #2677, turquoise #2850, yellow #2230, orange #2252, pink #2734, blue #2845, lime #2652, purple #2356, red #2390
- Size G/6 crochet hook or size needed to obtain gauge
- Yarn needle

Gauge

Rnds 1–3 = 2¾ inches; block = 8 inches

Check gauge to save time.

Pattern Notes

Weave in loose ends as work progresses.

Ch-3 counts as first dc throughout.

Join rnds with a sl st unless otherwise stated.

In using numerous color combinations on blocks, it is suggested changing colors only on Rnds 1–6, and Rnds 9 and 10, keeping black and white as instructed on remaining rnds for contrast.

Pattern Stitches

Popcorn (pc): 4 dc in indicated st, drop lp from hook, insert hook in first dc, pick up dropped lp and draw through st on hook.

Beg pc: Ch 3, 3 dc in same st, drop lp from hook, insert hook in 3rd ch of beg ch-3, pick up dropped lp and draw through st on hook.

Extended dc (edc): Yo, insert hook in indicated st, yo, draw up a lp, yo, draw through 1 lp on hook, [yo, draw through 2 lps on hook] twice.

Inverted dc shell: Holding back last lp of each dc on hook, work dc in each of next 8 sts, yo, draw through all 9 lps on hook.

Corner scallop: 7 dc in corner sp.

Beg corner scallop: Ch 3, 6 dc in corner sp.

Scallop: 5 dc in indicated st.

Block A

Make 6

Rnd 1: Beg at center with orange, ch 4, join to form a ring, ch 1, 6 sc in ring, join in beg sc. (6 sc)

Rnd 2: Ch 1, 2 sc in each sc around, join in beg sc, fasten off. (12 sc)

Rnd 3: Attach yellow in joining st of previous rnd, [ch 4, sc in 2nd ch from hook, hdc in each of next 2 chs, sl st in next sc of Rnd 2] 12 times, ending with last sl st at base of beg ch-4, fasten off. (12 rays)

Rnd 4: Attach green in tip of any ray of Rnd 3, ch 4 (counts as first hdc, ch-2 throughout), hdc in same st, *ch 2, [sc in tip of next ray, ch 2] twice **, [hdc, ch 2, hdc] in tip of next ray, rep from * around, ending last rep at **, join in 2nd ch of ch-4.

Rnd 5: Sl st in corner ch-2 sp, ch 2 (counts as first hdc throughout), [hdc, ch 2, 2 hdc] in same st as ch-2, *3 sc in each of next 3 ch-2 sps **, [2 hdc, ch 2, 2 hdc] in next corner ch-2 sp, rep from * around, ending last rep at **, join in 2nd ch of ch-2.

Rnd 6: Sl st in next hdc, sl st in corner ch-2 sp, ch 2, 2 hdc in same sp, *sc in each of next 13 sts **, 3 hdc in next corner ch-2 sp, rep from * around, ending last rep at **, join in 2nd ch of beg ch-2, fasten off. (64 sts)

Rnd 7: Attach white in 2nd hdc of any 3-hdc corner group, [beg pc,

Like the dazzling, fascinating color pattern in a kaleidoscope, this bright and cheery kid's afghan is sure to color any child's world with pure delight!

ch 2, pc] in same st, *ch 1, [sk 1 st, pc in next st, ch 1] 7 times, sk 1 st **, [pc, ch 2, pc] in next corner st, rep from * around, ending last rep at **, join in beg pc, fasten off.

Rnd 8: Attach black in any corner ch-2 sp, ch 3, 4 edc in same sp, *2 edc in each of next 8 ch-1 sps **, 5 edc in next corner ch-2 sp, rep from * around, ending last rep at **, join in 3rd ch of ch-3, fasten off.

Rnd 9: Attach turquoise in 3rd corner edc of any corner 5-edc group, ch 1, *3 sc in corner edc, [sc in each of next 6 sts, 3 sc in next st] twice, sc in each of next 6 sts, rep from * around, join in beg sc.

Rnd 10: Sl st in next corner sc, ch 3, 4 dc in same st, *hdc in next st, sc in each of next 2 sts, [sk next 2 sts, sc in each of next 3 sts, 3 sc in next st, sc in each of next 3 sts] twice, sk next 2 sts, sc in each of next 2 sts, hdc in next st **, 5 dc

in next corner st, rep from *
around, ending last rep at **, join
in 3rd ch of ch-3, fasten off.

Rnd 11: Attach white in 3rd (center) dc of any corner 5-dc group,
working fairly loosely for this
rnd, ch 1, *5 hdc in corner dc, ch
4, sk 1 st, [inverted dc shell, ch 3,
sc in next st, ch 3] twice, inverted
dc shell, ch 4, sk 1 st, rep from *
3 times, join in beg hdc.

Rnd 12: Sl st into 3rd (center) hdc
of corner group, ch 2, [hdc, ch 1, 2
hdc] in same st, *hdc in each of
next 2 hdc, 4 hdc in next ch-4 sp,
[hdc in eye of next inverted dc
shell, 3 hdc in next ch-3 sp, hdc in
next sc, 3 hdc in next ch-3 sp]
twice, hdc in eye of next inverted
dc shell, 4 hdc in next ch-4 sp, hdc
in each of next 2 hdc **, [2 hdc, ch
1, 2 hdc] in next corner hdc, rep
from * around, ending last rep at **,
join in 2nd ch of ch-2, fasten off.

Block B

Make 7

Work same as Block A, using yellow
for Rnds 1 and 2, lime for Rnd 3,
blue for Rnds 4–6, and red for
Rnds 9 and 10.

Block C

Make 6

Work same as Block A, using purple for Rnds 1 and 2, pink for Rnd
3, periwinkle for Rnds 4–6, and
lime for Rnds 9 and 10.

Block D

Make 5

Work same as Block A, using lime
for Rnds 1 and 2, blue for Rnd 3,
orange for Rnds 4–6, and yellow
for Rnds 9 and 10.

Block E

Make 6

Work same as Block A, using
turquoise for Rnds 1 and 2, red for
Rnd 3, yellow for Rnds 4–6, and
green for Rnds 9 and 10.

Block F

Make 5

Work same as Block A, using
orange for Rnds 1 and 2, purple for
Rnd 3, lime for Rnds 4–6, and pink
for Rnds 9 and 10.

Assembly

Following placement diagram,
with white, working through
both lps, sew motifs tog on WS
to make 7 rows of 5 blocks each.

Border

Rnd 1: Attach white in any corner
ch-1 sp, ch 3, [dc, ch 2, 2 dc] in
same corner sp, *dc in each st
across to next corner **, [2 dc, ch
2, 2 dc] in corner sp, rep from *
around, ending last rep at **, join
in 3rd ch of beg ch-3, fasten off.

*Note: Adjust spacing of sts as needed
when working between [ ] to accommodate st sequence, but keeping
number of scallops equal between
opposite sides.*

Rnd 2: Attach black in any corner
ch-2 sp, beg corner scallop in same
sp, *[sk next 2 sts, scallop in next
st, sk next 2 sts, sc in next st] rep
across, ending in 2nd st from next
corner sp, sk next st **, corner scallop in next corner ch-2 sp, rep from
* around, ending last rep at **, join
in 3rd ch of ch-3, fasten off.

Block afghan to size. ✄

B	D	C	A	E
F	A	E	B	D
C	B	D	F	A
A	F	C	E	B
B	E	A	D	C
D	C	B	E	F
E	A	F	C	B

Placement Diagram

Floral Vines

Continued from page 166

next horizontal st, rep from * across, slide all sts to opposite end of hook, turn. (297 lps on hook)

Rows 6–304: Rep Rows 2–5, ending after a Row 4.

Row 305: Bind off in the following manner. With green and working from right to left, ch 1, sk first vertical bar, sl st in next horizontal st, *sl st in next ch-1 sp, sl st in top of cl, sl st in next ch-1 sp, sl st in next horizontal st, rep from * across, fasten off.

Fringe

Cut yarn in 18-inch lengths. Working across short ends of afghan, place same-color fringe in the end of each 2-row section. For those rows that already have yarn ends, use 1 strand of yarn folded in half and incorporate the yarn ends into the fringe knot. For those rows that do not have yarn ends, use 2 strands of yarn folded in half and work a fringe knot. Trim ends evenly. ✂

Scrap Yarns

By Shirley Patterson

You have balls and balls of scrap yarn you can't seem to find a use for and you can't bring yourself to toss out. To hurriedly get rid of them, use your scraps for free-form designs. You don't have to fret over matching the colors; a finished project such as a throw rug, trivet, pot holder, chair pad, casserole tote, place mat or whatever you choose to make, will look like you planned each color. The best projects are those for which you can use 6–8 strands of yarn and a large hook such as a P or N.

To make a nice rug, hold 6–8 strands of any yarn colors together and work as follows:

Rnd 1: Ch 2, 6 sc in 2nd ch from hook, do not join rnds.

Rnd 2: 2 sc in each st around.

For rem rnds, sc around, inc 6 sc sts evenly sp on each rnd. When 1 color scrap ball of yarn ends, join another. Work to desired diameter or until all your scrap yarn is used.

These projects make extremely useful items and are good as gifts.

Northern Reflections

Design by Charlene Finiello

Gauge

15 dc = 6 inches; 8 dc rows = 6 inches

Check gauge to save time.

Pattern Notes

Weave in loose ends as work progresses.

Ch-3 counts as first dc throughout.

Join rnds with a sl st unless otherwise stated.

Work with 2 strands of yarn held tog throughout afghan and pillow.

Pattern Stitches

Front post tr (fptr): Yo hook twice, insert hook front to back to front again around vertical portion of indicated st, yo, draw up a lp, [yo, draw through 2 lps on hook] 3 times.

Bobble: [Yo, insert hook in indicated st, yo, draw up a lp, yo, draw through 2 lps on hook] 3 times in same st, yo, draw through all 4 lps on hook.

Afghan

Row 1 (RS): With 2 strands of off-white, ch 112, sc in 2nd ch from hook, sc in each rem ch across, turn. (111 sc)

Row 2: Ch 3, working in front lps only this row, dc in each st across, fasten off, turn.

Row 3: Attach dark country blue, ch 3, fpdc around next dc, sk dc directly behind fpdc, [working in back lps only, dc in each of next 2 sts, fpdc around next dc directly below, sk dc directly behind fpdc] rep across, ending with dc in 3rd ch of ch-3, turn.

Row 4: Ch 3, working in front lps only this row, dc in each st across, fasten off, turn.

Row 5: Attach country blue, rep Row 3.

Row 6: Rep Row 4.

Row 7: Attach light celery, rep Row 3.

Row 8: Rep Row 4.

Rows 9 & 10: Rep Rows 5 and 6.

Rows 11 & 12: Rep Rows 3 and 4.

Row 13: Attach off-white, rep Row 3.

Row 14: Rep Row 4.

Row 15 (RS): Attach light celery, ch 3, bobble in next dc, [working in back lps only this row, dc in each of next 2 sts, bobble in next dc] rep across, ending with dc in 3rd ch of ch-3, fasten off, do not turn.

Row 16 (RS): Attach off-white in top of beg ch-3 of previous row, ch 3, working in back lps only this row, dc in each st across, turn. (111 dc)

Row 17: Rep Row 4.

Rep Rows 3–17 until 5 fpdc section and 4-bobble section are completed.

At the end of last rep section of Row 17, do not fasten off.

The beautiful colors and softness of this gorgeous afghan make it a perfect gift idea. Stitch a matching pillow for a fabulous finishing touch!

Final row: Ch 1, working in front lps only this row, sc in each st across, fasten off.

Pillow

Front & Back

Make 2

Rnd 1 (RS): With 2 strands of light celery, ch 4, join to form a ring, ch 1, 16 sc in ring, join in beg sc. (16 sc)

Note: Work in back lps only throughout.

Rnd 2: Ch 3, 2 dc in next sc, [ch 1, tr in next sc, ch 1, 2 dc in next sc, dc in next sc, 2 dc in next sc] rep around, join in 3rd ch of beg ch-3, fasten off. (24 sts; 8 ch-1 sps)

Rnd 3: Attach country blue in 2nd dc to the right of a ch-1 sp, ch 3, dc in next dc, [2 dc in next ch-1 sp, fptr around next tr, ch 1, 2 dc in next ch-1 sp, dc in each of next 2 dc, fpdc around next dc, dc in each of next 2 dc] rep around, ending with fpdc, join in 3rd ch

Continued on page 188

Linked Shells

Design by Melissa Leapman

Skill Level: Beginner

Size: 49 x 57 inches

Materials

- Elmore-Pisgah Peaches & Crème cotton yarn (2½ oz per skein): 7 skeins each lemon #123 (A), light green #55 (B), persimmon #33 (C), 8 skeins white #1 (D)

- Size H/8 crochet hook or size needed to obtain gauge

- Tapestry needle

Gauge

[Sc, shell] twice = 1½ inches; 8 rows = 3 inches

Check gauge to save time.

Pattern Notes

Weave in loose ends as work progresses.

Work 2 rows each [A, B, C, and D] for pattern throughout.

Pattern Stitch

Shell: [Dc, ch 1, dc] in indicated st.

Afghan

Foundation Row (WS): With A, ch 182, sc in 2nd ch from hook, [ch 3, sk next 2 chs, sc in next ch] rep across, turn.

Row 1: Ch 3 (counts as first dc throughout), dc in same st as ch-3, sc in next ch-3 sp, [shell in next sc, sc in next ch-3 sp] rep across, ending with 2 dc in last sc, change color, turn.

Row 2: Ch 1, sc in first dc, ch 3, [sc in next ch-1 sp, ch 3] rep across, ending with sk next dc, sc in 3rd ch of turning ch-3, turn.

Rep Rows 1 and 2 in stripe pattern until afghan measures 56 inches from beg, ending after a Row 1 worked with A.

Final row: Ch 1, sc in first dc, ch 2, [sc in next ch-1 sp, ch 2] rep across, ending with sk next dc, sc in 3rd ch of turning ch-3, fasten off.

Edging

Rnd 1 (RS): Attach D with a sl st to upper right corner of afghan, ch 1, sc in same st, ch 3, *[sc in next st, sk ch sp, ch 3] rep across to corner, [sc, ch 3, sc] in corner st, working across side edge of rows, ch 3, [sc in side edge of next dc, ch 3] rep across working [sc, ch 3, sc] in corner st, rep from * around, ending with sc, ch 3 in same st as beg sc, join in beg sc.

This cotton afghan is worked in narrow stripes of color in a simple shell design. It's an ideal afghan to complement the decor of any room!

Rnd 2: Sl st into next ch-3 sp, ch 1, [sc, 2 dc, sc] in each ch-3 sp around, join in beg sc, fasten off. ✂

Scrap Bargello

Design by Diane Poellot

Stay warm and cozy at the end of a long winter day as you snuggle under this delightful afghan. Stitch it in masculine colors for the man who has everything!

Gauge

4 dc = 1 inch; 3 dc rows = 1 inch
Check gauge to save time.

Pattern Note

Weave in loose ends as work progresses.

Afghan

Row 1: With any scrap color, ch 259, sc in 5th ch from hook, sc in next ch, [hdc in each of next 2 chs, dc in each of next 3 chs, {2 tr, ch 1, 2 tr} in next ch, dc in each of next 3 chs, hdc in each of next 2 chs, sc in each of next 2 chs, sk next 2 chs, sc in each of next 2 chs] 14 times, sk next 2 chs, dc in last ch, fasten off, do not turn.

Row 2: Attach next color with a sc in 4th ch of skipped foundation chs at beg of Row 1, working in back lps only, ch 2, sk next 2 chs, [sc in each of next 2 sts, hdc in each of next 2 sts, dc in each of next 3 sts, {2 tr, ch 1, 2 tr} in next ch-1 sp, dc in each of next 3 sts, hdc in each of next 2 sts, sc in each of next 2 sts, sk next 4 sc] rep across, sk last 2 sc, dc in last dc, fasten off, do not turn.

Row 3: Attach next color with a sc in 2nd ch of beg ch-2 of previous row, working in back lps only, ch 2, sk next 2 sc, [sc in each of next 2 sts, hdc in each of next 2 sts, dc in each of next 3 sts, {2 tr, ch 1, 2 tr} in next ch-1 sp, dc in each of next 3 sts, hdc in each of next 2 sts, sc in each of next 2 sts, sk next 4 sc] rep across, sk last 2 sc, dc in last dc, fasten off, do not turn.

Rows 4–94: Rep Row 3.

At the end of Row 94, do not fasten off, turn.

Top Edging

Row 95: Sk first dc and next sc, [sl st in next 8 sts, {sl st, ch 1, sl st} in ch-1 sp, sl st in each of next 8 sts, sk next 2 sc] rep across, ending with sl st in 2nd ch of beg ch-2, fasten off.

Bottom Edging

Working on opposite side of foundation ch, with WS facing, attach matching yarn in 4th skipped foundation ch at beg of Row 1, [sl st in each of next 7 chs, sk next ch, sl st in each of next 7 chs, sl st in next ch, ch 1, sl st in next ch] rep across, ending with sl st in skipped ch, sl st in last dc of Row 1, fasten off. ✂

Reversible Rainbow

Design by Darla Fanton

Skill Level: Intermediate

Size: 47 x 67 inches

Materials

- Coats & Clark Red Heart Super Saver worsted weight yarn: 29 oz black #312, 27 oz various scrap colors
- Size K/10½ flexible double-ended crochet hook or size needed to obtain gauge
- Size J/10 crochet hook
- Tapestry needle

Gauge

3.85 sts = 1 inch; 5 rows = 1 inch
Check gauge to save time.

Pattern Notes

Weave in loose ends as work progresses.

Carry black along side edge; fasten off scrap colors after each 2-row section.

Afghan

Row 1: With double-ended hook and black, ch 177, insert hook in 2nd ch from hook, *yo, draw through ch, forming a lp on hook, keeping lps on hook, rep from * across foundation ch, slide all sts to opposite end of hook, turn. (177 lps on hook)

Row 2: Place scrap color on hook with sl knot, working from left to right draw sl knot through first lp, *yo, draw through 2 lps (1 lp each color), rep from * across until there is 1 lp left on hook, do not turn.

Row 3: With scrap color, ch 1, sk first vertical bar, *yo, insert hook under next vertical bar without working, [pick up lp under next vertical bar] twice, sl unworked st over last 2 sts, rep from * ending with yo, insert hook under next vertical bar without working, pick up lp under last vertical bar, pass unworked st over last st, slide all sts to opposite end of hook, turn. (177 lps on hook)

Row 4: Pick up black, yo and draw through 1 lp, *yo, draw through 2 lps (1 of each color), rep from * until 1 lp rem on hook, do not turn.

Row 5: With black, rep Row 3.

Row 6: With next scrap color, rep Row 2.

Rows 7–464: Rep Rows 3–6, ending after a Row 4.

Row 465: Bind off in the following manner: With black, ch 1, sk first vertical bar, *ch 1, insert hook under next vertical bar without working, [pick up lp under next vertical bar] twice, pass unworked lp over last 2 sts, yo, draw through all 3 lps on hook, rep from *, ending with ch 1, insert hook under next vertical bar without working,

Continued on page 188

Created with many different scrap colors, this reversible afghan is a wonderful way to use up all the extras in your scrap basket!

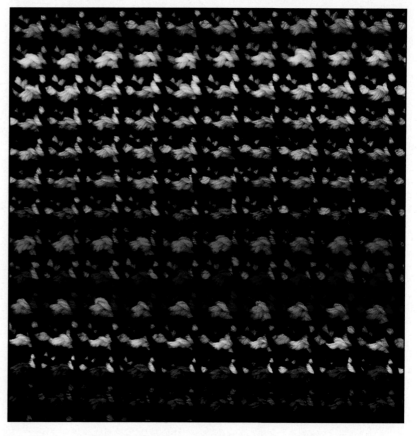

Country Wildflowers

Design by Carol Alexander

Gauge

With larger hook, motif = 4 inches; completed square = 10 inches; prickly wild rose = 2¾ inches in diameter; larkspur = 2¼ inches in diameter

With smaller hook, forget-me-not = 1½ inches in diameter; daisy = 2½ inches in diameter

Check gauge to save time.

Pattern Notes

Make 8 each Square A, Square B and Square C, joining as work progresses in Rnd 3 of edging.

You can almost smell the fresh air and feel the breeze as it blows across this field of wildflowers. Larkspur and daisies bloom together with forget-me-nots and wild roses in this stunning afghan.

Weave in loose ends as work progresses.

Ch-3 counts as first dc throughout.

Join rnds with a sl st unless otherwise stated.

Use larger hook unless otherwise stated.

To secure flowers to motif for sewing, arrange flowers on motif as indicated in photo, overlapping petals and leaves at various positions. Carefully lift edges of flowers and leaves and, leaving at least ¼ inch of petals and leaf tips free, place small dabs of fabric glue sparingly on under side. Smooth and gently press flowers and leaves back in place on motif, taking care not to move out of position. Let dry thoroughly. Once glue is dry, flowers and leaves can be securely stitched in place. Sew all pieces with soft navy, working from front side of square and underneath flowers; leave only the tips of flower petals and leaves free.

To change yarn color, draw new color through on last lp of last st of row; drop working color.

Pattern Stitches

Corner scallop: [Sc, 3 dc, ch 1, 3 dc, sc] in corner sp.

Shell: [Hdc, ch 3, hdc] in indicated st.

Scallop: [Sc, dc, ch 1, dc, sc] in indicated st.

P: Ch 2, sl st in top of last st made.

Dtr cl: *Yo hook twice, insert hook in indicated st, yo, draw up a lp, [yo, draw through 2 lps on hook] twice, rep from * twice, yo, draw through all 4 lps on hook.

Dtr: Yo hook 3 times, insert hook in indicated st, yo, draw up a lp, [yo, draw through 2 lps on hook] 4 times.

Trtr: Yo hook 4 times, insert hook in indicated st, yo, draw up a lp, [yo, draw through 2 lps on hook] 5 times.

First Square (A)

Diamond motif

Note: Make 4 motifs for each square.

Row 1: With soft navy, ch 2, sc in 2nd ch from hook, turn. (1 sc)

Row 2 (RS): Ch 1, 2 sc in first sc, sc in turning ch, turn. (3 sc)

Row 3: Ch 1, 2 sc in first sc, sc in each sc across to last sc, 2 sc in last sc, turn. (5 sc)

Row 4: Ch 1, sc in each sc across, inc 1 sc at center of row, turn. (6 sc)

Rows 5 & 6: Rep Rows 3 and 4. (9 sc)

Row 7: Rep Row 3. (11 sc)

Row 8: Ch 1, sc in each sc across, turn.

Rows 9–12: Rep Rows 3 and 4. (17 sc)

Row 13: Ch 2, dc in first sc, hdc in

next sc, 2 hdc in next sc, hdc in each of next 4 sc, sc in next sc, sc dec loosely over next 2 sc, hdc in each of next 4 sc, 2 hdc in next sc, hdc in next sc, dc in last sc, changing to light blue, turn. (19 sts)

Row 14: Ch 5, sk next st, sc in next st, [ch 3, sk next st, sc in next st] rep across to last 2 sts, ch 2, sk next st, dc in last st to form last ch sp, turn. (9 ch sps)

Row 15: Ch 4, sc in next ch sp, [ch 3, sc in next ch sp] rep across to last sp, ch 1, dc in last sp, turn. (8 ch sps)

Rows 16–21: Rep Row 15. (2 ch sps)

Row 22: Ch 3, sc in last ch sp, fasten off.

Gently shape motif into symmetrical square, defining corners.

Sew the 4 motifs tog on WS, carefully aligning rows, with soft navy sections joined at center to form a diamond.

Ruffle

Attach white in the skipped sc on Row 13 of diamond motif to left "of any corner joining, ch 1, [sc, 2 hdc, ch 1, 2 hdc, sc] in same sc, *[{sc, hdc, ch 1, hdc sc} in next skipped sc of Row 13] 7 times, [sc, 2 hdc, ch 1, 2 hdc, sc] in last skipped sc of Row 13 just before corner joining **, [sc, 2 hdc, ch 1, 2 hdc, sc] in next skipped sc of Row 13 just past corner, rep from * 3 times, ending last rep at **, join in beg sc, fasten off.

Prickly wild rose

Rnd 1: With pale yellow, ch 4, join to form a ring, ch 1, 10 sc in ring, join in beg sc, fasten off. (10 sc)

Rnd 2: Working in back lps only this rnd, attach light raspberry in any st of Rnd 1, *ch 3, [tr, dtr] in same st, ch 2, sl st in lp on center back of post of dtr just made, [dtr, tr, ch 3, sl st] in next st, sl st in next st, rep from * 4 times, fasten off. (5 petals)

Rnd 3: Working in rem front lps on Rnd 1, attach pale yellow in any st, ch 3, [sl st in next st, ch 3]

rep around, join in base of beg ch-3, fasten off.

Row 4: Attach medium sage to back of rose at base of and between any 2 petals, [ch 4, dtr, trtr, ch 2, sc around top of post of trtr just made, dtr, ch 4, sl st in same place] twice, fasten off. (2 leaf petals)

Smooth flower petals and arrange evenly.

Forget-me-not

Rnd 1: With smaller hook, with bright yellow, ch 2, 5 sc in 2nd ch from hook, join in beg sc, fasten off. (5 sc)

Rnd 2: With smaller hook, working in back lps only this rnd, attach blue, *ch 1, [2 dc, ch 1, sc around top of post of last dc made, dc, ch 1, sl st] in same st, sl st in next st, rep from * 4 times, fasten off. (5 petals)

Smooth and arrange petals evenly.

Daisy

Rnd 1: With smaller hook, with gold, ch 5, join to form a ring, working over beg tail, ch 1, 16 sc in ring, join in beg sc, fasten off. (16 sc)

Rnd 2: With smaller hook, attach bright yellow in any sc, *ch 3, [tr, p, ch 4, sl st] in same st, sl st in each of next 2 sts, rep from * 7 times, fasten off. (8 petals)

Pull beg yarn tail tightly to close center opening to approximately ¼ inch, weave in and secure on back.

Row 3: With smaller hook, attach medium sage to back of daisy at base of and between any 2 petals, [ch 5, {trtr, ch 2, sc around top of post of trtr just made, ch 5, sl st} in same place] twice, fasten off. (2 leaf petals)

Smooth flower petals and arrange evenly.

Larkspur

Rnd 1: With lavender, ch 2, 10 sc in 2nd ch from hook, join in beg sc. (10 sc)

Rnd 2: *Ch 3, [2 dc, p, dc, ch 3, sl st] in same st, sl st in each of next 2 sts, rep from * 4 times, fasten off.

(5 petals)

For stamen, with bright yellow, leaving a beg tail for sewing, ch 2, sl st in 2nd ch from hook, fasten off.

Thread beg yarn tail on needle and insert through flower center from front side; pull stamen firmly in place and sew securely on backside.

Row 3: Attach medium sage to back of flower at base of and between any 2 petals, [ch 4, dtr cl, ch 2, sl st in top of dtr cl, ch 4, sl st in same place] twice, fasten off. (2 leaf petals)

Smooth flower petals and arrange evenly.

Attach flowers to square.

Square edging

Rnd 1: Attach light blue in any corner ch-3 sp, ch 1, [2 sc, ch 2, 2 sc] in same sp, * 2 sc in each of next 7 ch sps, 2 hdc in each of next 2 ch sps (at corner of diamond motif), 2 sc in each of next 7 ch sps **, [2 sc, ch 2, 2 sc] in corner ch sp, rep from * around, ending last rep at **, join in beg sc, fasten off.

Rnd 2: Attach white in any corner ch-2 sp, ch 1, *[sc, ch 3, sc] in corner sp, ch 2, sk next 2 sts, [sc, ch 1, sc] in next st, ch 2, sk next 2 sts, [{sc, ch 3, sc} in next st, sk next 2 sts] 3 times, [sc, ch 3, sc] in next st, sk next st, [sc, ch 1, sc] in next st, sk next st, [sc, ch 3, sc] in next st, sk next st, [sc, ch 1, sc] in next st, sk next st, [{sc, ch 3, sc} in next st, sk next 2 sts] 3 times, [sc, ch 3, sc] in next st, ch 2, sk next 2 sts, [sc, ch 1, sc] in next st, ch 2, sk next st, rep from * 3 times, join in beg sc.

Rnd 3: Ch 1, *work corner scallop, ch 1, sk next ch-2 sp, shell in next ch-1 sp, ch 1, sk next ch-2 sp, scallop in each of next 4 ch-3 sps, ch 1, sl st in next ch-1 sp, ch 1, scallop in next ch-3 sp, ch 1, sl st in next ch-1 sp, ch 1, scallop in each of next 4 ch-3 sps, ch 1, sk next ch-2 sp, shell in next ch-1 sp, ch 1, sk next ch-2 sp, rep from * 3 times, join in beg sc, fasten off.

Second Square (B)

Make the same as first square (A) through Rnd 2 of square edging, except work flower colors as follows.

Prickly wild rose: Rnd 1 in pale yellow, Rnd 2 in lavender and Rnd 3 in pale yellow.

Forget-me-not: Rnds 1 and 2 in bright yellow.

Daisy: Rnd 1 in bright yellow and Rnd 2 in white.

Larkspur: Rnds 1 and 2 in delft blue and stamen with bright yellow.

Note: On the following joining rnd, rotate position of square ¼ turn when joining to previous square in order to alternate position and colors of flowers.

Rnd 3 (joining rnd): Work same as Rnd 3 of first square A to first corner of joining side. On joining side, work the ch-1 of each corner scallop as a sl st in the ch-1 sp of corresponding corner scallop on first square, and the ch-1 of each scallop along side as a sl st in ch-1 sp of corresponding scallop on first square; work the ch-3 of each shell as [ch 1, sl st in ch-3 sp of corresponding shell on first square, ch 1], complete rem of rnd same as for first square.

Third Square (C)

Follow instructions for 2nd square (B), except work flower colors as follows.

Prickly wild rose: Rnd 1 in pale yellow, Rnd 2 in white and Rnd 3 in pale yellow.

Forget-me-not: Rnd 1 in bright yellow, Rnd 2 in bright pink.

Daisy: Rnd 1 in gold, Rnd 2 in light plum.

Larkspur: Rnds 1 and 2 in light periwinkle and stamen with bright yellow.

Assembly

Following placement diagram, make and join 21 more squares in 6 rows of 4 squares each.

Afghan Border

Rnd 1: Attach white in corner ch-1 sp at right end of short side of afghan, ch 1, *[sc, ch 3, sc] in corner sp, [ch 3, sc in last sc of corner scallop, ch 3, sc in ch-3 sp of next shell, {ch 3, sc in ch-1 sp of next scallop} 9 times, ch 3, sc in ch-3 sp of next shell, ch 3, sc in first dc of next corner scallop, ch 3 **, sc in corner joining] 4 times, ending last rep at **, [sc, ch 3, sc] in corner sp, [ch 3, sc in last sc of corner scallop, ch 3, sc in ch-3 sp of next shell, {ch 3, sc in ch-1 sp of next scallop} 9 times, ch 3, sc in ch-3 sp of next shell, ch 3, sc in first dc of next corner scallop, ch 3 †, sc in corner joining] 6 times, ending last rep at †, rep from *, join in beg sc.

Rnd 2: Sl st in corner ch-3 sp, ch 3, [dc, ch 2, 2 dc] in corner sp, *3 dc in each ch-3 sp across to next corner sp **, [2 dc, ch 2, 2 dc] in corner sp, rep from * 3 times, ending last rep at **, join in 3rd ch of ch-3.

Rnd 3: Sl st to corner sp, [ch 3, dc, ch 2, 2 dc] in corner sp, *dc in each dc across to next corner sp **, [2 dc, ch 2, 2 dc] in corner sp, rep from * 3 times, ending last rep at **, join in 3rd ch of ch-3, fasten off.

Note: On Rnd 4, adjust spacing of sts as needed when working between brackets to accommodate st sequence, but keeping number of sts equal between opposite sides.

Rnd 4: Attach soft navy in any corner ch-2 sp, ch 1, *sc in corner sp, ch 5, sk next 2 dc, sc in next dc, [ch 5, sk next 3 dc, sc in next dc] rep across, ending in 3rd dc from next corner sp, ch 5, sk next 2 dc, rep from * 3 times, join in beg sc.

Rnd 5: Sl st in first 2 chs of next ch-5 sp, ch 1, sc in same ch-5 sp, *[ch 5, sc in next ch-5 sp] rep across, ending in the first of the 2 ch-5 sps forming next corner, ch 7 **, sc in 2nd ch-5 sp of corner, rep from *3 times, ending last rep at **, join in beg sc.

Rnd 6: [Sc, ch 1, 2 dc, ch 1, sc] in each ch-5 sp around and [{sc, ch 1, 2 dc, ch 1} 3 times, sc] in each corner ch-7 sp, join in beg sc, fasten off. ✂

A	B	C	A
C	A	B	C
B	C	A	B
A	B	C	A
B	C	A	B
C	A	B	C

Placement Diagram

Confetti Stars

Design by Martha Stein

Gauge

Square = 2¾ inches
Check gauge to save time.

Pattern Notes

Weave in loose ends as work progresses.

Join rnds with a sl st unless otherwise stated.

The more scrap colors used in this afghan the better. Each Rnd 1 with scrap color only required a few yards.

Square

Make 391

Rnd 1 (RS): With small hook and scrap color, ch 3, join to form a ring, ch 5 (counts as first dc, ch-2), dc in ring, ch 2, [dc in ring, ch 2] 5 times, join in 3rd ch of beg ch-5, fasten off. (8 dc; 8 ch-2 sps)

Rnd 2 (RS): With larger hook, attach black with sl st in any ch-2 sp, ch 3 (counts as first dc throughout), dc in same ch sp, *3 hdc in next ch-2 sp, [2 dc, ch 2, 2 dc] in next ch-2 sp, rep from * around, ending with 2 dc in beg corner sp, ch 2, join in 3rd ch of beg ch-3, leaving an 8-inch length of yarn, fasten off.

Assembly

Working in back lps only, whipstitch squares tog in 23 rows of 17 squares each.

Edging

Rnd 1: Working in back lps only this row, with larger hook, attach black in 2nd ch of any corner ch-2 sp, ch 1, sc in same st, * [sc in each of next 2 dc, sc in each of next 3 hdc, sc in each of next 2 dc, sc in ch sp, sk joining sts, sc in next ch sp] rep across to corner, sc in first ch of corner, ch 2, sc in 2nd ch of corner, rep from * around, join with hdc in beg sc to form last corner sp.

Rnd 2: Ch 1, sc in corner sp, ch 1, *[sk next sc, sc in next sc, ch 1] rep across to next corner, [sc, ch 2, sc] in corner ch-2 sp, ch 1, rep from * around, ending with sc in same corner sp as beg sc, join with hdc in beg sc.

Rnd 3: Ch 1, sc in corner sp, ch 1, *[sc in next ch-1 sp, ch 1] rep across to next corner, [sc, ch 3, sc] in corner ch sp, ch 1, rep from * around, ending with sc in beg corner sp, dc in beg sc.

Vibrant stars against a black background create a kaleidoscope effect with this gorgeous afghan!

Rnd 4: Ch 3, *[dc, ch 2, dc] in each ch-1 sp across to next corner, [dc, ch 3, 2 dc, ch 3, dc] in corner sp, rep from * around, ending with dc in same corner sp, join with dc in 3rd ch of ch-3.

Rnd 5: Ch 3, *[dc, ch 3, dc] in each ch sp across to next corner, [dc, ch 4, dc] in each of 2 corner ch-3 sps, rep from * around, join with tr in 3rd ch of beg ch-3.

Rnd 6: Ch 3, *[dc, ch 4, dc] in each ch sp to next corner, [dc, ch 5, dc] in each of 2 corner ch-4 sps, rep from * around, ending with dc in 2nd ch-4 sp, ch 5, join in 3rd ch of beg ch-3, fasten off. ✄

Autumn Leaves

Design by Martha Stein

Cool, crisp fall days are just around the corner. Leaf motifs worked in beautiful autumn colors create a stunning work of art in this delightful granny square pattern!

Gauge

Granny square = 2¾ inches

Check gauge to save time.

Pattern Notes

Weave in loose ends as work progresses.

Ch-2 counts as first dc.

Join rnds with a sl st unless otherwise stated.

Solid Granny Square

Note: Make 239 Aran and 4 of each leaf color.

Rnd 1: Ch 4, join to form a ring, ch 2, 2 dc in ring, [ch 2, 3 dc in ring] 3 times, hdc in 2nd ch of beg ch-2.

Rnd 2: Ch 2, 2 dc in corner sp, *ch 1, [3 dc, ch 2, 3 dc] in next ch-2 sp, rep from * twice, ch 1, 3 dc in beg corner sp, ch 2, join in 2nd ch of beg ch-2, leaving an 8-inch length of yarn, fasten off.

Two-Color Granny Square

Note: Make 4 of each of 9 leaf color.

Rnd 1: With Aran, ch 4, join to form a ring, ch 3, sl st in 2nd ch from hook, holding lp made to right of chs, [2 dc, ch 2, 3 dc] in ring, leaving a 3-inch length, fasten off, pick up leaf color, leaving

a 3-inch length at beg, draw lp through st on hook, ch 1, [3 dc, ch 2, 3 dc] in ring, join in side lp of beg ch-3, fasten off.

Tie ends of first color change in square knot.

Rnd 2: In last corner joined, sl st with Aran, ch 3, sl st in 2nd ch from hook, 2 dc in same corner sp, ch 1, [3 dc, ch 2, 3 dc] in next corner sp, ch 1, 3 dc in next corner sp, leaving a 3-inch length, fasten off, draw a lp of color through lp on hook, ch 1, 3 dc in same corner sp, ch 1, [3 dc, ch 2, 3 dc] in next corner sp, ch 1, 3 dc in beg corner sp, join in side lp of beg ch-3, leaving an 8-inch length, fasten off.

Tie ends of first color change in a square knot.

Assembly

Whipstitch all squares tog in back lps only.

Following diagram for placement, make 19 leaf blocks.

Sew rem Aran granny squares in 9-block squares as indicated in diagram.

Sew sections tog with vertical seams first and then sew horizontal seams.

Sew rem granny squares around outer edge of afghan.

Edging

Rnd 1: Working in back lps only this rnd, attach Aran in 2nd ch of any corner ch-2 sp, ch 1, sc in same st, *[sc in each of next 3 dc, sc in next ch-1 sp, sc in each of next 3 dc, sc in next ch-1 sp, sk joining sts, sc in next ch-1 sp] rep across to corner, in corner work sc in first ch, ch 2, sc in 2nd ch of same corner, rep from * around, join with hdc in beg sc.

Rnd 2: Ch 1, sc in beg corner, ch 1, *[sk next sc, sc in next sc, ch 1] rep across to next corner sp, [sc, ch 2, sc] in corner ch-2 sp, ch 1, rep from * around, ending with ch 1, sc in beg corner, ch 1, join in beg sc, fasten off.

Note: Edging should rem flat; if you find edging begs to curl, slightly, change to a larger hook to keep edging flat.

Rnd 3: Attach leaf color in any ch-1 sp on side edge, ch 1, sc in same ch-1 sp, ch 1, *[sc in next ch-1 sp, ch 1] rep across to corner ch-2 sp, [sc, ch 2, sc] in corner ch-2 sp, ch 1, rep from * around, join, fasten off.

Rnd 4: With Aran, rep Rnd 2.

Rnd 5: With another leaf color, rep Rnd 2.

Rnd 6: With Aran, rep Rnd 2, do not fasten off.

Rnd 7: Sl st into next ch sp, ch 3,

*[sl st in next ch-1 sp, ch 3] rep across edge, [sl st, ch 3] 3 times in corner ch-2 sp, rep from * around, fasten off. ✂

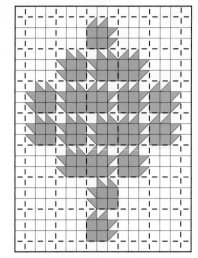

Make 19 leaves, sewing sections together as numbered.

Placement Diagram

Northern Reflections

Continued from page 172

of beg ch-3. (40 sts; 8 ch-1 sps)

Rnd 4: Ch 3, dc in each of next 3 sts, [dc in next ch-1 sp, ch 1, tr in next tr, ch 1, dc in next ch-1 sp, dc in each of next 9 sts] rep around, join in 3rd ch of beg ch-3, attach dark country blue, fasten off country blue. (48 sts; 8 ch-1 sps)

Rnd 5: Ch 3, dc in next dc, fpdc around next dc, dc in each of next 2 dc, *dc in next ch-1 sp, ch 1, fptr around next tr, ch 1, dc in next ch-1 sp, [dc in each of next 2 dc, fpdc around next dc] 3 times, dc in each of next 2 dc, rep from * around, join in 3rd ch of beg ch-3.

Rnd 6: Ch 3, dc in each of next 5 dc, [2 dc in next ch-1 sp, ch 1, tr in

tr, ch 1, 2 dc in next ch-1 sp, dc in each of next 13 dc] rep around, join in 3rd ch of beg ch-3, attach off-white, fasten off dark country blue.

Rnd 7: Ch 3, dc in next dc, fpdc around next dc, dc in each of next 2 dc, fpdc around next dc, dc in each of next 2 dc, *dc in next ch-1 sp, ch 1, fptr around tr, ch 1, dc in next ch-1 sp, [dc in each of next 2 dc, fpdc around next dc] 5 times, dc in each of next 2 dc, rep from * around, join in 3rd ch of beg ch-3.

Rnd 8: Ch 3, dc in each of next 8 dc, *2 dc in next ch-1 sp, ch 1, tr in next tr, ch 1, 2 dc in next ch-1 sp, dc in each of next 18 dc, rep from * around, join in 3rd ch of

beg ch-3, attach light celery, fasten off off-white.

Rnd 9: Ch 3, dc in next dc, [bobble in next dc, dc in each of next 2 dc] 3 times, *dc in next ch-1 sp, ch 1, bobble in next tr, ch 1, dc in next ch-1 sp, dc in next dc, [bobble in next dc, dc in each of next 2 dc] 7 times, rep from * around, join in 3rd ch of beg ch-3, fasten off.

Note: At the end of Rnd 9 on 2nd pillow section, do not fasten off.

Assembly

With WS of pillow tog and matching sts, sc in each st around, inserting pillow form before closing, join in beg sc, fasten off. ✂

Reversible Rainbow

Continued from page 176

pick up lp under next vertical bar, pass unworked lp over last st, yo, draw through both lps on hook. Transfer last lp of black to crochet hook and continue with edging.

Edging

Rnd 1: Ch 2 (counts as first hdc throughout), 2 hdc in same spot as final bind-off st, hdc evenly sp

around all 4 sides, working 3 hdc in each corner, sl st to join in 2nd ch of beg ch-2.

Note: You should have an odd number of sts along each side between the 3 corner sts.

Rnd 2: Sl st in next hdc, ch 2, hdc, ch 2, 2 hdc] in same st, *ch 1, sk next st, hdc in next st, rep from

* around working [2 hdc, ch 2, 2 hdc] in each corner sp, sl st to join in 2nd ch of beg ch-2.

Rnd 3: Attach scrap color with a sc in any st, [hdc in st below ch sp, sc in next st] rep around, sl st to join in beg sc, fasten off. ✂

General Instructions

Please review the following information before working the projects in this book. Important details about the abbreviations and symbols used are included.

Hooks

Crochet hooks are sized for different weights of yarn and thread. For thread crochet, you will usually use a steel crochet hook. Steel crochet-hook sizes range from size 00 to 14. The higher the number of the hook, the smaller your stitches will be. For example, a size 1 steel crochet hook will give you much larger stitches than a size 9 steel crochet hook. Keep in mind that the sizes given with the pattern instructions were obtained by working with the size thread or yarn, and hook given in the materials list. If you work with a smaller hook, depending on your gauge, your project size will be smaller; if you work with a larger hook, your finished project's size will be larger.

Gauge

Gauge is determined by the tightness or looseness of your stitches, and affects the finished size of your project. If you are concerned about the finished size of the project matching the size given, take time to crochet a small section of the pattern and then check your gauge. For example, if the gauge called for is 10 dc = 1 inch, and your gauge is 12 dc to the inch, you should switch to a larger hook. On the other hand, if your gauge is only 8 dc to the inch, you should switch to a smaller hook.

If the gauge given in the pattern is for an entire motif, work one motif and then check your gauge.

Understanding Symbols

As you work through a pattern, you'll quickly notice several symbols in the instructions. These symbols are used to clarify the pattern for you: brackets [], curlicue brackets {}, asterisks *.

Brackets [] are used to set off a group of instructions worked a number of times. For example, "[ch 3, sc in ch-3 sp] 7 times" means to work the instructions inside the [] seven times. Brackets [] also set off a group of stitches to be worked in one stitch, space or loop. For example, the brackets [] in this set of instructions, "Sk 3 sc, [3 dc, ch 1, 3 dc] in next st" indicate that after skipping 3 sc, you will work 3 dc, ch 1 and 3 more dc all in the next stitch.

Occasionally, a set of instructions inside a set of brackets needs to be repeated, too. In this case, the text within the brackets to be repeated will be set off with curlicue brackets {}. For example, "[Ch 9, yo twice, insert hook in 7th ch from hook and pull up a loop, sk next dc, yo, insert hook in next dc and pull up a loop, {yo and draw through 2 lps on hook} 5 times, ch 3] 8 times." In this case, in each of the eight times you work the instructions included in brackets, you will work the section included in curlicue brackets five times.

Asterisks * are also used when a group of instructions is repeated. They may either be used alone or with brackets. For example, "*Sc in each of the next 5 sc, 2 sc in next sc, rep from * around, join with a sl st in beg sc" simply means you will work the instructions from the first * around the entire round.

"*Sk 3 sc, [3 dc, ch 1, 3 dc] in next st, rep from * around" is an example of asterisks working with brackets. In this set of instructions, you will repeat the instructions from the asterisk around, working the instructions inside the brackets together.

Buyer's Guide

Caron International Inc.
Customer Service
P.O. Box 222
Washington, SC 27889
(800) 868-9194
www.caron.com

Coats & Clark
Consumer Service
P.O. Box 12229
Greenville, SC 26912-0229
(800) 648-1479
www.coatsandclark.com

DMC Corp.
Hackensack Ave. Bldg. 10A
South Kearny, NJ 07032
(800) 275-4117
www.dmc-usa.com

Lion Brand Yarn Co.
34 W. 15th St.
New York, NY 10011
(800) 795-5466
www.lionbrand.com

Patons Yarns
Box 40
Listowel, Ontario
N4W 3H3 Canada
(519) 291-3780
www.patonsyarns.com

STITCH GUIDE

Front Loop (a) Back Loop (b)

Chain (ch)

Yo, draw lp through hook.

Slip Stitch Joining

Insert hook in beg ch, yo, draw lp through.

Front Post/Back Post Dc

Fpdc (a): Yo, insert hook from front to back and to front again around the vertical post (upright part) of next st, yo and draw yarn through, yo and complete dc.
Bpdc (b): Yo, reaching over top of piece and working on opposite side (back) of work, insert hook from back to front to back again around vertical post of next st, yo and draw yarn through, yo and complete dc.

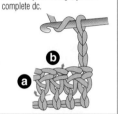

Single Crochet (sc)

Insert hook in st (a), yo, draw lp through (b), yo, draw through both lps on hook (c).

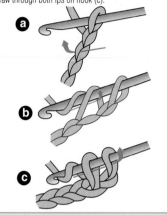

Half-Double Crochet (hdc)

Yo, insert hook in st (a), yo, draw lp through (b), yo, draw through all 3 lps on hook (c).

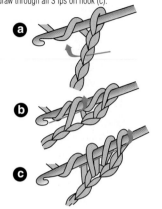

DECREASING

Single Crochet Decrease

Dec 1 sc over next 2 sts as follows: Draw up a lp in each of next 2 sts, yo, draw through all 3 lps on hook.

Double Crochet Decrease

Dec 1 dc over next 2 sts as follows: [Yo, insert hook in next st, yo, draw up lp on hook, yo, draw through 2 lps] twice, yo, draw through all 3 lps on hook.

Double Crochet (dc)

Yo, insert hook in st (a), yo, draw lp through (b), [yo, draw through 2 lps] twice (c, d).

Treble Crochet (tr)

Yo hook twice, insert hook in st (a), yo, draw lp through (b), [yo, draw through 2 lps on hook] 3 times (c, d, e).

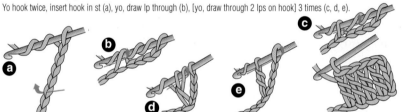

SPECIAL STITCHES

Chain Color Change (ch color change)

Yo with new color, draw through last lp on hook.

Double Crochet Color Change (dc color change)

Drop first color, yo with new color, draw through last 2 lps of st.

Reverse Single Crochet (reverse sc)

Working from left to right, insert hook in next st to the right (a), yo, draw up lp on hook, complete as for sc (b).

Stitch Abbreviations

The following stitch abbreviations are used throughout this publication.

beg	begin(ning)
bl(s)	block(s)
bpdc	back post dc
ch(s)	chain(s)
cl(s)	cluster(s)
CC	contrasting color
dc	double crochet
dec	decrease
dtr	double treble crochet
fpdc	front post dc
hdc	half-double crochet
inc	increase
lp(s)	loop(s)
MC	main color
p	picot
rem	remain(ing)
rep	repeat
rnd(s)	round(s)
RS	right side facing you
sc	single crochet
sk	skip
sl st	slip stitch
sp(s)	space(s)
st(s)	stitch(es)
tog	together
tr	treble crochet
trtr	triple treble crochet
WS	wrong side facing you
yo	yarn over

Crochet Hooks

METRIC	US
.60mm	14 steel
.75mm	12 steel
1.00mm	10 steel
1.25mm	8 steel
1.50mm	7 steel
1.75mm	5 steel
2.00mm	B/1
2.50mm	C/2
3.00mm	D/3
3.50mm	E/4
4.00mm	F/5
4.50mm	G/6
5.00mm	H/8
5.50mm	I/9
6.00mm	J/10

Yarn Conversion

OUNCES TO GRAMS

1	28.4
2	56.7
3	85.0
4	113.4

GRAMS TO OUNCES

25	⅞
40	1⅜
50	1¾
100	3½

Crochet Abbreviations

US	INTL
sc—single crochet	dc—double crochet
dc—double crochet	tr—treble crochet
hdc—half-double crochet	htr—half treble crochet
tr—treble crochet	dtr—double treble crochet
dtr—double treble crochet	trip—triple treble crochet
sk—skip	miss

YARNS

Bedspread weight	No. 10 cotton or Virtuoso
Sport weight	3-ply or thin DK
Worsted weight	thick DK or Aran

Check tension or gauge to save time.

Special Thanks

Sandy Abbate
Country Mini Stocking, Jolly Snowman Ornament

Carol Alexander
Dappled Blossoms Table Runner Country Wildflowers Kid's Kaleidoscope

Kathryn Clark
Balloon Appliqués

Donna Collinsworth
Baby's Bowling Set, Beautiful Butterfly, Country Heart Table Set, Cuddly Buddies, Snow People

Dot Drake
Floral Heart Picture, Lilac Fantasy Doily, Tulipmania Table Topper

JoHanna Dzikowski
Cozy Pet Bed, Floral Harvest Doily

Katherine Eng
Holiday Scrap Ornaments, Mini Poinsettia Wreath, Thirty-Minute Cloche

Darla Fanton
Floral Vines, Reversible Rainbow, Reversible Tote Bag

Nazanin Fard
Beaded Coin Purse, Pansies Barrette, Roses Photo Frame

Charlene Finiello
Mexican Serape Place Mat & Napking Ring, Northern Reflections

Valmay Flint
Rose Trellis Doily

Connie Folse
Christmas Star Hot Pad, Gold Cross Ornament, Little Gray Mouse

Kathleen Garen
Teen Totes & Topper

Lillian Gimmelli
Floral Coaster Set

Gloria Graham
Dainty Floral Coasters

Tammy Hildebrand
Denim Skirt Trim, Girls Scrap Poncho, Scrap Country Rug, V-Stitch Rug

Jewdy Lambert
Dawn to Dusk Sweater

Melissa Leapman
Linked Shells, Pretty Pastels Sweater, Spicy Vest

Beverly Mewhorter
Fishbowl Place Mat

Jennifer Moir
Pansies & Heart Cards

Margaret Nobles
Block Party T-Shirt, Floral Tissue Box Cover, Flower Time Headband & Pin

Shirley Patterson
Rainbow Stripes Table Runner

Rose Pirrone
Blue Skies Pot Holder, Cherry Jubilee Dish Towel, Coaster Crazy

Diane Poellot
Scrap Bargello, Striped Throw Rug

Janet Rehfeldt
Set of Ornaments
American Pride Rug

Sandy Scoville
Cross-Stitch Bookmark

Cynthia See
Bunny Bath Mitt, Fruit Napkin Rings

Ann E. Smith
Dozens of Dots Sweater, Granny Square Shawl, Hooded Jacket, Raindrops on Windowpanes Pullover, Santa Star Ornament

Martha Stein
Autumn Leaves, Confetti Stars

Vicky Tignanelli
Little Miss Mary

Paula Wendland
Heart Photo Frame Magnet

Michele Wilcox
American Flag Rug, Delightful Dishcloths, Dragon Puppet, Floral Hot Pad, Granny Square Rug, Kitty Dishcloth, Ladybug Hot Pad, Lucky Duck, Patchwork Kitty, Summer Place Mat Set, Pumpkin Hat, Tomato Pincushion

Lori Zeller
Americana Bookmarks, Dainty Blues Doily, Checkerboard Rug, Holiday Pins, Little Critter Finger Pals

Notes